Total School
Cluster Grouping
&Differentiation

Total School Cluster Grouping &Differentiation

Second Edition

A Comprehensive, Research-Based Plan for Raising Student Achievement and Improving Teacher Practices

Marcia Gentry

WITH **Kristina Ayers Paul, Jason McIntosh, C. Matthew Fugate, & Enyi Jen**

PRUFROCK PRESS INC.
WACO, TEXAS

Library of Congress Cataloging-in-Publication Data

Gentry, Marcia Lynne.
 Total school cluster grouping and differentiation : a comprehensive, research-based plan for raising student achievement and improving teacher practice / by Marcia L. Gentry, Ph.D. -- 2nd edition.
    pages cm
 ISBN 978-1-61821-161-3 (pbk.)
 1. Gifted children--Education--United States. 2. Ability grouping in education--United States. 3. Academic achievement--United States. I. Title.
 LC3993.9.G43 2014
 371.95--dc23
                        2014000224

Edited by Bethany Johnsen

Cover and layout design by Raquel Trevino

ISBN-13: 978-1-61821-161-3

At the time of this book's publication, all facts and figures cited are the most current available. All telephone numbers, addresses, and website URLs are accurate and active. All publications, organizations, websites, and other resources exist as described in the book, and all have been verified. The authors and Prufrock Press Inc. make no warranty or guarantee concerning the information and materials given out by organizations or content found at websites, and we are not responsible for any changes that occur after this book's publication. If you find an error, please contact Prufrock Press Inc.

Prufrock Press Inc.
P.O. Box 8813
Waco, TX 76714-8813
Phone: (800) 998-2208
Fax: (800) 240-0333
http://www.prufrock.com

TABLE OF CONTENTS

ACKNOWLEDGEMENTS

I would like to acknowledge and thank my graduate school mentors, Sally M. Reis, Joseph S. Renzulli, Robert K. Gable, Steven V. Owen, Karen Westberg, and E. Jean Gubbins, whose guidance, teaching, and support made the work on this model possible. I am fortunate and proud to have studied with each of you. Sally, your encouragement resulted in this work; thank you. I would also like to thank the many school district administrators and teachers who have successfully implemented this model; they have added to our knowledge base concerning how to effectively use Total School Cluster Grouping, and I draw from their experience in this book.

Special recognition goes to my research team members, colleague Kristina Ayers Paul, and Ph.D. candidates Jason McIntosh, C. Matthew Fugate, and Enyi Jen, who each contributed chapters and their best thinking to this book. They provide an invaluable source of inspiration to me. A very special thanks goes to Dr. Bill Asher, Professor Emeritus from Purdue University and Gifted Education Research Institute advisory board member, whose generosity and encouragement allowed us to continue our research, even when grant funds were cut. I credit Bessie Duncan, whose work with cluster grouping in the Detroit Public Schools in the 1980s laid the foundation for the development of this model.

I am grateful for the support of my family and friends. I dedicate this book to my daughter, Gentry Lee, whose journey though school provides me daily with a fresh perspective of our educational system. This work is for her and other students who, like her, deserve the best education that we can provide them.

—Marcia Gentry

FOREWORD

I am delighted that this important, practical, easy-to-read manual has been so well received, and that the author has agreed to revise and update it with all of the new information about how cluster grouping can be implemented. This edition provides new and updated information as well as new research for teachers and administrators who are interested in using cluster grouping. This type of grouping can be an essential service for gifted and high potential students as well as a method for more effectively and efficiently meeting the broad instructional needs of all students. Why is this so critical? My colleague Janine Firmender and I studied reading levels in fourth-grade classrooms across the country, finding that in most, reading levels range across 11 grades! How can one teacher handle such a broad range of reading achievement levels? The answer is simple—he cannot—unless he uses a strategy such as cluster grouping.

The author of this book points out a critical truth about cluster grouping: Grouping alone has little, if any, effect on academic gains and other outcomes. Educators must first group and then differentiate with appropriate enrichment and acceleration activities and strategies. The more limited range of achievement levels in a classroom (four rather than 11 grade levels, for example) will enable teachers to focus and differentiate the curriculum, materials, process, and products specifically to meet all of their students' needs and characteristics. Marcia Gentry's research on cluster grouping has proven that this practice raises achievement and promotes talent development in a broader range of students. When grouped appropriately and given differentiated instruction, students are able to make continuous progress.

The strategies discussed in this book are based on sound educational research, research that is sorely missing in too many books and articles about educational and instructional interventions. I recommend it to all educators who are interested in challenging and engaging their students and in ensuring that every student makes continuous progress in school.

Sally Reis, Ph.D.
University of Connecticut

INTRODUCTION

My work with what has become the Total School Cluster Grouping Model (TSCG) began in earnest in the late 1980s with the implementation, development, and refinement of the model. I studied the model in the 1990s and found that all students in schools where the model was implemented benefited from the model by achieving at higher levels and by having their teachers recognize them as higher achieving. I also found that classroom teachers implemented strategies and curriculum typically reserved for use in gifted programs with all students. Since then, I have helped many school districts across the country implement this model. My original research has served as a foundation for larger-scale research, program implementation, and evaluation studies conducted by myself and by other researchers. We have received evaluation, research, clinical and anecdotal reports of achievement, identification, and teacher practice results similar to those we found and reported. Due to the continued popularity and increased implementation across the country, we have continued to study and evaluate the effects of TSCG, each time finding strikingly similar results. Additionally, we have developed a website filled with resources based on what we have learned in the past 25 years to assist educators in their implementation efforts (http://www.purduegeri.org).

Total School Cluster Grouping offers educators a common-sense, whole-school approach to student placement, staff development, and differentiation. This model uses talent-development approaches typically found in gifted education programs to improve the achievement and performance of all of the children in the school. As such, this model focuses on what students can do and how educators can enhance every student's strengths, skills, and confidence by using grouping and enriched instruction.

The second edition of this book represents the culmination of our knowledge to date of the best way to implement this model in elementary schools with two or more classes per grade level. In it, we provide the rationale for and specifics of the TSCG model together with suggestions for staff development, evaluation, and differentiating curriculum and instruction. Part I is devoted to the specifics of the Total School Cluster Grouping Model. In Chapter 1, we define cluster grouping, examine the theory and research that supports the model, define terms, and consider cluster grouping in the wider context of ability grouping. In Chapter 2, we define the Total School Cluster Grouping model, describe how to flexibly identify the performance levels of all students in the school, and then discuss how to thoughtfully place them in classrooms in a manner that increases the odds that their educational needs will be met. We conclude this chapter with a discussion of teacher selection, teacher practices, data collection, talking with parents, and general suggestions for successful implementation. In Chapter 3, we address all aspects of professional development from initial training to ongoing and in-depth support. In Chapter 4, we have added a simulation using case studies that is designed to help teachers broaden their views of students' potentials. In Chapter 5, we explain how the Total School Cluster Grouping Model fits with other gifted and school-based initiatives. Part I concludes with a thoughtful chapter on the importance of and steps for program evaluation.

In Part II, we address implementing differentiation strategies, compacting curriculum, working with twice-exceptional learners, and developing student resilience in the cluster-grouped classroom. Beginning with Chapter 7, we define differentiation and provide exemplary practices for immediate use with students. Chapter 8 deals with curriculum compacting and how by implementing compacting, teachers can increase the level of challenge in their classrooms. In Chapter 9, we tackle the special needs of twice-exceptional learners, offering instructional strategies for use with these children, with the knowledge that many students will benefit from these strategies. Chapter 10 deals with affective needs, specifically developing resilience among high-ability learners, by focusing on strategies that can be incorporated into the daily classroom activities. Finally, in Chapter 11, we introduce the concept of student-focused differentiation, a brand of differentiation that is designed to increase student motivation and decrease teacher preparation by putting the student in charge of his or her learning.

Appendix A provides an interview protocol, and Appendix B contains an observation form tied to this interview protocol. Appendix C contains the epilogues of the simulation presented in Chapter 4. This list is not meant to be definitive, but rather a place to begin, in that it contains high quality materials, websites, and recommendations that we know work for teachers and their students. These resources can be helpful in developing a multifaceted, well-rounded program. Finally, Appendix D contains recommendations of quality resources that teachers can use to continue their quest toward effective differentiation in their classrooms.

We believe that Total School Cluster Grouping *and* effective curricular and instructional differentiation using principles of talent development can benefit all students and staff. Our research findings support this belief. This book offers educators a model for rethinking traditional approaches to classroom placement and grouping. This model can, quite simply, help teachers more effectively meet the educational needs of all students.

PART I

DEVELOPING A TSCG PROGRAM

CHAPTER 1

WHAT IS CLUSTER GROUPING?

An Introduction to Total School Cluster Grouping

Total School Cluster Grouping (TSCG) is a specific form of cluster grouping that has a research base, theoretical rationale, and model for successful implementation in elementary schools. The book focuses on why an elementary school staff would want to consider developing a TSCG program, followed by how to implement this model successfully in schools and effective strategies for differentiating in the cluster-grouped classroom. TSCG is guided by the following goals:

- Provide full-time services to high-achieving and high-ability elementary students.
- Help all students improve their academic achievement and educational self-efficacy.
- Help teachers more effectively and efficiently meet the diverse needs of their students.
- Weave gifted education and talent development "know-how" into the fabric of all educational practices in the school.
- Improve representation of traditionally underserved students identified over time as above average and high achieving.

Prior to discussing the details of the TSCG Model, we will consider the model in the context of general cluster grouping and other ability grouping practices to provide you with information concerning what Total School Cluster Grouping is and what it is not.

GENERAL CLUSTER GROUPING

Cluster grouping is a widely recommended and often used strategy for meeting the needs of gifted, high-achieving students, and/or high-ability students in the general elementary classroom. (In the Total School Cluster Grouping Model, we identify students not as "gifted," but rather by their current achievement level; hence the use of the term "high achieving.") Its use has gained popularity because of the move toward inclusive education, budget cuts, and heterogeneous grouping policies that have eliminated programs for gifted students (Purcell, 1994; Renzulli, 2005b; National Association for Gifted Children & Council of State Directors of Programs for the Gifted, 2013). When viewed in the larger context of school reform and extending gifted education services to more students, cluster grouping can reach and benefit teachers and students beyond those in traditional gifted programs.

Many variations in definitions and applications of cluster grouping have been noted, but three nonnegotiable components consistently prevail (Gentry, 1999; Gentry, 2013). First, groups of students (varying in number from three to more than 10) identified as gifted, high-achieving, or high-ability are placed in classrooms with students of other achievement levels. Second, teachers differentiate curriculum and instruction for the high-achieving students in the clustered classroom. Third, successful teachers of the high-ability students have an interest or background in working with gifted students. These three components drive the success of cluster grouping and serve as the foundational touchstones for this book. In order to understand the philosophical and structural nuances of cluster grouping, one first needs to consider definitions, history, research, misconceptions, and theoretical underpinnings of such programming.

Cluster grouping is generally defined as placing a group of gifted, high-achieving, or high-ability students in an elementary classroom with other students. Many experts in the field of gifted education recommend this approach. They often suggest a specific number of high-ability children—say six to eight—to comprise the cluster, and they specify that the rest of the class should be heterogeneous. Further, many applications of cluster grouping are frequently only concerned with the identified high-ability children and what occurs in their designated classroom. Composition of and practices within the other classrooms are frequently ignored when cluster grouping is implemented, as the perceived purpose of cluster grouping is to serve the identified high-ability children.

However, because cluster grouping places the highest-achieving students in one classroom and affects the composition of all other classrooms, it affects all students and teachers in the school. Therefore, cluster grouping should not only be viewed as a program for gifted students, but also as a total school program. Through staff development, flexible placement, and grouping integrated with the regular school structure, cluster grouping offers a means for improving curriculum, instruction, and student achievement. Total School Cluster Grouping provides a system and framework for student placement and education that extends general cluster grouping and addresses the needs of all students and teachers.

The benefits of a thoughtfully implemented TSCG program include:

- challenging high achievers by placing them together in one classroom, thus enabling new talents to emerge among students in the other classrooms and allowing them opportunities to become academic leaders;
- increasing the ability of all teachers to meet the individual academic needs of their students by reducing the range of student achievement levels in all classrooms;
- improving how teachers view their students with respect to ability and achievement;
- improving student achievement among students from all achievement levels;
- increasing the number of students identified as high achieving and decreasing the number of students identified as low achieving;
- extending gifted education services to more students in the school and beyond those students formally identified as "gifted and talented";
- bringing gifted education staff development, methods, and materials to all of the teachers in a school;
- providing full-time placement and services for students identified as high achieving;
- providing a seamless fit with a continuum of gifted and talented services for students;
- helping teachers work together to plan effective differentiated curriculum and instruction for students at various levels of achievement and readiness;

- engaging in ongoing assessment and identification of student strengths and abilities; and
- offering students the opportunity to grow and develop by receiving services that match their current levels of achievement in various subjects.

THEORETICAL UNDERPINNINGS

In educational settings across the country, meeting the needs of high-achieving students is a perpetual struggle. Staff, budget, and resource constraints frequently limit or exhaust the possibility of programming for the highest achievers. Further, identifying and serving gifted and potentially gifted students often take a back seat to other educational reforms and priorities. Cluster grouping is a widely recommended and popular strategy for meeting the needs of high-achieving, gifted, or high-ability students in elementary school classrooms (Balzer & Siewert, 1990; Brown, Archambault, Zhang, & Westberg, 1994; Coleman & Cross, 2005; Davis & Rimm, 2004; Gentry, 2013; Hoover, Sayler, & Feldhusen, 1993; Kulik, 2003; LaRose, 1986; Renzulli, 1994; Rogers, 2002). The practice has become popular in recent years due to heterogeneous grouping policies and financial cutbacks that have eliminated special programs for gifted and talented students (Purcell, 1994; Renzulli, 2005; National Association for Gifted Children & Council of State Directors of Programs for the Gifted, 2013). Research findings have showed improved achievement test scores of students of all achievement levels (Brulles, Peters, & Saunders, 2012; Brulles, Saunders, & Cohn, 2010; Gentry & Owen, 1999; Matthews, Ritchotte, & McBee, 2013; Pierce et al., 2011). District personnel across the country are searching for a way to improve student performance on tests, and cluster grouping has the potential to help them achieve this goal.

UNDERSTANDING CLUSTER GROUPING IN THE CONTEXT OF ABILITY GROUPING

Cluster grouping is an organizational model that should be discussed in the broader context of ability grouping. Thousands of studies have been conducted on the positive and negative effects of full-time ability grouping. Since 1982, at least 13 meta-analyses have been conducted on the topic of ability grouping with variable results (i.e., Goldring, 1990; Henderson, 1989; Kulik, 1985; Kulik & Kulik, 1982, 1984, 1987, 1992; Lou et al., 1996; Mosteller, Light, & Sachs, 1996; Noland & Taylor, 1986; Slavin, 1987a, 1990, 1993). Conflicting results, conclusions, and opinions exist regarding ability grouping. The practice has been both touted as an effective means for promoting student achievement (Kulik, 2003) and decried as an evil force contributing to the downfall of America's schools (Oakes, 1985). However, the "real" answer lies somewhere in the middle and depends largely upon the context and application of the ability grouping. Throughout this controversy, teachers are doing their best to meet students' individual needs within their classrooms. With the recent emotional calls for full-scale elimination of ability grouping, the advent of full inclusion, the addition of few resources, increased class sizes, and increased accountability for student test performance, many teachers have found meeting the continuum of individual students' needs in the regular classroom nearly impossible. Despite its mixed reception, analyses of National Assessment of Educational Progress data suggest that the use of ability grouping has markedly increased since the turn of the last century (Loveless, 2013). Most researchers tend to agree that when teachers adjust their curriculum and instruction to the achievement and skill level of the child, students of all achievement levels benefit. This is the approach to achievement grouping that cluster grouping embraces.

Unfortunately, the issues and intricacies surrounding ability grouping have been continually relegated to one side of an ugly argument: Ability grouping is either "bad" or "good." Neither could be further from the truth—thus the conflicting results. However, ability grouping is not an easily investigated topic, nor are answers clearly documented. The difficulty is due to the wide range of variables found in the school settings under which ability grouping should be studied if the study is to yield meaningful results. Most teachers know that what goes on within the ability grouping makes it an effective or ineffective tool. The same can be said for whole-group instruction, cooperative learning, inclusion, or resource rooms.

Research on tracking has shown that students in higher tracks benefited from this placement, but students in the lower tracks did not (Slavin, 1987a). Some researchers concluded that placing the students in the higher tracks caused the poor achievement of students in lower tracks (Oakes, 1985). One must question whether this is indeed the case. Might other factors have caused the performance in both groups, such as the quality of the teachers, their expectations, or the curriculum? Indeed, recent research reveals a trend of classes in which lower achieving students are placed being more likely to be led by lower quality and more novice teachers, and of these classrooms having fewer resources (Kalogrides & Loeb, 2013).

Renzulli and Reis (1991) explained an important delineation between tracking and ability grouping when they described tracking as "the general and usually permanent assignment of students to classes taught at a certain level" and ability grouping as "a more flexible arrangement that takes into account factors *in addition* to ability, and sometimes in the place of ability" (p. 31). Even so, research regarding tracking has become generalized to include all forms of ability grouping, although the terms tracking and ability grouping are not synonymous (Tieso, 2003). Cluster grouping is used with elementary students, and tracking is a practice used with high school students.

GROUPING TERMINOLOGY DEFINITIONS

Because terms surrounding grouping are often attributed with different, conflicting definitions, and these definitions often overlap or carry emotional weight, I offer the following definitions to clarify terms used throughout this chapter.

GENERAL CLUSTER GROUPING

Cluster grouping has a variety of definitions based on how it is implemented, but can generally be defined as placing several high-achieving, high-ability, or gifted students in a regular classroom with other students and with a teacher who has received training or who has a desire to differentiate curriculum and instruction for these "target" students (Gentry, 2013).

TOTAL SCHOOL CLUSTER GROUPING (AS APPLIED BY THE SCHOOLS IN THE STUDIES REFERENCED IN THIS BOOK)

Total School Cluster Grouping takes general cluster grouping several steps further to consider the placement and performance of *every* student in the school together with the students who might traditionally be identified as gifted and placed in the cluster classroom under the general model. Since cluster grouping affects the whole school, the focus of this book is on the application of Total School Cluster Grouping, which differs from general clustering in the following important ways:

1. Identification occurs yearly on the basis of student performance, with the expectation that student achievement will increase as students grow, develop, and respond to appropriately differentiated curricula.
2. Identification encompasses the range of low-achieving to high-achieving students, with all student achievement levels identified.
3. The classroom(s) that contain clusters of high-achieving students contain no above-average-achieving students, as these students are clustered into the other classrooms.
4. Some classrooms may contain clusters of special needs students with assistance provided to the classroom teacher.
5. Teachers may flexibly group between classes or among grade levels as well as use a variety of flexible grouping strategies within their classrooms.
6. All teachers receive professional development in gifted education strategies and have the opportunity for more advanced education in gifted education and talent development through advanced workshops, conferences, and coursework.
7. The teacher whose class has the high-achieving cluster is selected by an enrichment team or his or her colleagues and provides differentiated instruction and curriculum to these students as needed to meet their educational needs.

ABILITY GROUPING

Students of similar ability are placed together in groups for the purpose of modification of pace, instruction, and curricula to address the needs of individual students who have different abilities in different curricular areas (Tieso, 2003). Kulik (1992) warned, "Benefits are slight from programs that group children by ability but prescribe common curricular experiences for all ability groups" (p. 21). He also stressed that students from all ability levels gain when curriculum and instruction are adjusted to meet their learning needs. Ability grouping can be done by subject, within classes or between classes, and for part of the day or throughout the day. In some applications of ability grouping, the composition of the groups changes, while in others it does not.

ACHIEVEMENT GROUPING

Similar to ability grouping, achievement grouping focuses on demonstrated levels of achievement by students, with achievement viewed as something dynamic and changing. Like ability grouping, achievement or skill-level grouping can be done by subject, within or between classes, and for part of the day or all day. It very often takes place in a flexible manner as performance and achievement levels of students change (Renzulli & Reis, 1997). Throughout this book, the term "achievement grouping" is used rather than the term "ability grouping" due to its more fluid and manifest definition. Ability is often equated to intelligence and viewed as latent and fixed, whereas achievement is more likely to be viewed as changeable or to be affected by effective educational opportunities. Further, high-achieving students inherently have high ability; however, not all high-ability students achieve at high levels.

BETWEEN-CLASS GROUPING

This occurs when students are regrouped for a subject area (usually within an elementary grade level) based on ability or achievement. It is one application of ability or achievement grouping. Teachers instruct students working at similar levels with appropriately challenging curricula, at an appropriate pace, and with methods most suited to facilitate academic gain. For example, in mathematics, one teacher may be teaching algebra to advanced students, while a colleague teaches prealgebra to students not as advanced, and yet another teacher works with students for whom math is a struggle, employing strategies to enhance their success and understanding. Between-class grouping arrangements by subject areas usually require that grade-level teachers teach the subject at the same time to facilitate the grouping arrangements.

WITHIN-CLASS GROUPING

Within-class grouping refers to different arrangements teachers use within their classes. Groups may be created by interest, skill, achievement, job, ability, self-selection—either heterogeneous or homogeneous—and can include various forms of cooperative grouping arrangements. Flexible arrangements for within-class grouping are desirable.

FLEXIBLE GROUPING

Flexible grouping calls for use of various forms of grouping for instruction, pacing, and curriculum in such a manner that allows student movement between and among groups based on each student's progress and needs. Flexible grouping takes place (a) when there is more than one form of grouping used (e.g., class, project, job, skill, heterogeneous, homogeneous) and (b) when group membership, in some or all of these groups, changes according to the form of grouping used. Keep in mind that groups are formed and modified based on the academic needs of the students. Both critics and supporters of grouping agree that grouping should be flexible (Gentry, 1999; George, 1995; Renzulli & Reis, 1997; Slavin, 1987b).

TRACKING

Tracking is full-time placement of students into ability groups for instruction—usually by class and at the secondary level. In a tracked system, there is very little opportunity to move between the various tracks, and some form of "objective" testing often determines placement in the tracks. "[Tracking is] the practice of grouping students according to their perceived abilities . . . most noticeable or more commonly found in junior and senior high schools . . . the groups are sometimes labeled college bound, academic, vocational, general, and remedial" (McBrien & Brandt, 1997, pp. 97–98). Tracking has very little to do with ability or achievement grouping in elementary grades, although it has frequently been generalized to elementary school settings and used to discourage grouping with young children.

Table 1.1 contains a summary of the grouping terminology definitions.

ABILITY GROUPING CONSIDERATIONS

Slavin (1987b; 1990; 2006) listed three important advantages to regrouping students for selected subjects over class assignments in which students are homogeneously grouped by ability: (a) identifying and placing students in the setting for most of the day reduces labeling effects; (b) achievement in reading or math determines group placement—not ability level; and (c) regrouping plans tend to be flexible. In their meta-analyses, Kulik and Kulik (1991) reported that within-class programs specifically designed to benefit gifted and talented students raised the achievement scores of these students. Slavin (1987a) reported that within-class ability grouping had a positive effect (.34 standard deviations) on the mathematics achievements of all students, with the most positive effect for students who initially achieved at low levels. He also stated that the within-class use of grouping for reading instruction might be necessary. After reviewing the effects of 13 different research syntheses on grouping, Rogers (1991; 2002) concluded that grouping students on the basis of academic ability and on the basis of general intellectual ability has "produced marked academic achievement gains as well as moderate increases in attitude toward the subjects in which these

TABLE 1.1
GROUPING TERMINOLOGY SUMMARY

Term	Definition
Cluster Grouping	The placement of several high-achieving, high-ability, or gifted students in a regular classroom with other students and a teacher who has received training or has a desire to differentiate curriculum and instruction for these "target" students.
Total School Cluster Grouping	Cluster grouping model that takes into account the achievement levels of all students and places students in classrooms yearly in order to reduce the number of achievement levels in each classroom and facilitate teachers' differentiation of curriculum and instruction for all students and thus increase student achievement.
Ability Grouping	Students are grouped for the purpose of modification of pace, instruction, and curriculum. Groups can be flexible and arranged by subject, within classes, or between classes.
Achievement Grouping	Focuses on demonstrated levels of achievement by students and is viewed as something dynamic and changing. Groups can be arranged by subject, within classes, or between classes.
Between-Class Grouping	Students are regrouped for a subject area (usually within an elementary grade level) based on ability or achievement. Teachers instruct students working at similar levels with appropriately challenging curricula, at an appropriate pace, and with methods most suited to facilitate academic gain.
Within-Class Grouping	These groups are different arrangements teachers use within their classes. Groups may be created by interest, skill, achievement, job, ability, self-selection—either heterogeneous or homogeneous—and can include various forms of cooperative learning grouping arrangements. Groups are intended to be flexible.
Flexible Grouping	The use of various forms of grouping for instruction, pacing, and curriculum in such a manner to allow for movement of students between and among groups based on their progress and needs.
Tracking	The full-time placement of students into ability groups for instruction—usually by class and at the secondary level. Little opportunity exists to move between tracks.

students are grouped" (1991, p. xii). Despite many arguments for and against ability grouping, it appears from reviews of the research that grouping can help to improve the academic performance of students of all achievement levels if implemented with appropriate curricula, instruction, and expectations.

For grouping to positively affect the academic achievement of students, more than a simple administrative grouping plan must exist. As demonstrated by the varied results from the meta-analytic studies on grouping, there is more to grouping than simply assigning students to groups on the basis of their ability or achievement levels. The studies that reported the largest effects were of programs that provided *differentiation* within ability groups (Kulik, 1992,

2003; Rogers, 1991, 2002). Rogers (1991) suggested that it was unlikely that grouping itself caused the gains. Kulik (2003) noted that bright, average, and low-achieving youngsters benefited from grouping programs if the curriculum was appropriately adjusted to the aptitude levels of the groups. Accordingly, he recommended schools use various forms of flexible ability grouping. In discussing their meta-analyses findings on grouping practices, Kulik and Kulik (1992) concluded:

> If schools eliminated grouping programs with differentiated curricula, the damage to student achievement would be great, and it would be felt broadly. Both higher and lower aptitude students would suffer academically from the elimination of such programs. The damage would be truly great if, in the name of de-tracking, schools eliminated enriched and accelerated classes for their brightest learners. The achievement level of such students would fall dramatically if they were required to move at the common pace. No one can be certain that there would be a way to repair the harm that would be done. (p. 73)

WHAT THE RESEARCH SAYS ABOUT CLUSTER GROUPING

It is clear that a discrepancy exists between what takes place in schools for students with regard to challenge and instructional strategies and what should take place if American students are to compete in a global marketplace (Renzulli, 2005). "We know that all students' learning improves when schools are perceived as being enjoyable, relevant, friendly places where students have some role . . . deciding what they will learn, and how they will pursue topics in which they may have a special interest" (Renzulli, 1994, pp. 20–21). Restricting the range of student achievement levels in classrooms results in more time for teachers to work with individual students. Cluster grouping has been found to be beneficial to students in that it allows students of similar achievement levels to work together and challenge each other (Gentry, 2013). For high-ability learners, cluster grouping also allows them the opportunity to compare themselves to their intellectual peers and form a more accurate perception of their own abilities. In a cluster-grouped classroom, these individuals are not always the "best." By not always being best or first academically, they learn to work, to fail, and to strive for excellence, and they have others' high-quality work with which to compare their own work. These elements are essential for high-ability students to learn to work to their potential (Robinson, Reis, Neihart, & Moon, 2002).

Researchers have noted benefits from grouping gifted students. These benefits include improved academic achievement (Brulles et al., 2010; Brulles et al., 2012; Gentry, 1999; Matthews et al., 2013; Tieso, 2005; Pierce et al., 2011), realistic perception of abilities when compared to peers (Marsh, Chessor, Craven, & Roche, 1995), appropriate levels of challenge (Kulik, 2003; Rogers, 2002; Gentry, 1999), the opportunity for teachers to address unique social and emotional needs of gifted students (Peterson, 2003), and the ability of the teacher to better address individual strengths and weaknesses (Gentry, 2013; Moon, 2003). Research findings reveal the following major benefits of cluster grouping.

1. Gifted students regularly interact both with their intellectual peers and their age peers (Delcourt & Evans, 1994; Gentry, 1999; Rogers, 1991; Slavin, 1987a).

2. Full-time services are provided for gifted students without additional cost (Gentry & Owen, 1999; Hoover et al., 1993; LaRose, 1986).

3. Curricular differentiation is more efficient and likely to occur when a group of high-achieving students is placed with a teacher who has expertise, training, and a desire to differentiate curriculum than when these students are distributed among many teachers (Brulles et al., 2010; Bryant, 1987; Gentry, 1999; Kennedy, 1995; Kulik, 1992; Rogers, 2002).

4. Removing the highest achievers from most classrooms allows other achievers to emerge and gain recognition (Gentry & Owen, 1999; Kennedy, 1989).

5. Student achievement increases when cluster grouping is used (Brulles et al., 2010; Brulles et al., 2012; Gentry & Owen, 1999; Pierce et al., 2011).

6. Over time, fewer students are identified as low achievers and more students are identified as high achievers (Gentry, 1999; Gentry, 2011; Gentry, 2012; Brulles et al., 2012).

7. Cluster grouping reduces the range of student achievement levels that must be addressed within the classrooms of all teachers (Coleman, 1995; Gentry, 1999; Delcourt & Evans, 1994; Rogers, 1993).

Several analyses of studies regarding ability grouping in elementary schools have been completed (Goldring, 1990; Henderson, 1989; Kulik, 1985, 1992; Kulik & Kulik, 1982, 1984, 1985, 1987, 1992; Lou et al., 1996; Mosteller et al., 1996; Noland & Taylor, 1986; Nomi, 2010; Rogers, 1991; Slavin, 1987a, 1990, 1993); however, only a handful of published studies and several dissertations from the past 30 years could be found that examined the effects of ability grouping on gifted students in schools where a cluster grouping model was used (e.g., Bear, 1998; Brulles, 2005; Brulles et al., 2010; Brulles et al., 2012; Delcourt & Evans, 1994; Delcourt, Loyd, Cornell, & Goldberg, 1994; Gates, 2011; Gentry, 1999; Gentry & Keilty, 2004; Gentry & Owen, 1999; Hoover et al., 1993; LaRose, 1986; Lou et al., 1996; Marotta-Garcia, 2011; Matthews el al., 2013; Miller, Latz, Jenkins, & Adams, 2011; Pierce et al., 2011; Porcher, 2007). Most of these studies were concerned with the effects of cluster grouping on gifted students, and only our work, the work of Brulles et al., the work of Matthews et al., and the work of Pierce et al. examined effects on students of other achievement levels.

Although cluster grouping is commonly suggested as a programming option for gifted students, surprisingly little evidence exists regarding its effects on these students. In our seminal study, we examined the effects of cluster grouping on all students and on teachers' perceptions of other students' performance (Gentry & Owen, 1999). Gentry (1999) and Gentry and Owen (1999) reported that, for two entire classes (i.e., graduation years) of students when compared to similar students in a longitudinal, quasi-experimental study, student achievement increased among all students in the cluster-grouped school. Standardized achievement scores in math, reading, and the total battery on the Iowa Tests of Basic Skills (Hieronymus, Hoover, & Lindquist, 1984) improved for two entire classes as the students progressed from grade 3 through grade 5. Further, the cluster-grouped students began with lower total achievement than the comparison school students and ended with significantly higher total achievement than the comparison school students. These achievement trends are depicted in Figures 1.1 and 1.2. The gains in achievement and the differences in achievement were both statistically and practically significant with medium to large effect sizes.

Additionally, more students in the treatment school were identified as above average or high achieving, whereas fewer students were identified as low achieving during the 5-year span of the study. Changes in the achievement categories are depicted in Figures 1.3 and 1.4. Gentry also reported qualitative findings concerning teacher practices, administrative leadership, and the various uses of grouping that helped to explain the achievement and identification findings.

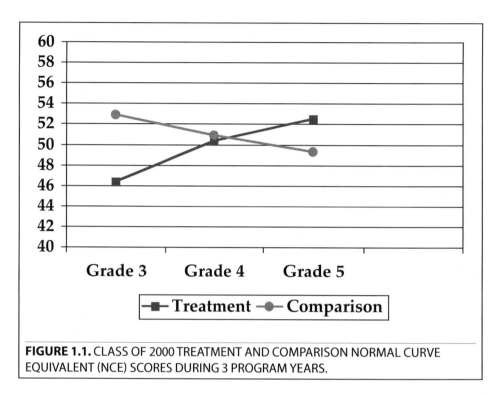

FIGURE 1.1. CLASS OF 2000 TREATMENT AND COMPARISON NORMAL CURVE EQUIVALENT (NCE) SCORES DURING 3 PROGRAM YEARS.

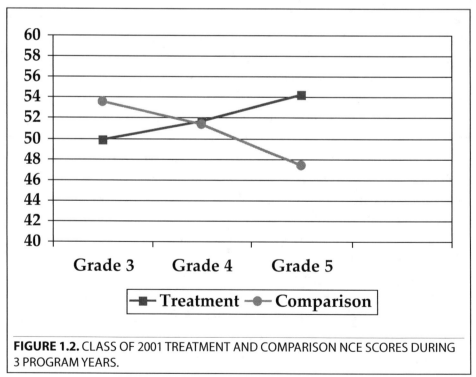

FIGURE 1.2. CLASS OF 2001 TREATMENT AND COMPARISON NCE SCORES DURING 3 PROGRAM YEARS.

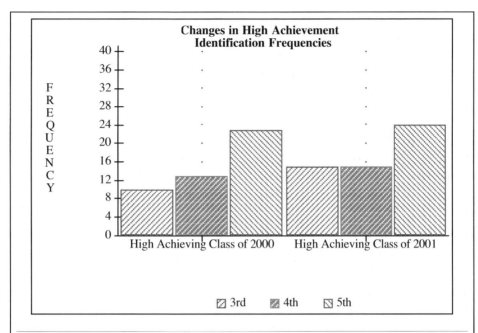

FIGURE 1.3. CHANGES IN FREQUENCIES OF STUDENTS IDENTIFIED AS HIGH ACHIEVING DURING 3 PROGRAM YEARS.

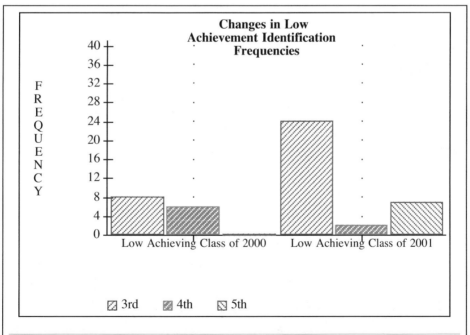

FIGURE 1.4. CHANGES IN FREQUENCIES OF STUDENTS IDENTIFIED AS LOW ACHIEVING DURING 3 PROGRAM YEARS.

Since this research was published, this model has been widely recommended and implemented. Although school districts using the model may conduct program evaluations, they typically have little interest in publishing the results. There are several unpublished evaluation studies and anecdotal information concerning the efficacy of implementation in these varied sites (e.g., Teno, 2000). In fact, I found increased student achievement and improved representation of students from underserved populations in the high achievement category in two recent evaluation studies (Gentry, 2011; Gentry, 2012). Additionally, my 2012 evaluation of the Total School Cluster Grouping program in five treatment schools detailed gains in Normal Curve Equivalent (NCE) mathematics scores for students from all achievement groups, as well as increased achievement in reading for those students in average and higher achieving groups among students. These results are summarized in Figures 1.5–1.9 and in Table 1.2.

Additionally, the 1999 study has been replicated with similar findings reported in dissertations (Bear, 1998; Brulles, 2005; Gates, 2011; Marotta-Garcia, 2011; Porcher, 2011). Other researchers have recently added to the literature on the efficacy of cluster grouping (Brulles et al., 2010; Brulles et al., 2012; Matthews et al., 2013; Pierce et al., 2011) as well as contributed a book that advocates for a schoolwide approach that is loosely based on TSCG (Winebrenner & Brulles, 2008). In fact, Brulles et al. (2010; 2012) reported achievement gains by students who were from low-income families or who were learning English as a new language.

Our research team is involved in ongoing evaluation and longitudinal research on the model, and we post updates regularly to the TSCG website (http://www.purduegeri.org). Results from this work mirror those found in the original study (Gentry, 1999). The TSCG model that I studied in the mid-1990s and which we are currently replicating serve as the conceptual basis for the remainder of this book.

TOTAL SCHOOL CLUSTER GROUPING

Total School Cluster Grouping operates on the premise that gifted education practices will enhance the educational experiences within an entire school. As noted by Tomlinson and Callahan (1992), Renzulli (1994), Reis, Gentry, and Park (1995), and the U.S. Department of Education (1993), the use of gifted education "know-how" has the potential to improve general education practices.

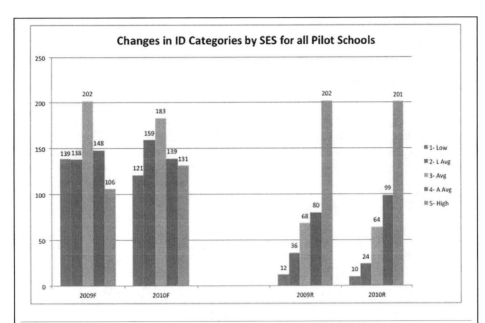

FIGURE 1.5. CHANGES FROM 2009–2010 FOR STUDENTS ELIGIBLE FOR FREE/ REDUCED PRICED MEALS (F) AND STUDENTS NOT ELIGIBLE FOR FREE/REDUCED PRICED MEALS (R).

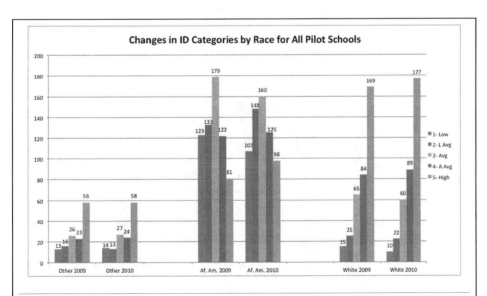

FIGURE 1.6. CHANGES IN IDENTIFICATION CATEGORIES BY RACE FOR ALL PILOT SCHOOLS (*NOTE.* "OTHER" INCLUDES ASIAN, HISPANIC, AND MULTIRACIAL STUDENTS COMBINED).

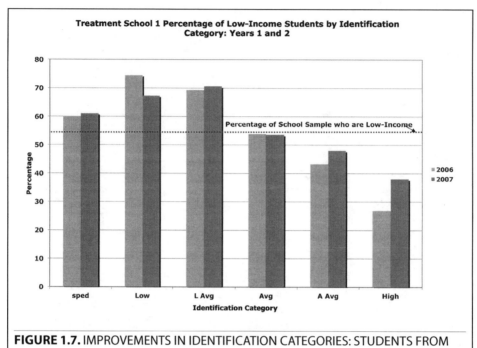

FIGURE 1.7. IMPROVEMENTS IN IDENTIFICATION CATEGORIES: STUDENTS FROM LOW-INCOME FAMILIES.

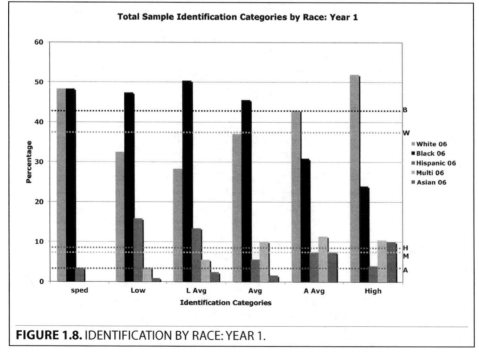

FIGURE 1.8. IDENTIFICATION BY RACE: YEAR 1.

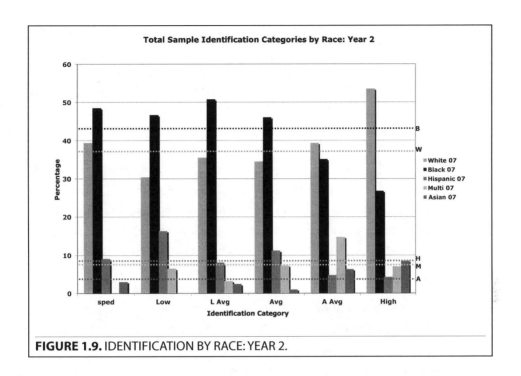

FIGURE 1.9. IDENTIFICATION BY RACE: YEAR 2.

TABLE 1.2
STATE TEST NCE MATH MEANS FROM 2009–2011 BY 2009 ACHIEVEMENT CATEGORY

Achievement Category	2009 PSSA Math NCE	2010 PSSA Math NCE	2011 PSSA Math NCE	Number of students
Low-Achieving	17.62 (9.89)	22.36 (13.82)	**28.03 (+10.41)** (12.69)	*n*=42 (2009) *n*=61 (2010) *n*=69 (2011)
Low-Average	27.52 (11.98)	33.79 (15.92)	33.00 **(+5.48)** (15.82)	*n*=60 (2009) *n*=99 (2010) *n*=94 (2011)
Average	35.45 (11.29)	40.82 (14.34)	40.00 **(+4.55)** (15.48)	*n*=62 (2009) *n*=125 (2010) *n*=124 (2011)
Above-Average	44.10 (15.75)	51.93 (15.99)	**52.25 (+7.83)** (16.86)	*n*=59 (2009) *n*=105 (2010) *n*=98 (2011)
High	61.49 (18.97)	69.29 (19.59)	**69.81 (+8.32)** (17.98)	*n*=97 (2009) *n*=163 (2010) *n*=153 (2011)
TOTAL	41.11 (21.41)	48.03 (23.03)	47.93 **(+6.82)**	*n*=320 (2009) *n*=553 (2010) *n*=538 (2011)

Note. Standard deviations are in parentheses; increased scores from 2009–2010/2011 are bolded.

The long-term study conducted by Gubbins et al. (2002) found that by employing strategies typically used in gifted programs, academic needs were more likely to become the focus of the curriculum than the typical topic-based units (e.g., watermelons, apples, pumpkins) that had previously existed in many classrooms. Total School Cluster Grouping, when designed appropriately, can simultaneously address the needs of high-achieving students *and* those of other students in the school.

Professional development of all teachers—not just those with the high-achieving cluster of students—increases the use of gifted education strategies within all classrooms. In my research, I have found that training focused on instructional strategies from gifted education prompted teachers to integrate higher order thinking skills, develop critical thinking skills, compact curriculum, use open-ended questions, accelerate students in content areas, and incorporate several other instructional strategies, which, teachers reported, enabled them to address the specific needs of their students (Gentry & Owen, 1999). According to one third-grade teacher who taught the high-achieving cluster students:

> We had so many high [achieving] math students who weren't in a high cluster [for high-achieving students]. We thought, to really meet the needs of the grade-level, we would have a cluster group strictly for math. We also had the high [achieving] cluster reading group to meet the needs of other children who may not have been identified or who had strengths that weren't evident across the board. We were able to target more children for high reading by regrouping within the grade level for reading. (Gentry & Owen, 1999, p. 234)

Kulik and Kulik (1992) and Rogers (1991) suggested that grouping by ability, when used in conjunction with appropriate differentiated instruction, can enhance achievement for students at all levels. When placed together, gifted students are given the opportunity to see the level at which their academic peers are performing. When in heterogeneous groups, these students may be able to perform at a subpar level and still be seen as excelling beyond their classmates, when in truth, they are capable of much more (Kulik, 2003; Rogers, 2002). Therefore, by grouping more homogeneously, the façade of effort and ability can be removed and replaced with more appropriate challenge and rigor.

In turn, the same phenomenon occurs in the other classrooms. Students who previously sat quietly, able to avoid participation, are now free to engage in and contribute to the learning process. As expectations are raised for all students, accountability increases, attention focuses, and productivity begins to rise. By regrouping the student population according to achievement levels, educators are better able to meet the diverse academic needs of the students and the nonnegotiable budget restrictions (Gentry, 1999). As one fourth-grade teacher explained:

> Maybe cluster grouping has a lot to do with it. The cluster grouping may give the lower achieving students more self-confidence, because I think they become more involved in class when the high [achieving] kids are removed. And you know that those high [achieving] kids are competitive and tend to dominate class sometimes. Also, the average student or high-average student really blossomed, too, which may be due to cluster grouping. (Gentry & Owen, 1999, pp. 228–229)

Administrators and teachers noted the merit of TSCG, as it provided positive results for teachers and for students. The teachers liked the program, and 95% of them believed it helped them better meet the needs of the students in their classrooms (Gentry, 1999). One teacher explained how she came to view the program:

> One thing—I remember how skeptical I was at the beginning because I am not a risk-taker. I thought the same thing a few other people thought—oh, you take those top kids out and I'm not going to have any spark. And that was far from being true. I see lots of sparks in my room . . . and having my daughter in [the program] . . . there's such a difference in her attitude and her love for school is back . . . before being placed in the high-achieving cluster, she wasn't being challenged in school, now to see her doing research projects as an 8-year-old . . . she's doing projects so beyond what I ever thought and she is so excited about school. (p. 238)

The reason for grouping is to facilitate learning. Achievement grouping allows teachers to adjust curricula based on the skill level of the students, and other forms of grouping are equally effective tools to enhance student learning.

Teachers in our study were not afraid to use grouping. In fact, the teachers came to use a variety of grouping strategies, including:

- Between-class groups, which included regrouping by achievement levels for reading and math 4–5 days per week. In this manner and for these two subjects, one teacher taught the advanced students, another teacher taught the struggling students, and the remaining teachers taught the average students using appropriately leveled materials that were high quality and interesting to the students at each level. The teacher who taught the students struggling with math or reading had help from a special education teacher-consultant and from a Title I aide.

- Within-class groups, which included grouping students by interest, in cooperative learning groups, as peer learning dyads, and by achievement levels in subjects other than math and reading—as those subjects were addressed in the between-class arrangements.

Key to both the within-class and between-class configurations of grouping was flexibility in the groups. As students gained in skills in the between-class arrangements, they were moved to higher skill groups, with some students being moved to higher grades. Whereas a cluster-grouped classroom of high-achieving students might have had 10 students who excelled in both math and reading, the high-achieving reading section had 24 students who excelled in reading. The addition of 14 new students to the original 10 advanced readers created a new group of students with strengths in reading. By definition, this is a form of flexible grouping, which then provided advanced reading curriculum to able readers in a grade level. These procedures were also used for math instruction.

When teachers regrouped students for instruction, they added to the core groups of students who excelled in math and reading other students who excelled in math *or* reading. Within the classes, grouping strategies used by the teachers were also flexible. Cooperative learning was used in both homogeneous and heterogeneous applications, and students in these classes worked with a variety of their classmates on all types of schoolwork. Teachers also gave students the choice to opt out of group work if they would rather work alone.

When academically struggling students worked together in their achievement-grouped class in either math or reading, the teacher who instructed these groups used quality curriculum, had high expectations that these students would succeed, and presented the material at a pace and depth that facilitated student understanding. These students didn't have to worry about being behind or having other kids snicker if they asked a question because they didn't understand, and as a result, they began asking more questions. As they developed skills, they developed confidence, and as they developed confidence, they began to achieve. These instructional groups, formed by grouping students of similar achievement levels in the specific content areas, served as an intervention for the low-performing students. Similar students in other settings or schools might have remained low-performing and fallen further behind, but the students in this achievement-grouped setting began to make progress.

In summary, Total School Cluster Grouping is a model with a growing body of research to support its effectiveness in raising the achievement of students at all levels. Our research and evaluation studies have highlighted some of the ways that teachers have effectively incorporated gifted education instructional strategies to meet the needs of students at all levels, as well as the multiple forms of flexible within-class and across-grade grouping they have used to more efficiently manage their efforts to target the subject-specific learning needs of students. Total School Cluster Grouping serves as an intervention for meeting the academic needs of gifted and talented students, while at the same time helping all students achieve at high levels. In the next chapter I discuss, in detail, how to implement the model.

CHAPTER 2

TOTAL SCHOOL CLUSTER GROUPING MODEL

Implementation and Practice

Total School Cluster Grouping provides an organizational framework that places students into classrooms on the basis of achievement, flexibly groups and regroups students as needed for instruction (based on interest and needs), and provides appropriately challenging learning experiences for all students. In this chapter, I describe the details and considerations necessary for successfully implementing the Total School Cluster Grouping Model. The specific research-based application of cluster grouping that the remainder of this book addresses aims to:

1. Provide full-time services to high-achieving elementary students.
2. Help all students improve their academic achievement and educational self-efficacy.
3. Help teachers more effectively and efficiently meet the diverse need of their students.
4. Weave gifted education and talent development "know-how" into the fabric of all educational practices in the school.

5. Improve representation of traditionally underserved students identified, over time, as above average and high achieving.

IDENTIFICATION

Identification is a key component for all programming, and in Total School Cluster Grouping, formal identification takes place yearly, with the expectation that students will improve in their achievement performance over time as they respond to appropriately differentiated curriculum and instruction delivered by skilled teachers. Criteria are not fixed, but rather determined by consensus in a manner that builds in flexibility to accommodate individual students and their needs. In addition to yearly identification and placement of students into classrooms, the model includes flexible grouping and regrouping of students for instruction once they are placed into classrooms. Following are the general categories of achievement that facilitate yearly identification for classroom placement.

CATEGORIES OF ACHIEVEMENT

Identification in a traditional gifted program can be fraught with problems of accountability, testing, elitism, exclusion, equity, and limited space in the program. These issues do not exist in the Total School Cluster Grouping Model, as the achievement levels of *all* students are identified. This is done using a combination of student performance in the classroom, as identified by their teachers, and achievement testing results. In this model there is no set number or percentage of students to identify for gifted services. Rather, *all* students are identified yearly based on their performance and using five categories defined as follows:

1. *High Achieving*: These students are great at math *and* reading when compared to their age peers.
2. *Above-Average Achieving*: These students are great at math *or* reading, or they are pretty good at math and reading, but not as advanced as students identified as high achieving.
3. *Average Achieving*: These students achieve in the middle when compared to others in their grade level. This might be "on grade level" in

many schools, but in an impoverished area, they might be achieving below grade level, but at an average level for the school population.

4. *Low-Average Achieving*: These students may struggle with math or reading, or be slightly behind their peers in both areas. However, it also appears that with some extra support of their work, these students are not at risk of failure.

5. *Low Achieving*: These students struggle with school and face risk of failure in school. In many schools, the longer they attend, the further behind they fall in their performance. Despite remedial efforts, schools often fail to reach these students.

A word about students who are identified for and who receive special education services: Another category could be developed for special needs students. However, these students have already been identified, so placing them where they can succeed becomes the only concern. To facilitate this placement, the achievement levels of these students should be noted. Many students served by special education are not low achieving. Additionally, many students may have more than one label, such as ADHD *and* gifted or learning disabled *and* gifted. If a student has a dual exceptionality, placement should be made in the high achieving cluster, so that the twice-exceptional student's strengths become the educational focus.

Teachers, counselors, and administrators need to understand these identification category definitions and that the categories are based on the population attending their school. By using a local frame of reference, the system of identification can work in any type of school. If a school is "average" (is there such a school?), then an average student would be on grade level, whereas if a school is high performing, an average student might be achieving above grade level. These categories are based on relative performance.

The HOPE Scale (Peters & Gentry, 2010; 2013) might be helpful in guiding teachers in their identification of academic and social aspects of giftedness. With only 11 items and empirical evidence of construct validity from more than 10,000 participants, the HOPE+ scale is a useful new tool for adding teacher nominations to the identification process. Additionally, it is invariant among income and ethnic groups, showing promise for helping to increase representation of underserved students in gifted programs. Similarly, The Scales for Rating the Behavioral Characteristics of Superior Students (Renzulli et al., 2002) might assist teachers in understanding characteristics of academically high-performing students, although the ratings should *never* be summed and used in an identification matrix. It is also important to understand the following:

1. Identification categories are designated to assist with placement of students into classrooms in this model, not as definitive, permanent labels or indicators of expectations.
2. Categories change as students grow, learn, and develop. A specific identification category might not drive instructional placement for students identified in average, low-average, or low-achieving categories.
3. Identification takes place yearly for classroom placement, and students will improve as they progress through school.

IDENTIFICATION PROCEDURES AND GUIDELINES

Once definitional categories are established and explained, the process of identifying the achievement levels of the students for placement in classrooms can begin. This process is labor intensive and involves several steps. First, try to have the teachers identify the performance of their students prior to them examining any test performance data on the students. This is important, as together the teacher designations and the test performance will be used to identify and place students in the classrooms. If teachers check the tests to see if they are "right," and then adjust their assessments of student achievement based on test results, the information used for placement will have too much test emphasis rather than a balance of information from both teachers and test results. This model uses tests for means of *inclusion* in the program, not for means of *exclusion* from the program. In many identification systems, tests are used as a gateway, with a certain test score required for entry. In TSCG, students are never excluded as high achieving based on a test score.

Teachers will identify students who fail to test well but who perform well in class. Teachers, in general, know their students well. Occasionally, teachers will fail to identify as gifted (or high achieving) students who fail to do their work, who are unorganized, or who are defiant. There are many reasons for not identifying this type of student, not the least of which is that such a child might take a spot away from a more "deserving" child. In TSCG, there is no limit to the number of spaces in the high-achieving cluster. If a child scores well on the test, but not in class, he or she will be placed in the high-achieving cluster in virtue of his or her scores; thus the test is used to *include* students whom the teachers might not otherwise identify for placement. I suggest using a local norm of 90th to 95th percentile or greater in math and reading for automatic inclusion into the high-achieving cluster. Other high achievers will be so designated by their teachers regardless of their test scores. In the event of a teacher who overnominates, have that teacher rank the nominated students in order of greatest need. Our experience has shown that overnomination is a phenomenon that disappears with time as teachers in grade-level teams discuss their students and begin to understand the model, placement, and characteristics of student achievement.

To *include* students as above-average achieving, use a local norm of 90th percentile or greater percentile in math *or* reading or 75th percentile in math *and* reading. Again, teachers will include others who exhibit (but do not test at) above-average performance.

By using both teacher ratings and achievement scores, a system of checks and balances is developed. Through this method, it is possible for a student who did not test well to be identified, and conversely, a student whose classroom performance did not reflect his or her ability could be identified as *high achieving* or *above average* on the basis of achievement scores. Due to the holistic approach and flexible nature of this identification process, cut-off scores and matrices should not be employed. The use of cut-off scores may cause educators to misidentify students by placing too much emphasis on one factor. Using a matrix focuses on a combination of rigid factors, magically summed, rather than on fluid pathways to identification. In TSCG, students are identified and placed into classes by the people who know them best and who have their best interests in mind.

OTHER CONSIDERATIONS

When teachers designate the achievement levels of their students, they should also designate which students need to be separated from each other, which students have behavior problems, and which students receive special assistance in areas such as math, reading, language, and speech. Principals might consider sending information home to explain the program to parents. If parent requests for placing children in specific classrooms are usually honored, it needs to be made clear (for reasons that will be explained later in this chapter) that placement into the classroom with a cluster of high-achieving students might not be possible.

STUDENT DATA CARDS: AN EXAMPLE FROM PRACTICE HIGHER ACHIEVING GROUPS AMONG STUDENTS

Participants at one site developed a Student Data Card based on these identification procedures, and they found the cards to work quite effectively. The teachers used the cards to record all the information pertinent to placement, and they brought the completed cards to a grade-level placement conference. A sample Student Data Card is depicted in Figure 2.1. This card can be adapted for use in other districts based on local information and placement considerations.

DEVELOPING A TEMPLATE

I have found through practical experience in many schools that developing a template of the number and identification category based on the total number of students for each grade helps to facilitate placement into classrooms during the placement conference. To develop the template, teachers bring their current class lists and identification cards to a meeting. One person then uses a chart, similar to the one depicted in Table 2.1, to gather the number of high-, above-average-, average-, low-average-, and low-achieving students for each teacher's current class. The group then sums these numbers to provide an overview of how many students of each achievement category exist within the entire grade and how many students are in the grade. Dividing the total number of students by the number of teachers for the following year determines the number of students to place in each teacher's classroom. Finally, using the actual numbers of students, a template specifying the number of students in each category can be developed and used to guide placement of the students in the classroom. In developing the template, follow these simple guidelines:

- place high-achieving students in one cluster and above-average students in other classrooms;
- reduce the ranges of achievement levels by not placing every level in each classroom;
- avoid placing low-achieving students in the classroom in the class with the high-achieving students (too wide of a range); and
- ensure each teacher has about the same number of students who achieve at average or above.

Student Data Summary Card

School Year _____

Name _____ Current Grade _____ Projected Grade _____

Gender: M   F   Race: _____

	Language Arts	Math	Science
State test			
NWEA			

Final Reading Grade: _____   Running Record A-Z: _____

Final Math Grade: _____

Identification Category (circle)

  High Achieving   Above Average   Average   Low Average   Low

Special Education (achievement level) _____

English Proficiency Level   1   2   3   4   5   N/A

Kingore Inventory Yes (include score) _____ No _____

Discipline Issues   Never   Seldom   Often

Attendance Issues Never   Seldom   Often

Other Comments _____

_____

_____

_____

FIGURE 2.1. SAMPLE DATA CARD USED BY ONE SCHOOL.

Developing and using this template will make the actual placement of students into classes move more swiftly and help teachers focus on the students rather than on how many students go in which classroom when they are developing the lists. If the template does not work because of the need to separate students, student/teacher personalities, or other reasons, it can easily be adjusted. See Table 2.2 for an example of how the data from Table 2.1 was used to create a placement template.

The sample template depicted in Table 2.2 provides some important considerations. First, note that each classroom contains about the same number of students who achieve at or above average. This is important, as it helps everyone

TABLE 2.1
SAMPLE GRADE LEVEL IDENTIFICATION DATA AND NUMBERS COLLECTED FROM THIS YEAR'S TEACHERS

	TOTAL	Classroom 1	Classroom 2	Classroom 3	Classroom 4	Classroom 5
High Achieving	12	2	3	1	4	2
Above-Average	25	5	5	5	5	5
Average	44	11	8	9	7	9
Low-Average	25	5	5	5	5	5
Low	11	1	2	4	1	3
Special Educ.	8	1	2	1	3	1
TOTAL	125	25	25	25	25	25

TABLE 2.2
PROPOSED GRADE-LEVEL PLACEMENT TEMPLATE FOR NEXT YEAR, BASED ON DATA COLLECTED IN TABLE 2.1

	TOTAL	Classroom 1	Classroom 2	Classroom 3	Classroom 4	Classroom 5
High Achieving	12	12	0	0	0	0
Above-Average	25	0	6	6	6	7
Average	44	5	10	10	10	9
Low-Average	25	7	9	9	0	0
Low	11	0	0	0	5	6
Special Educ.	8	1*	0	0	4	3
TOTAL	125	25	25	25	25	25

*Note. This student is twice exceptional, LD, and gifted.

see that no classroom is without high performers. Also notice that each teacher has fewer achievement groups in the cluster-grouped data than from the data in Table 2.1. Finally, special needs students are clustered in two rather than spread across five classrooms, with an exception of one twice-exceptional student placed in Classroom 1. This sample template provides an example of taking the total number of students from each identification category prior to the placement process and creating a plan for how to place the students during that process.

DEVELOPING CLASS LISTS

The information gathered in Step 1, Identification, is used to develop class lists for the following school year. This process usually involves teachers and other educators (e.g., specialists, administrators, coordinators, coaches) using the template numbers to place student cards in classroom groups. Teachers have used index cards or sticky notes with all the information on each student included, which enables them to easily move students among classes by placing the cards in classroom groups on a table or by sticking them to a wall or door until an ideal solution is reached by the grade-level team. Other teachers have computerized the information, and still other educators simply work from a printed class list. Whatever the method in developing class lists, the process is undertaken with the following goals:

1. Reduce the number of achievement groups that each teacher has in his or her classroom while still maintaining some heterogeneity.
2. Cluster the *high-achieving* students in one classroom (or more classrooms if there are a large number of classes per grade level or a large number of high-achieving students in a particular grade level).
3. Place a group of *above-average* students in every other teacher's classroom.
4. Cluster the students needing special services (if appropriate) in classrooms with resource personnel assistance.
5. Honor parental requests for specific teachers when possible and if this follows building or district policy.
6. Evenly distribute students with behavior problems among all classrooms so that no teacher has more than his or her fair share of difficult students.
7. Involve the teachers in developing the class lists.

Using these goals, the identification category information, and the template they developed, teachers work through the placement process to build ideal classrooms for next year's teachers. It is also possible to have an administrator, secretary, counselor, or coordinator use the information to develop the draft class lists and then review the draft lists with the current grade-level teachers to solicit their input. These draft lists will be changed based on teacher suggestions. During this placement conference, which can initially take an hour or two, the teachers (who know their colleagues and their students) either create or review the lists for appropriateness. Teachers should feel free to suggest and to make student placement changes. The only rule concerning moving students is that like-labeled students must be "traded" among the classrooms. For example, an average-achieving student from classroom A might be traded for an average-achieving student from classroom B to create better teacher–student fit, or to separate two students who should not be in the same classroom. An average-achieving student cannot be traded for an above-average achieving student or a student from any other category than average achieving. Once all the changes have been made, the class lists can be finalized.

I recommend using an asterisk to designate any students who are placed in a classroom for a specific reason. This asterisk denotes that these students may not be moved, and it will reduce the number of changes made to the lists after they have been "finalized." The asterisk captures the conversations that occur during the placement conference in a simple manner. It does not require explanation, but serves as a reminder that during the conference, there was a reason this student was placed in that classroom, and that he or she should not be moved. By using the asterisk system, when a request for change is made (usually to someone in the office), the person taking the request can quickly glance at the class lists and easily change unasterisked students of the same identification categories. If a request comes in for a change that would require moving a student denoted with an asterisk, I recommend that the school personnel tell the parent or guardian that making a change is not currently an option, but that it would be possible to revisit the request after 6–8 weeks of school. Usually, the student will acclimate to the class during that time period. If after 6–8 weeks of school the placement is not working for the student, a change should be considered.

The goals for developing the class lists can be met by using these procedures for placing students into classrooms each year. Tables 2.3–2.6 depict how the placement might look for a particular grade level in schools with two to five classrooms per grade level. If the number of classrooms exceeds five per grade level, then school personnel can consider designating two classrooms per grade level in which to place high-achieving students. In large schools of 10 or more classrooms per grade level, three or more high-achieving cluster classrooms might be needed. Please keep in mind that the number of high-achieving students will vary from year to year, as will the numbers of students in all achievement categories. Because one of the goals of the model is to increase the achievement of more students over time, and because the model uses a total school approach to identification and placement, any number of high-achieving students can be accommodated.

As students progress through the grade levels, and as teachers identify more students who begin to achieve at higher levels, it may be necessary to add additional classrooms to accommodate the increased numbers of high-achieving students. By grade 5 in one study school, teachers faced a decision about whether to have one self-contained classroom of high-achieving students or to have two classrooms with clusters of high-achieving students. Such a situation presents a positive problem in a school—what to do with all of the students who achieve at such high levels. In this school, the fifth-grade team of teachers discussed the situation and decided to have one teacher teach *all* of the high-achieving students, which created a self-contained class in the fifth grade. Had there been another fifth-grade teacher who wanted a cluster of high-achieving students, and who was qualified to teach them, they could have just as easily decided to create two cluster classrooms in grade 5. Each solution would have worked, and I recommend involving the teachers who will be responsible for the students in the decision-making process when these situations arise. Had there been another fifth-grade teacher who wanted a cluster of high-achieving students, creating a second classroom would have involved this teacher. I should note that the other four classrooms each had a large number of above-average students and a small number of low-achieving students, as student achievement had increased during the 3 program years.

As displayed in Tables 2.3–2.6, the range of ability levels has been significantly reduced from what one would likely find in a typical heterogeneous classroom that was computer generated, or in a classroom in which the students were distributed evenly in order to be "fair" to the teachers. The philosophy behind TSCG is that having a similar number of different types of students in classrooms is not fair, as it creates too wide a range of achievement levels for teachers to effectively meet the diverse needs of their individual students. TSCG creates a reduction in range of achievement levels for teachers, allowing for more focused and academically appropriate curricular approaches, and thus increasing the chances that individual students' academic needs will be met.

As noted in Tables 2.3–2.6, a cluster of students with learning disabilities is placed in one classroom, but assistance is provided to the classroom teacher. This manner of inclusion brings the special education teacher into the classroom, integrating him or her into the general education classroom. The students who receive special services are, in effect, clustered as well, and this affords them a peer group rather than singling them out as the only students in class who are different and who receive special services. In turn, the special education teacher is a master of differentiation and can help ensure that methods and materials are

TABLE 2.3
STUDENTS CLUSTERED INTO FIVE CLASSROOMS

ID Category	3rd Grade Classroom 1	3rd Grade Classroom 2	3rd Grade Classroom 3	3rd Grade Classroom 4	3rd Grade Classroom 5	3rd Grade Total Grade
High-Achieving	11	0	0	0	0	11
Above-Average	0	7	7	7	7	28
Average	10	10	10	10	10	50
Low-Average	3	4	8	8	0	23
Low	0	0	0	0	8	8
Sp. Educ.	1*	4**	0	0	0	5
Total	**25**	**25**	**25**	**25**	**25**	**125**

*Note. This student is Learning Disabled *and* Gifted.

**Note. These students see the same teacher consultant, who spends 4 half-days per week working in this classroom

TABLE 2.4
STUDENTS CLUSTERED INTO FOUR CLASSROOMS

ID Category	2nd Grade Classroom 1	2nd Grade Classroom 2	2nd Grade Classroom 3	2nd Grade Classroom 4	2nd Grade Total Grade
High-Achieving	8	0	0	0	8
Above-Average	0	7	7	7	21
Average	10	10	10	10	50
Low-Average	5	0	5	5	15
Low	0	8	0	3	11
Sp. Educ.	2*	0	3**	0	5
Total	**25**	**25**	**25**	**25**	**100**

*Note. These students are Learning Disabled *and* Gifted.

**Note. These students see the same teacher consultant, who also helps the classroom teacher.

appropriate for the varied achievement levels of the students. The decision to cluster special needs students is a local one.

It should be noted that each year presents a new continuum of student needs. Some years will seem "normal" in their distribution of students achieving at various levels (e.g., a few students at each end of the normal curve and most students near the center). But other years may present quite a different situation, such as those depicted in Tables 2.7 and 2.8. These tables contain actual data from a school in which the numbers of students achieving at the various achievement levels did not follow a normal distribution. The school depicted in Table 2.7 had an unusually high number of both high- and low-achieving students.

TABLE 2.5
STUDENTS CLUSTERED INTO THREE CLASSROOMS

ID Category	4th Grade Classroom 1	4th Grade Classroom 2	4th Grade Classroom 3	4th Grade Total Grade
High-Achieving	6	0	0	6
Above-Average	0	7	6	13
Average	10	10	10	30
Low-Average	8	0	6	14
Low	0	8	0	8
Sp. Educ.	1*	0	3**	4
Total	**25**	**25**	**25**	**75**

*Note. This student is twice-exceptional.
**Note. These students see the same teacher consultant, who also helps the classroom teacher.

TABLE 2.6
STUDENTS CLUSTERED INTO TWO CLASSROOMS

ID Category	5th Grade Classroom 1	5th Grade Classroom 2	5th Grade Total Grade
High-Achieving	6	0	6
Above-Average	0	7	7
Average	10	10	20
Low-Average	7	0	7
Low	0	6	6
Sp. Educ.*	2	2	4
Total	**25**	**25**	**50**

*Note. Placement of special education students will need to be done based on individual students' needs.

Teachers agreed at the placement conference to reduce the number of students in Classroom 5 to help this teacher attend to a large cluster of low-achieving students. The special education teacher worked beside the teacher in this classroom and helped her differentiate for the special education students. In addition, this teacher had full-time services from a Title 1 aide. Because she only had two achievement levels, she was able to provide differentiated services to both groups of children.

Table 2.8 shows an example of three first-grade classrooms. Due to the make-up of this grade level, each teacher's class had two achievement levels, rather than the more common range of five achievement levels. This made planning, teaching, and differentiation easier for these three teachers. First-grade teachers often choose to keep their own students rather than regrouping within

TABLE 2.7
STUDENTS CLUSTERED INTO FIVE CLASSROOMS IN AN ATYPICAL YEAR

ID Category	3rd Grade Classroom 1	3rd Grade Classroom 2	3rd Grade Classroom 3	3rd Grade Classroom 4	3rd Grade Classroom 5	3rd Grade Total Grade
High-Achieving	10	10	0	0	0	20
Above-Average	0	0	7	7	7	21
Average	0	8	8	8	0	24
Low-Average	16	0	0	9	0	24
Low	0	6	10	0	10	26
Sp. Educ.	0	2*	0	2	4**	10
Total	**26**	**26**	**26**	**26**	**21**	**125**

*Note. These students are Learning Disabled *and* Gifted.
**Note. These students are LD and see the same teacher consultant, who spends 4 half-days per week working in this classroom, the teacher consultant will work in the classroom with the teacher. Her class size has been reduced.

TABLE 2.8
STUDENTS CLUSTERED INTO THREE CLASSROOMS IN AN ATYPICAL YEAR

ID Category	1st Grade Classroom 1	1st Grade Classroom 2	1st Grade Classroom 3	1st Grade Total Grade
High-Achieving	6	0	0	6
Above-Average	0	5	5	10
Average	14	0	0	14
Low-Average	0	15	0	15
Low	0	0	15	15
Sp. Educ.	0	0	0	0
Total	**20**	**20**	**20**	**60**

the grade level with colleagues; however, they could still choose to work together. In this example, no children had been identified for special education services; hence their absence from the table.

Note that in these situations, some teachers only had two distinct achievement groups in their classrooms. My advice is to maintain flexibility and creativity to place students after assessing the numbers of students who achieve at the different levels in the entire grade. The unique aspect of the TSCG Model is that there are no preconceived notions about how many students can or must be identified as "gifted."

Admittedly, time and energy are involved in identifying students and developing class lists. The payoff occurs the following year, when each teacher can more effectively reach his or her students due to the decrease in the number of achievement levels in each classroom. Having fewer achievement levels leads to an environment in which teachers can efficiently use differentiation strategies discussed at length in Part II of this book.

A realistic timeline for identifying and making placements is depicted in Figure 2.2. Some districts set aside an afternoon for placement conferences, others hold these conferences after school or during a staff meeting, and still others have used common grade-level planning time. One school has teachers from all grade levels sit at tables in the cafeteria during a half-day work time. Such an arrangement facilitates discussion about students among the various grade levels. Despite taking more time than computer-generated class lists, I have found that teachers appreciate being involved in the process and developing placements for the coming school year.

PLACING NEW STUDENTS AFTER SCHOOL BEGINS

All schools receive new students at the beginning of the school year, and students enroll throughout the year. Because records often take several days—or even weeks—to reach new schools, resulting in an absence of information about the academic skills of a new student, I suggest conducting a quick assessment of reading and math skills when new students enroll. Educators can then place new students tentatively into classrooms until records arrive and student performance can be more fully assessed. Teachers should explain to parents or guardians that the initial classroom placement is temporary and that a permanent placement will be made within 2 or 3 weeks. In the majority of cases, the initial placement works just fine. In cases of extremely low or high achievement, a move might be necessary.

WHAT TO DO WITH KINDERGARTEN STUDENTS

Kindergarten is a special place, with the widest range of development, readiness, and skills of all the grades. Additionally, kindergarten students rapidly grow and change. I am frequently asked whether to use cluster grouping in kindergarten, because unlike the other students, achievement data often do not exist when they begin school. Depending on whether kindergarten is full-day or half-day and how teachers are assigned, it may be possible to implement a modified form of cluster grouping beginning in kindergarten. I suggest doing so with caution, focusing on clustering those students who come to school already reading. Clustering these students in one classroom gives them a peer group and allows the teacher to focus on their advanced needs. Assessments given to students before school begins may or may not yield accurate data concerning the students' readiness. Kindergartners grow and change so quickly, and as weeks pass the results may not reflect the students' true capabilities when they enter school in the fall. It is also possible that the examiner might intimidate some students taking the assessment, and these students may not perform to their potentials. For these reasons and more, I suggest assessing the students during the first 2 weeks of school and creating the high-achieving cluster after school begins. It is important to remain flexible, as some students who did not start school reading may learn it very quickly and need to work with those students who were initially clustered at the beginning of the year. By beginning clustering in kindergarten, the odds increase that kindergarten teachers will have more time to focus on the group of advanced students.

TEACHER SELECTION AND APPOINTMENT

One perceived challenge in the initial implementation of a Total School Cluster Grouping program might involve which teachers teach which classrooms of students. In examining schools that have implemented cluster grouping, I have recognized some basic "truths" concerning how to select and appoint teachers to teach the high-achieving (and other) cluster classrooms.

First, the teacher of the high-achieving classroom must want to work with these students, commit to differentiating curriculum, and provide these students with appropriately challenging curriculum and instruction. Second, this individual must commit to learning about how to work with these students through coursework, workshops, licensure, or degree programs. Third, if selected to teach this classroom, the appointment is not a lifetime appointment, but it will last for a minimum of 3 years. Three years provides the teacher with a first year to learn how to facilitate the high-achieving students, a second year to perfect it, and a third year to enjoy it. Of course, during those 3 years, if a teacher finds that this is not his strength or if someone leaves the position, another interested teacher can fill the position. At the end of 3 years, the appointment will be revisited in the context of the grade level, and consideration will be given to other teachers who have an interest in working with the high-achieving students. I recommend a rotating appointment to offer others the opportunity to teach the high-achieving students and to reduce the appearance of exclusivity of these appointments. However, change at the end of 3 years occurs only if another teacher wants the opportunity and commits to training.

In this model, if implemented as described, more students will likely be identified each year as talented; thus the demand for teachers to work with high-achieving students will increase over time. Further, districts that implement between-class grouping in math and/or reading will need more teachers who have the desire and skills to teach the high-achieving clusters, high-achieving math groups, and high-achieving reading groups. The high-achieving cluster teacher need not also teach both advanced math and advanced reading. In fact, by involving more than one teacher at each grade level in the delivery of advanced instruction and content, more teachers will develop skills in working with high-achieving students, and perceptions of one classroom as the advanced class are diminished.

I suggest setting some parameters and application processes for initially designating teachers who will teach the high-achieving cluster classrooms. Parameters would include knowledge and background, experience and skills, and willingness to engage in additional educational training concerning gifted child education. One district used the simple application depicted in Figure 2.3 to document interest by teachers in teaching this cluster classroom.

The interview protocol we use in our student programs at Purdue University might be helpful in selecting the appropriate teachers (see Appendix A: Interview Protocol), and it is tied to an observation protocol useful in evaluating teachers' effectiveness in working with gifted students (see Appendix B: Teacher Observation Form). We have tested and used this protocol to hire high-quality teachers for our Saturday and summer enrichment programs for many years, and because we also use the Teacher Observation Form as an evaluation tool, the interview and position expectations are aligned with the evaluation observations. I have included both of these instruments in the appendices and encourage you to use them.

I also suggest that grade-level teachers sit together and openly discuss who is interested in teaching this classroom. Often the grade-level educators, working

---

Name:

Detail your experience working with high-achieving students.

List relevant education and background in working with high-achieving students (include coursework, workshops, conferences, degrees, certifications, etc.).

Grade levels you are willing to teach: K 1 2 3 4 5 6

Are you willing to wait 3 years for this appointment? Yes No

If yes, during that time, what actions would you take to increase your knowledge in this area?

Explain why teaching this group of students interests you.

FIGURE 2.3. SAMPLE TEACHER APPLICATION.

---

together, can and will make the designation. If they do, such a discussion can avoid the appearance of special treatment or questions surrounding the process of who was selected and why he or she was chosen to teach this class. Buy-in to the classroom assignment by one's colleagues increases the chances for success and reduces misperceptions and jealousy. Further, once a teacher has a classroom with a cluster of high-achieving students, I recommend that grade-level teachers meet on a regular basis to discuss and plan together. I also recommend that that teacher be candid with her colleagues about exactly how hard she works to keep up with the high-achieving students. Occasionally, perceptions might exist that somehow the high-achieving students are easy and well-behaved. However, these perceptions are far from the truth. It would be a mistake for the teacher of the high-achieving cluster to give the impression that she has all the great kids and is having a delightful year when in fact she is working harder than ever before.

Ideally, some teachers on staff will have certification, licensure, *and* experience in working with gifted or high-achieving students. In reality, this is often not the case. In selecting educators to teach the high achievers, the first criterion needs to be willingness to engage with these students, followed closely by a willingness to obtain expertise about working with them. If licensure or certification exists in the state, then the teacher should be given a window of time in which to obtain it.

Obtaining expertise need not be dictated simply by what exists in a geographic region, although many areas around the country have on-campus degree or licensure programs in gifted education and talent development. Additionally,

Purdue University offers a certificate in gifted, creative, and talented studies, which requires a series of four three-credit online courses at a reasonable in-state tuition rate, as well as a campus-based master's degree (see http://www.purdue.edu/geri). The Gifted Education Resource Institute at Purdue University also offers professional development modules for subscription. These modules, when completed, result in certificates of completion and documentation of hours spent completing the work. They are centered on the TSCG Model, differentiation, social and emotional needs, and specific content areas. The University of Connecticut offers a master's degree in gifted education online (http://www.gifted.uconn.edu). Most states offer state conferences in the area of gifted education, and several top-quality summer institutes that provide in-depth study in gifted education exist. These include the University of Connecticut's Confratute (http://www.gifted.uconn.edu), Minnesota's Hormel Gifted and Talented Education Symposium (http://www.austin.k12.mn.us/educationalservices/GTsymposium/Default.aspx), and Boise State University's Edufest (http://www.edufest.org). A current listing of gifted education conferences is maintained at http://www.hoagiesgifted.org/conferences.htm.

Each district should discuss and set criteria for these positions collaboratively with their grade-level teachers. If more teachers want to teach high-achieving clusters than these classrooms exist, we suggest encouraging expertise attainment by all of those teachers interested in teaching high-achieving students. Ultimately, the general education program will benefit, and a 3-year cycle can be developed. As the model continues over the course of several years, the need for additional cluster teachers will increase, and qualified teachers will become available.

Occasionally, the opposite problem exists, one in which no teachers want to teach the high-achieving students. If this is the case, the administrator should speak individually to each teacher at that grade level to determine reasons for the lack of interest. Teachers may fear jealousy from colleagues, they may feel unqualified, or they may be afraid of trying something new. Often someone really does want to take on the challenge, but may not want to say so in front of the group. If this is the case, then the administrator can "appoint" the teacher to teach this class and allay any fears the teacher may have about the position. If, on the other hand, no one wants to teach these children, then it might be possible to reassign a teacher from another grade level. However, if teachers from other grade levels feel the same way, then this administrator needs to do more work to create buy-in before attempting the model. Perhaps taking a year in which staff would read and discuss this book and other articles together would offer time for discussion, problem solving, and ultimately encourage buy-in.

IMPLEMENTATION CONSIDERATIONS

As with any educational program, a model is only as strong as its theoretical underpinnings, research basis, and the people who implement it. This statement holds true for Total School Cluster Grouping. In order for this model to succeed, it requires knowledge of the students for whom the model is provided, a willingness to collaborate, and continuous, responsive professional development. The rationale, research, and goals have been outlined and serve as the conceptual basis for developing a site-specific application of Total School Cluster Grouping. The implemented model should reflect the community and cultures of the school in which it is developed. As Renzulli (1986) described, common goals and unique means provide a solid foundation for a successful model.

THE ROLES OF THE TEACHERS

TSCG demands that various things take place in a classroom simultaneously. The role of the teacher expands to include facilitation, mediation, implementation, and inspiration. Methods and means for meeting these challenges are detailed in Part II of this book. For the greatest successes with the students in these classrooms, there must be a positive environment and high, yet realistic, teacher expectations (Gentry, 1999):

> The cluster teachers plan activities of a progressively challenging nature. These learning activities may be considered "instead of" rather than "in addition to" the regular curriculum. We suggest to teachers that it can be interpreted as not "more of the same" but something "instead." For example, instead of answering a number of low-level comprehension questions at the end of a story, the student may be asked to describe the story's theme and analyze how it could apply to his/her own life. In another situation, cluster teachers may pretest their students on the content of the math unit to be covered during the next 2 weeks. Students who demonstrate mastery of that content on the pretest might then be directed toward an independent research study facilitated by a teacher. In some classrooms the teacher may design a lesson with sufficient depth and breadth to challenge all of

his/her students. In some cases students might be accelerated through a portion of the curriculum. In other situations, teachers may decide to provide an enrichment unit that extends the learning into higher levels and newer horizons. These strategies may be used in any subject area with just the cluster students, a mixture of cluster students and other students, or the whole class. The plans may be shared with other teachers (Gentry & Keilty, 2004, p. 154).

It can be realistically said that any educational model is only as strong as the teacher who implements it. When teachers practice the following elements of practice, cluster grouping can yield impressive results.

1. **Foster and maintain a positive classroom environment.** Kids are observant beings. If teachers do not orchestrate a positive classroom environment from the start, students may recognize each other only for their different abilities, instead of focusing on strengths and interests. When teachers work to adjust assignments, help students achieve success, and create classrooms where students want to be, positive results are likely (Gentry, 1999). Facilitating acceptance and understanding among classroom members creates a positive learning community in which risk taking is safe.

2. **Possess high, yet realistic, expectations of all students.** Students perform based on the expectations of those around them. Teachers' expectations have profound influence on student performance. Therefore, by teachers maintaining high yet realistic expectations, students are more likely to reach their full potential. A focus on both long-term process and incremental success along the way not only helps to encourage students, but also provides them with an inherent sense of progress that is likely to stay with them beyond that specific classroom experience.

3. **Implement strategies to challenge students and meet students' needs in the cluster-grouped classroom.** What is good for gifted students may benefit other students. However, the reverse does not necessarily hold true. It is imperative that educators use foundational strategies that have proven successful in challenging gifted students. A wealth of research exists regarding strategies that work for this population, and these strategies should be fully

integrated within cluster grouping programs. Part II of this book explores in depth appropriate and effective differentiation strategies.

4. **Participate in ongoing professional development opportunities.** There is always more to be learned concerning good classroom practices and curricular development, regardless of level of experience in education. Professional development can come in a variety of forms, from a more formal in-service program to regularly scheduled, focused conversations between colleagues. The regularity of such self-advancement is an essential piece in meeting the needs of all of learners. Professional development is discussed in detail in Chapter 3.

THE ROLE OF ADMINISTRATORS

Strong administrative support is essential for effective implementation. The identification process alone will require time outside of class for teachers to identify and assign students to classrooms. With administrative support, this time can be made available. Administrators also play a key role in that this model affects the entire grade level and school. Unlike pull-out or self-contained gifted programs, which focus only on the identified gifted students, TSCG involves the placement and concern for students of all achievement levels. Without the leadership and support of the school's administrative team, from the school counselor to the principal, TSCG cannot be successfully implemented.

Administrators work closely with the public, and they should consider the role of parents in the support of this model. I suggest that parents be a part of the planning committee to help facilitate communication and understanding of the model and how it will help teachers better meet the needs of students of all achievement levels. Some districts have developed a pamphlet that they send home to families (see Figure 2.4), others hold meetings, and still others answer parent questions as they arise. The administrator, working with her staff, can determine what will be most appropriate in the context of the school and community.

What about other clusters besides high achieving?

By adopting the cluster model for elementary classroom assignment, the needs of all groups of students are taken into account.

Students in classrooms that do not have high achievers included will benefit because they will not be overshadowed, perhaps, by the high-achieving students. In that way, other students can find that they, too, can achieve at higher levels.

The methods of addressing the needs of all students will be the same—differentiating of instruction and assessment in order to meet the needs of everyone.

Teachers will be able to differentiate more effectively with fewer skill levels in the same classroom, and all students will benefit. This model maximizes learning for all students.

If I continue to have questions, where do I go?

The building principal of the school your child attends is in the best position to answer any questions you might have.

Converse Elementary: Valree Kinch, Principal 395-
Sweetser Elementary: Mike Keaffaber, Principal 385-
Awayzee Elementary: Terry Renberger, Principal 922-

Oak Hill United School Corporation

An Explanation of the Total School Cluster Grouping Model to Determine Classroom Assignment

---

Outside pages (1 and 4) of brochure

The Model
A group of parents, teachers, and administrators was formed in 2005 to study the issue of providing focused services for high-achieving students.

As a result of that study and the assistance of professionals in the field, the "cluster grouping" model was selected as the preferred method of differentiating instruction and serving students at the elementary level in the Oak Hill United School Corporation.

Benefits of Total School Cluster Grouping

- Research shows that cluster grouping improves student achievement among students from all achievement levels.
- This model allows students with similar academic needs to work together during part of every day.
- Clustering provides teachers with structure for adjusting the curriculum and instruction to the achievement and skill level of the child.
- This tool allows teachers to serve all students effectively and differentiate instruction to meet the needs of all students.
- This model maximizes learning for all students.

How are students placed in a cluster?
All students are identified for small-group instruction in a cluster group. Results from several grade-level-appropriate assessments such as NWEA, ISTEP, DIBELS, STAR Math, and teacher recommendations all play a role in this determination, as well as the special needs of individual students.

Will students stay in the same cluster throughout their elementary experience?
While cluster groups are generally sWW, the assessment of students is an ongoing part of providing the best educational experience. These groups are flexible enough to allows changes as needed to better meet the needs of the student. Reevaluation of all students is done annually.

How will instruction be differentiated for students who have demonstrated that they are ready to handle much more challenging work?
Most students at a particular grade level fall within a fairly narrow range around what most professionals would define as grade-level skills. This will vary within the content area, the skill, and the student. Some students enter a grade level already having mastered many of the skills typically taught at that grade. Those high-achieving students need additional challenge.

Instruction for students in the high-achieving cluster in grades 1 and 2 will focus primarily on mathematics and literacy development. In grades 3–5, students will have more opportunities to integrate and apply skills in the content areas of science and social studies as well. In grade 6, expectations for students in this cluster will be defined by the content areas of mathematics, science, reading, writing, and social studies.

An annual plan for mathematics instruction for this group of learners will be determined through the use of a thorough preassessment of skills already mastered. Once the grade-level skills yet to be mastered have been identified, students will move through the work at a faster pace. They will then study skills that are outlined in the Indiana Standards for the next grade level, using above-grade-level materials. In addition, students will be challenged to solve more complex, difficult problems and will be pushed to develop higher level thinking skills. These students will progress through above-level materials as time allows, but will not necessarily be expected to master all of the standards at the next grade level.

In the areas of language arts, science, and social studies, additional challenges will be provided through project selection, the choices offered to the students, and the materials used for instruction. These students will also be expected to read and discuss more advanced literature. Curriculum for this group will be extended to develop the depth of understanding of a topic or theme in keeping with the students' strengths and capabilities.

Inside pages (2 and 3) of brochure

FIGURE 2.4. SAMPLE PAMPHLET.

THE ROLE OF DATA COLLECTION

Districts that take the time, effort, and energy to implement a TSCG Model should not do so without a plan to evaluate the effects and efficacy of the program. Developing such a plan is discussed in detail in Chapter 5. Here I discuss the need to maintain data related to cluster grouping to enable you to conduct meaningful program evaluation. In this era of accountability, all school districts gather data throughout the year and annually, so data collection need not be additional, as existing data can be used. To fully understand the program effects on all students, data from all students, not just those identified as high achieving, must be examined. I recommend maintaining records of identification categories to help understand if the program results in more students being identified as achieving at higher levels and fewer students being identified at lower levels. This data point will be lost unless you make the effort to enter it into the student data file. Because one of the goals of TSCG is to improve the representation of typically underserved students as high achieving, it is important to keep track of the yearly identification categories so that you can examine changes over time for different groups of students. This is as simple as setting up an Excel workbook of students and their identification categories over time, or adding a column or field to the district database on each student, if such a database exists. The identification data coupled with individual student achievement scores can provide an informative picture of how the program functions. Comparing these data with baseline data or data from a school in the district not using cluster grouping can provide more insights into the actual effects of cluster grouping. Identification data and achievement data examined together with classroom practices and school climate data can provide a comprehensive program evaluation from which adjustments and improvements can be made.

Meeting with staff to discuss what works and what needs to be improved and soliciting their written suggestions can be a valuable source of data resulting in program improvements. For example, in our study school, teachers suggested clustering the students with learning disabilities and team-teaching, which turned out to be an effective addition to the program that allowed colleagues to work together to address the special needs of these students.

UNDERREPRESENTED GROUPS IN THE HIGH ACHIEVING CATEGORY

Another important consideration involves whether the students identified as high achieving proportionally represent the demographic student population of the district and school in which the program exists. The field of gifted education is plagued by the underidentification of children from certain minority groups (i.e., African American, Latino/a, Native American) and of children living in poverty (Gentry & Fugate, 2012; Yoon & Gentry, 2009). Such underidentification is not acceptable; however, in this model it is easily dealt with, as no limits are placed on how many children can be "identified." In other, more exclusive models with limits on the number of seats in the gifted program, identifying a child from poverty who has potential might result in services denied to another child who already achieves at high levels. In Total School Cluster Grouping, both of these children can be identified *and* receive services. An examination of who is identified at the beginning of program development (as a baseline) will provide valuable information concerning the equity of access to programming efforts. Over time, as they develop skills and confidence, more children should be identified as high achieving. The proportion of children from diverse cultural backgrounds and children from poverty should increase and mirror the population of the school as a whole. If the program does not develop in this manner, then school personnel should intervene, include children who show potential in the high-achieving clusters, and provide these children with the extra support they need to reach their individual potentials.

REACHING OUT TO PARENTS

In our work with this program during the past two decades, we have found that educators are often worried about how to explain this model to parents. First, let us say that concerned parents are an asset and not a liability. Schools often have as a goal to increase parent involvement, yet educators may seem uncomfortable when parents question practices. Often the questions parents ask can serve to increase accountability and educational quality. Parents can become strong advocates for effective programs like Total School Cluster Grouping if they are provided with information about the program. Total School Cluster Grouping is a program that has relevant theory, promising research, and effective practices as its cornerstones. Thus, developing brochures and presentations that explain the program to parents is a very good idea.

I have found in my work that the best approach in dealing with parents is one of open and honest communication. I have also found that several questions commonly arise. First, parents want to understand how (and why) students are identified for placement in particular classrooms. School personnel should begin by explaining that *all* classroom teachers differentiate curriculum and instruction, and that the Total School Cluster Grouping Model enables *all* teachers to better address the educational and affective needs of *all* their students. Program leaders can explain the achievement categories to parents similarly to how they explain them to teachers, but without the educational jargon. Stress that the categories:

- are not fixed,
- are used for placement purposes,
- reflect children's achievement in school at that time and relative to others in the same grade, and
- are a combination of observed performance and achievement measures that are used to include, not exclude, students in achievement groups.

Next, they can explain that students will be grouped for instruction based on skill levels in reading and math to promote optimal learning and growth. If the school supports regrouping among classes within the grade, parents will want to know about that practice as well. Program leaders should describe how all classrooms will have students who achieve at above-average levels, and explain how this arrangement and regrouping by skill level promotes academic growth for all levels of students. School personnel should ensure that parents understand that students will be reidentified each year and that the number of students who can be identified at high-achieving levels is not limited. In addition, many parents like to hear about accountability; therefore, program leaders should be sure to stress the research findings on the model and the school's plan for tracking program effects.

Second, sometimes issues arise concerning parents requesting placement in the classroom that has been designated as the one for the high-achieving students. This presents a problem only when the student for whom the placement is requested achieves at an above-average level and the parents are requesting placement in the high-achieving cluster classroom. In this model, it is important to place above-average achieving students into *other* classrooms (i.e., not in the high-achieving classroom). When the high-achieving students are separated from the above-average students, the above-average students are given an opportunity to shine within their own classrooms. When such requests occur, we suggest that school personnel explain to parents how their son or daughter's achievement level compares with other students who will be in the cluster of high-achieving students. Even though their child has been identified as above-average, he or she will likely fall at the bottom of the high achievers. A year of being in another classroom among his or her academic peers may contribute to academic growth and boost academic self-confidence. In fact, the child may be among the top students in the class. School personnel can remind parents that differentiation will occur in every classroom and all students will be challenged. In addition, students will be reidentified each year for appropriate placement. Finally, if the parent is not satisfied, school personnel can schedule another meeting after 6 weeks to assess whether the student is thriving in his or her placement. We have found that after about 6 weeks, most students, and thus most parents, are happy with their classroom experience. But, if after 6 weeks the placement does not appear to appropriately address the child's needs, then a move should be considered.

Third, issues can arise when perceptions exist that all of the quality educational experiences occur in the classroom with the cluster of high-achieving students. These issues and questions underscore the need for quality in all classrooms. For a successful implementation of this model, all classroom teachers must offer students appropriately challenging and engaging learning experiences and proudly display the results of those experiences. All classroom teachers should employ differentiation strategies and engage in gifted education pedagogy. All classroom teachers must have high expectations of their students. A trip down the hall in an effectively cluster-grouped school should reveal few differences among classrooms to the casual observer. In other words, all classrooms should be enriched, and all students should be engaged in projects and learning experiences that address their interests and talents. Such engagement will help promote achievement among all students in the school. These strategies are addressed in Part II of this book. Conversely, if the only place that enrichment, field trips, independent study, and interest-based learning occurs is the classroom with the high-achieving students, then parents would have every right to be concerned.

Finally, once students are in the cluster-grouped classrooms, sometimes parents raise concerns about the work being too hard or their children experiencing frustration. This initial bump in the road is a normal occurrence. Teachers should emphasize that it presents an opportunity for students to learn to work hard and rise to meet challenging curriculum. It is much better for students to be challenged and receive marks below 100% than for them to move through school obtaining great grades with little effort (Robinson et al., 2002).

FIDELITY CHECKS FOR IMPLEMENTATION

The identification and placement of students is an important and time-consuming task. Likewise, assigning teachers to classes is vitally important to program success and buy-in. However, it is what occurs after placing students in and assigning teachers to particular classes that really makes the model successful. Early in the model implementation process, we want teachers to become comfortable, experience the identification and placement process, and enjoy working more deeply with students less varied in ability than previous years' classes. Later in implementation, we expect to see nuanced practices and refinement of the model based on the context of the school and its teachers and students. A few fidelity checks along the way serve to provide direction for implementation. In the first 2 years of implementation, the following should be achieved:

1. All homeroom classes contain children who achieve at above-average levels.
2. High-achieving and above-average children are not in same homeroom.
3. Teachers are actively involved in class list development.
4. Asterisks are used to capture placement conference conversations, designating students who should not be moved to a different classroom.
5. Even distribution of students with frequent/severe behavioral problems exists.

In years 3–5 of implementation, the following should occur:
1. Every teacher uses gifted education practices.
2. Differentiation is made easier with grouping.
3. Regrouping can occur among classes and grade levels.
4. Test scores for inclusion only (move students up but not down) in designating yearly identification categories during yearly identification.
5. No language about "low" or "high" classes exists, as each room is a cluster room with enriched learning opportunities.

Ultimately, after 5 years of programming, a casual observer walking down the hall should not be able to identify which class contains the highest achieving students, as every classroom should appear to be a gifted education classroom.

CHAPTER **3**

DEVELOPING A PROFESSIONAL LEARNING PLAN TO SUPPORT TSCG IMPLEMENTATION

Supporting Teachers and Educating the Community*

The adoption of Total School Cluster Grouping may require a cultural shift among school staff and the community of stakeholders supporting the school. This change will not happen automatically. One only has to look at the mission statements posted in nearly every school across the country and compare them to the contrary practices within the school to realize that the best-laid plans for cultural change are not likely to matter without planning, dialogue, and buy-in from the school community (Fullan, 2004; Senge, 1991). Educational initiatives

---

*   The author cowrote this chapter with Kristina Ayers Paul.

usually take 3–5 years to be implemented at a high level (Hall & Hord, 2001), and a variety of professional learning activities will be needed to support the shifts in attitude, knowledge, and skill that will be necessary for successful TSCG adoption. This chapter will address the different types of professional learning topics and approaches that can support this change with the school community. We will discuss research-based components for providing effective professional learning opportunities, the different types of learning needs that staff will have during TSCG adoption and implementation, and ways of building differentiated learning experiences for teachers.

KEYS TO DESIGNING EFFECTIVE PROFESSIONAL DEVELOPMENT EXPERIENCES

Even though in-service training days and one-time workshops are the default mode of professional development in many schools, research and practical wisdom tell us that these are not necessarily the most effective formats for facilitating professional learning. In *Powerful Designs for Professional Learning* (Easton, 2008), 19 formats for professional development are described in detail and serve as alternatives to the one-time workshop. Although there is a time and place for informational sessions presented in the workshop format, other methods of delivering professional development are better aligned with the research-based elements of effective professional development, which are: a) intensive, sustained experiences connected to practice, b) meaningful content focused on specific academic content, c) coherence with other school initiatives, and d) opportunities for collaboration with other teachers (Darling-Hammond, Wei, Andree, Richardson, & Orphanos, 2009). From research we also know that professional development is most directly related to positive student achievement outcomes when it is intensive and sustained over time (Garet, Porter, Desimone, Birman, & Yoon, 2001). Therefore, a few days of in-service training at the beginning of TSCG adoption will not suffice. The ideas and suggestions that we provide in this chapter incorporate these research-based effective practices and are rooted in our own experiences implementing and researching the Total School Cluster Grouping Model in many different schools with real students and their teachers (Gentry, 1999; Gentry & Keilty, 2004).

STAGES OF PROFESSIONAL DEVELOPMENT TO SUPPORT TOTAL SCHOOL CLUSTER GROUPING

An essential component of successful TSCG is delivering an effective, sustained program of professional development to support the teachers involved in the program. Each stage of TSCG adoption requires a different set of training topics and formats. Furthermore, educators will bring various levels of knowledge, skills, and attitudes to the table, thus prompting the need for a carefully planned program of differentiated professional development that will support team members at different stages and of different levels of readiness as they work to adopt the TSCG model. In this section, we describe different types of professional development experiences that will be needed at various stages of TSCG implementation. A description of each type is provided below, and Table 9 provides examples of specific topics and delivery ideas to complement the narrative of this chapter.

SETTING THE STAGE FOR ADOPTION

In Gentry and Keilty's (2004) investigation of professional development opportunities offered in schools implementing cluster grouping, one of the key findings was that initial discussions to develop vision and buy-in among staff were vital to successful TSCG implementation. Teachers and community members may have emotionally charged opinions of grouping. As discussed in Chapter 1, the history of the tracking movement has led many to form strong opinions against any form of grouping, although research supports the appropriate use of grouping such as in the Total School Cluster Grouping model. It will be important that the school team engage in open and honest dialogue about existing ideas about grouping and discuss research regarding the use of TSCG as an effective strategy for meeting the needs of high-ability students while at the same time increasing achievement among all student groups. Research that supports the appropriate use of the TSCG Model as outlined in Chapter 1 and found on the TSCG website (http://www.purduegeri.org) will aid in these discussions.

PLANNING FOR ADOPTION

There are several ways that teachers will need support in getting started with the Total School Cluster Grouping Model. The most obvious needs that teachers will have are information needs—the *why*, *what*, *where*, and *how* of the model. The entire school staff will need to learn about what the TSCG model is, how

TABLE 3.1
ANTICIPATED PROFESSIONAL LEARNING NEEDS AND SUGGESTED PROFESSIONAL
DEVELOPMENT FORMATS FOR EACH STAGE OF PROGRAM IMPLEMENTATION.

Stage of Implementation	Anticipated Professional Learning Needs	Possible Learning Formats
Setting the Stage for Adoption	Knowledge of the philosophy and structure of the TSCG Model	**Book study** – Educators independently read the first two chapters of this book and meet regularly for discussion. Facilitators of the book study provide focus questions for reflection and discussion. **Workshop presentation** – Consultant or staff member knowledgeable in TSCG presents an interactive workshop that builds teachers knowledge of the philosophy and structure of the model. **Online Professional Development Module** – Teachers participate in Unit 8: Total School Cluster Grouping of Gifted Education Resource Institute's Online Professional Development Program, *Developing Student Strengths and Talents*.
	Opportunity to consider/reconcile personal philosophies in relationship to TSCG Model	**Examining data** – Facilitators gather survey data from educators to gauge where team members stand philosophically. Facilitators present data to educators to consider and discuss in light of TSCG model adoption.
Planning for Adoption	TSCG - nuts and bolts of model adoption	**Planning/Work Sessions** – Facilitators present information about how the TSCG model operates and what work will need accomplished to get started. Educators actively contribute to the planning work during this designated time. Training materials to use when explaining the nuts and bolts of TSCG are provided on the Gifted Education Resource Institute's Total School Cluster Grouping Website.
	Menu of training opportunities to match educators' individualized needs.	**Training workshops** – Facilitators present basic training in curriculum compacting, differentiated instruction, and the enrichment triad model. Facilitators acknowledge that educators, like students, have different levels of pre-existing knowledge and skill regarding these topics. Facilitators use pre-assessments to determine if educators can be compacted out of basic training workshops. **Online Professional Development Modules:** Teachers participate in online professional development modules focused on the nature and needs of gifted, creative, and talented youth, differentiation, curriculum compacting, and other topics related to TSCG. The modules are available through Purdue University's Gifted Education Resource Institute. See http://www.geri.education.purdue.edu.

TABLE 3.1 CONTINUED

Stage of Implementation	Anticipated Professional Learning Needs	Possible Learning Formats
Early implementation	Menu of training opportunities to match educators' individualized needs. Topics may include: 1. integrating higher order thinking skills; 2. developing critical thinking, teaching students to use creative thinking skills and think divergently; 3. integrating problem solving; 4. assigning long-term and high-level projects; 5. using acceleration; 6. adjusting assignments based on student skills; 7. grouping students so they could spend time with like-ability peers; 8. developing and implementing curricular extensions to challenge their students; 9. providing students with choices of partners or groups; 10. providing students with choices to work alone or together; 11. using open-ended questioning; 12. offering students independent study options; 13. using challenging questions; 14. implementing Curriculum Compacting (Reis, Burns, & Renzulli, 1992); 15. providing students choices of problems and assignments; 16. providing enrichment experiences to students; and 17. having high expectations for student achievement.	**Needs assessment:** Facilitators conduct a needs assessment to identify groups of teachers who have different learning needs regarding instructional strategies that correspond with TSCG implementation. As a result of the needs assessment, a menu of learning opportunities are planned. The Classroom Practices Survey, available on the Gifted Education Resource Institute's Total School Cluster Grouping website, may be of assistance in this process. **Personalized learning plans:** Individual educators review the results of their own needs assessment, review the menu of planned learning opportunities, and develop a personalized plan for obtaining the knowledge and skills they need to be an effective adopter of the TSCG model. **Workshop series with tuning protocols:** Facilitators coordinate a series of two or more active-learning workshops in which the following occurs: ◆ Workshop 1: Information and examples are provided, and time is given to educators to think through how the information can be applied in their own practice. Teachers return to the classroom and implement the new strategy. ◆ Workshop 2+: Teachers return to subsequent workshops in the series to discuss their experiences implementing the new strategy. A tuning protocol can be used to structure the conversations and maximize the productivity of conversations. See Allen and Blythe (2004) and McDonald, Mohr, Dichter, and McDonald (2007) for in-depth information about the use of tuning protocols to structure conversations about teachers' experiences in the classroom. **Professional learning communities:** Small groups of educators meet on a regular basis to develop professional learning goals and work together to learn and apply strategies of interest. **Coaching:** An educator who is experienced and skilled in differentiated instructional techniques is designated as a part-time or full-time coach to meet with teachers, observe and offer constructive feedback, and provide a safe place for teachers to learn and grow in a one-on-one environment without fear of formal evaluation. **Drop-in troubleshooting sessions:** The facilitator advertises a once-per-week drop-in troubleshooting session before or after school when teachers can stop by and informally ask for advice and recommendations for challenges they are facing in implementing the TSCG model in their classrooms.

TABLE 3.1 CONTINUED

Stage of Implementation	Anticipated Professional Learning Needs	Possible Learning Formats
Advanced Implementation	Menu of training opportunities to match educators' individualized needs.	In addition to the strategies suggested for the early implementation stage, the following advanced professional learning formats are also suggested as possible formats appropriate during advanced implementation of TSCG. **Lesson study** – Educators examine the learning process that results from a specific instructional strategy by observing and analyzing the components of lessons. Educators in the lesson study group engage in a formalized peer observation, feedback, and debriefing process to learn from one another's experiences and work toward mutual improvement of specific instructional skills. **Mentoring** – Educators who show advanced skill with implementing specific instructional techniques are partnered with other educators who are novices with the technique and express an interest in learning through a mentoring relationship. The mentoring relationship is less formal than a coaching relationship in that the mentor is there to serve as a resource and source of advice rather than a one-on-one coach with a specific plan for facilitating improvement. **Independent study using professional trade materials** – Teachers with advanced skills and confidence access professional trade materials that are provided through the TSCG resource library. This library includes books and professional journals such as those recommended in Appendix B. **Online professional learning and networking** – Teachers actively participate in online professional learning and networking to enhance their knowledge of information and resources related to TSCG. Recommendations for appropriate online professional learning and networking outlets include: ◆ The Gifted Education Resource Institute's Professional Development Modules from Purdue University: http://www.geri.education.purdue.edu ◆ Total School Cluster Grouping Facebook Group ◆ Twitter Conversations at #GTChat ◆ LinkedIn Groups: National Association for Gifted Children and the World Council for Gifted and Talented Children ◆ The Teaching Channel: http://www.teachingchannel.org ◆ Edmodo Communities: http://www.edmodo.com
Ongoing orientation for new faculty	Knowledge of philosophy and structure of the TSCG Model	**Mentoring** – New educators independently read the first two chapters of this book and meet with their assigned mentor for discussion. Program facilitators provide focus questions for reflection and discussion. **Online Professional Development Modules:** New educators participate in the Total School Cluster Grouping online professional development available through Purdue University's Gifted Education Resource Institute. See http://www.geri.education.purdue.edu.
	Menu of training opportunities to match educators' individualized needs	**Personalized learning plans** – Individual educators complete a personal needs assessment, review the menu of planned and self-directed learning opportunities, and develop a personalized plan for obtaining the knowledge and skills they need to be an effective adopter of the TSCG model.

it operates, and how each classroom will be affected. Gentry & Keilty (2004) found that, during this stage of the staff development, it was important to partner the nuts and bolts topics with research supporting TSCG and effectiveness of the practices incorporated in the TSCG model.

First, the entire staff needs an introduction to Total School Cluster Grouping. The Gifted Education Resource Institute's Total School Cluster Grouping Research website (http://www.purduegeri.org) includes a resource page with a slideshow presentation keyed to the content of this book. These presentations are designed to be used in a staff meeting and to stimulate further exploration and discussion of the model by staff.

Sometimes it is necessary to hire a professional consultant or expert in the model, enroll in online training, or send a team to a workshop to develop understanding and buy-in of the model. Likewise, it is possible to develop the understanding and buy-in by presenting the model to staff, engaging them in reading, discussion, and planning, to implement the model. However, it is important to recognize that understanding the model, identifying students, and placing them in classes represents only the beginning step of effective implementation.

In addition to the *why, what, where, and how* of the TSCG Model, we highly recommend that all teachers in the school be provided with a general overview of gifted education and talent development, as we did in the TSCG Model studies (Gentry, 1999; Gentry & Keilty, 2004). Several teachers in our study explained how valuable the staff development in gifted education had been for them.

We recommend that teachers be introduced to the three-ring conception of giftedness (Renzulli, 1978) and the Enrichment Triad Model (Renzulli, 1977; Renzulli & Reis, 1997) because the work of Renzulli and Reis fits seamlessly with the model. These topics are described below, and those interested in more in-depth information can visit http://www.gifted.uconn.edu.

In his three-ring conception of giftedness, Renzulli (1978) proposed giftedness as a behavior that results from the interaction of three traits: above-average ability, task commitment, and creativity. When the three traits interact and are brought to bear upon a specific human endeavor such as, for example, science, fine arts, or public service, gifted behavior occurs. Renzulli believes that gifted behaviors can be developed in students who are given appropriate opportunities, resources, and encouragement to develop their strengths and interests.

Renzulli proposed the Enrichment Triad Model (Renzulli, 1977; Renzulli & Reis, 1997) as a means for developing talent in more students than those who are traditionally identified for gifted programs. In this model, three types of enrichment activities are provided for students, and there is an interaction among these types of enrichment, with each leading to and reinforcing the others. Type I Enrichment consists of exploratory activities designed to expose students to a variety of topics and areas of study not ordinarily covered in the regular curriculum. Type II Enrichment consists of group training in thinking and feeling processes; learning-how-to-learn skills; research and reference skills; and written, oral, and visual communication skills. Type III Enrichment consists of firsthand investigations of real problems.

The Enrichment Triad Model is based on ways in which people learn in a natural environment, rather than the artificially structured environment that characterizes most classrooms. We encourage the use of the Enrichment Triad Model schoolwide and in all classrooms. The wide implementation of gifted education strategies in all classrooms lessens the stigma of a "gifted class" that engages in "better" learning activities. Then the school climate can become one of talent development in the school as a whole, with each classroom teacher focusing on student strengths, talents, and interests.

SUPPORTING EARLY IMPLEMENTATION

Even though each classroom teacher will be dealing with a narrower range of student achievement levels, these students will still present a variety of needs. Therefore, professional development focusing on differentiation will be required for the entire staff. Findings from the cluster grouping study (Gentry, 1999) indicate that all teachers should be involved in learning strategies for meeting the needs of high-achieving students. It is also helpful to have a resident teacher who is an expert in gifted education. This teacher serves as a resource for other teachers in the building. The teachers in the study reported that when they had questions about what to do with their high-achieving students, it was helpful to have a colleague in the building with whom they could discuss questions and ideas. We encouraged the gifted education staff to serve as a resource for all teachers, whether or not they were directly responsible for high-achieving students. As a result, we found that all teachers at the study site had participated in some level of professional learning concerning strategies for working with high-achieving children.

Teachers in the study who had clusters of high-achieving students used most of the strategies listed below:
1.   integrating higher order thinking skills,
2.   developing critical thinking,
3.   teaching students to use creative thinking skills and think divergently,
4.   integrating problem solving,

5. assigning long-term and high-level projects,
6. using acceleration,
7. adjusting assignments based on student skills,
8. grouping students so they could spend time with like-ability peers,
9. developing and implementing curricular extensions to challenge their students,
10. providing students with choices of partners or groups,
11. providing students with choices to work alone or together,
12. using open-ended questioning,
13. offering students independent study options,
14. using challenging questions,
15. implementing Curriculum Compacting (Reis, Burns, & Renzulli, 1992),
16. providing students choices of problems and assignments,
17. providing enrichment experiences to students, and
18. having high expectations for student achievement.

Most noteworthy was that the other teachers in the studies also used these strategies. In this manner, the types of curricula, instruction, and strategies that might most often be reserved just for students in a gifted program permeated the school in the cluster grouping study and likely led to the overall increase in student achievement, reflecting what Ward (1981, p. 76) termed "a radiation of excellence."

These 18 strategies can serve as the basis for developing a menu of professional development topics. Part II of this book provides detailed information on differentiating instruction, which will also serve as an excellent source of information when planning a comprehensive menu of professional development opportunities. See Table 3.2 for ideas on the format that these professional development experiences might take.

Not all teachers in the cluster grouping study used all strategies, which underscores the fact that teachers are as different from each other as are their students. Any discussion concerning professional development ought to include the notion of differentiation for teachers, as they differ from each other in their teaching methods, materials, and styles. For this reason, the 18 strategies listed above, as well as those in Part II of the book, should be provided as a menu of topics from which teachers might choose. Also, the format ideas described in Table 3.2 respond to the need for differentiated professional learning experiences, experiences that respect teachers' differences and honor their time.

TABLE 3.2
PROVIDING SELF-DIRECTED LEARNING OPPORTUNITIES FOR ALL STAKEHOLDERS

Professional Learning Needs	Venues for Providing Self-Directed Learning	Audiences
Philosophy behind TSCG	School website	Administrators
	Link to research and resources available at the Gifted Education Resource Institute's TSCG website: http://www.purduegeri.org	School board members
	Brochure in multiple languages	Instructional leaders
	Total School Cluster Grouping and Differentiation: A Comprehensive, Research-Based Plan for Raising Student Achievement and Improving Teacher Practices (Second Edition)	Parents
		Teachers
	Online professional development modules available through the Gifted Education Resource Institute at Purdue University	Specialists
Research to support TSCG	Information posted to school website	Administrators
	Link to research and resources available at the Gifted Education Resource Institute's TSCG website: http://www.purduegeri.org	School board members
		Instructional leaders
	Online professional development modules available through the Gifted Education Resource Institute at Purdue University	Parents
		Teachers
		Specialists
Nuts and bolts of TSCG implementation	Manual with site-specific information, forms, and procedures	Administrators
	Slideshow or recorded webinar	Instructional leaders
	Online professional development modules available through the Gifted Education Resource Institute at Purdue University	Teachers
		Specialists

TABLE 3.2 CONTINUED

Professional Learning Needs	Venues for Providing Self-Directed Learning	Audiences
Strategies for differentiating instruction	School subscription to professional journals such as Gifted Child Today and Teaching for High Potential	Instructional leaders
		Teachers
	Online professional development modules available through the Gifted Education Resource Institute at Purdue University	Specialists
	Teacher resource website with links to free, online learning networks and opportunities, such as:	
	• The Gifted Education Resource Institute's Professional Development Modules from Purdue University: http://www.geri.education.purdue.edu	
	• Twitter conversations at #GTChat	
	• LinkedIn groups: National Association for Gifted Children and the World Council for Gifted and Talented Children	
	• The Teaching Channel: http://www.teachingchannel.org	
	• Edmodo Communities: http://www.edmodo.com	
	School-organized, closed, online networking groups where teachers can informally share strategies, issues, concerns, and resources as a professional learning community (e.g., Edmodo, Google group, Facebook group, LinkedIn group)	
Data to tell the story of your school's TSCG implementation	Small "Did you know?" data figures or articles printed in school newsletter	Administrators
		School board members
	Data dashboard on district or school website	Parents
	Data checkups sent through your school Twitter or Facebook account	Teachers
	Annual report posted to school website and provided in multiple formats (e.g., slideshow, one-page overview, full report)	Specialists
	Links to annual report provided through your school Facebook or Twitter account	

DELIVERING ADVANCED OPPORTUNITIES FOR PROFESSIONAL LEARNING

Initially the school may need to seek help from professional consultants to conduct or facilitate the types of training recommended in the previous sections. Online learning developed to support TSCG implementation also exists and can take the place of on-site consultants (see http://www.geri.education.purdue.edu for more information). As the program develops and teachers become more skillful in implementing the instructional strategies that work well in the cluster-grouped classroom, the need for outside presenters will fade, and more reflective, practice-based professional learning experiences will become more important. Strategies such as lesson study, professional mentoring, independent study using professional trade materials, and the development of online personal learning networks (PLNs) will promote reflection grounded in practice. However, the occasional consultation with professionals outside of the local school program should still be considered to ensure that fresh perspectives, new strategies, and cutting-edge ideas are continually incorporated into the program.

Good professional development is perpetual and grounded in the needs of the educators involved. Even the best models and strategies continually need to be revisited and updated to fit the needs of a school's current population. At the research implementation site, staff development initiatives often originated from teachers' requests or questions. In other words, once the program begins, it will be important to ask teachers what they need.

PROVIDING ONGOING OPPORTUNITIES FOR NEW STAFF MEMBERS

As new staff members join your school, you will need to provide them with orientation types of knowledge about TSCG. Plan for these additions to your staff by developing self-directed learning opportunities through which teachers can build their knowledge of TSCG nuts and bolts independently or through mentorships. At the very least, new staff members should be provided with a copy of this book, either a desk copy or through a school lending library. The first two chapters are most important for orienting new staff members to the model.

We also suggest that you create a how-to manual that is specific to your school context. The manual might include the timeline used for grouping decisions, a list of teachers according to classroom composition, descriptions of teaching strength profiles that complement different types of classroom compositions, TSCG resources specific to your school context, and other information that addresses specifically the details of TSCG implementation in your school context.

Another idea is to record a slideshow that provides an overview of the Total School Cluster Grouping in your school. The desktop versions of Microsoft PowerPoint for PC and Mac have a feature that allows you to record a voiceover of your slides, and there are several free and fee-based software programs that also include this feature (e.g., Camtasia Studio, TouchCast, Adobe Presenter). These recorded slideshows and presentations can be added to your self-serve menu of professional development opportunities to support TSCG implementation, which we discuss in the following section.

DEVELOPING SELF-DIRECTED OPPORTUNITIES FOR CONTINUOUS LEARNING AMONG STAFF AND COMMUNITY

Professional learning can occur in informal settings just as easily as it does in formally delivered presentations or workshops. As you move forward with TSCG implementation, consider developing a self-service menu of professional development opportunities from which staff can choose to work independently on topics of interest. It is also important to consider how these learning opportunities can be extended to other stakeholders within your school community, such as school board members, parents, community groups that partner with your school, and regional service agencies. There are many different individuals and groups connected with schools that are typically left out of formal professional learning opportunities, but it is often valuable information for them to have as they build their understanding of your school programs and culture. Table 3.3 provides a list of professional learning needs, possible venues for providing self-directed learning, and the audiences that you should consider when developing self-service learning opportunities to support TSCG implementation.

LEARNING THROUGH REFLECTION

Finally, Gentry and Keilty (2004) recommended several steps to maintain and grow the program, including evaluation, research, and reflective practices that consider the achievement and growth of all students in the school. Effective implementation of Total School Cluster Grouping involves a combination of professional development and effective teacher practices. Recognizing that implementing any model requires work, evaluation, and changes to create the best fit of the model into the specific school context will enhance the quality of the implementation. Chapter 5 outlines strategies for evaluating your Total School Cluster Grouping program so that your educational community can learn through reflection. Involving the entire staff in the development and improvement of the program, as well as in the identification of areas for supportive staff

TABLE 3.3
PROVIDING SELF-DIRECTED LEARNING
OPPORTUNITIES FOR ALL STAKEHOLDERS

Professional Learning Needs	Venues for Providing Self-Directed Learning	Audiences
Philosophy behind TSCG	School website Link to research and resources available at the Gifted Education Resource Institute's TSCG website: http://www.purduegeri.org Brochure in multiple languages *Total School Cluster Grouping & Differentiation: A Comprehensive, Research-Based Plan for Raising Student Achievement & Improving Practices* (2nd Edition) Online professional development modules available through the Gifted Education Resource Institute at Purdue University	Administrators School Board Members Instructional leaders Parents Teachers Specialists
Research to support TSCG	Information posted to school website Link to research and resources available at the Gifted Education Resource Institute's TSCG website: http://www.purduegeri.org Online professional development modules available through the Gifted Education Resource Institute at Purdue University	Administrators School Board Members Instructional leaders Parents Teachers Specialists
Nuts and bolts of TSCG implementation	Manual with site-specific information, forms, and procedures Slideshow or recorded webinar Online professional development modules available through the Gifted Education Resource Institute at Purdue University	Administrators Instructional Leaders Teachers Specialists

Strategies for differentiating instruction	School subscription to professional journals such as *Gifted Child Today* and *Teaching for High Potential*
	
	Professional library that includes books such as those recommended in Appendix C
	
	Online professional development modules available through the Gifted Education Resource Institute at Purdue University
	
	Teacher resource website with links to free, online learning networks and opportunities, such as:
	  • The Gifted Education Resource Institute's Professional Development Modules from Purdue University: http://www.geri.education.purdue.edu
	  • Total School Cluster Grouping Facebook Group
	  • Twitter Conversations at #GTChat
	  • LinkedIn Groups: National Association for Gifted Children and the World Council for Gifted and Talented Children
	  • The Teaching Channel: http://www.teachingchannel.org
	  • Edmodo Communities: http://www.edmodo.com
	
	School-organized, closed, online networking groups where teachers can informally share strategies, issues, concerns, and resources as a professional learning community (e.g., Edmodo, Google Group, Facebook Group, LinkedIn Group)
		Instructional Leaders
		Teachers
		Specialists

Data to tell the story of your school's TSCG implementation	Small "did you know?" data figures or articles printed in school newsletter Data dashboard on district or school website Data checkups sent through your school Twitter or Facebook account Annual report posted to school website and provided in multiple formats (e.g., slideshow, one-page overview, full report) Links to annual report provided through your school Facebook or Twitter account	Administrators School Board Members Parents Teachers Specialists

development, will go a long way to creating buy-in and support of the model. Finally, recognizing benefits that this model has for all students and teachers will create a positive school climate and learning environment.

CHAPTER 4

THE PURDUE SIMULATION*

Understanding and Identifying Students Across the Gifted Spectrum†

TSCG requires that teachers maintain high expectations of their students and believe that students, no matter where they come from or how they achieve, can achieve at high levels. It also requires a broadened understanding of what giftedness is and who is capable of gifted behaviors. It is critical that teachers believe that their students are capable and that they have potential for growing up into someone who might just change the world, regardless of their situation as a child. Developing these beliefs requires that stereotypes are challenged and that assumptions about talent and achievement are discussed. It is with this in mind that we suggest engaging in a simulation of "real life" kids, and follow this simulation with in-depth, heartfelt discussion about what it means to educate students and to believe in their capabilities.

---

*   The author acknowledges Heather Carmody for her initial work on this simulation.

†   This chapter was contributed by C. Matthew Fugate.

As Forrest Gump says, "Life is like a box of chocolates . . . you never know what you're gonna get" (Finerman & Starkey, 1994). Much like those chocolates, no two gifted students are alike, and you never know what that young mind in your classroom today will go on to become tomorrow. The profiles in this chapter are intentionally brief, containing approximately the amount of information that teachers receive about their students when they first receive their class lists. These profiles are fictionalized accounts of the school experiences of famous people whose identities are revealed in Appendix C: Purdue Simulation Case Study Epilogues. (All biographical information found was collected from reliable sources, and fictionalized accounts are based upon the data in those source materials.) Also included in Appendix C are additional resources for teachers and students to learn more about the lives of these famous figures. As you read through each of the profiles, take a moment to reflect on what you now know about Total School Cluster Grouping and answer the following questions:

1. What strengths do you see in this student?
2. What are the areas of concern?
3. What additional information would you request?
4. Would this child qualify for the current gifted program at your school?
5. What cluster grouping recommendations (i.e., high, above-average, average, low-average, or low achieving) would you make for this child and why?
6. Are there any community resources you would access?

Once you have identified the famous figure, think about the following questions:

1. Should the student have received additional/different services than what you originally considered?
2. Does your school typically make recommendations based on information that is this limited?
3. What are the implications of this simulation that schools implementing Total School Cluster Grouping should consider?

STUDENT 1, NATHAN KASUN (SERBIAN)

Nathan Kasun is a profoundly gifted 4-year-old child with an IQ above 150. His physical development and health are excellent, although he has been described as eccentric in nature. His advanced visual-spatial perception and metacognitive skills make him highly imaginative. He spends most of his waking hours during the night, preferring to sleep only during the day. His parents have often stated that an electrical storm hit at midnight just as he was born, and he can often be heard talking to himself for hours throughout the night, particularly during lightning storms. They think the weather conditions at the time of his birth may have contributed to Nathan's passion for inventing and building electrical devices, and have noted that he can often be heard talking through an entire invention during a storm. In fact, his latest invention was a crude water wheel without paddles using a twig for the axel. He was intrigued at how smoothly the wheel turned in the water. Nathan has very acute senses and claims to be able to detect the presence of objects in a pitch-dark room by a "peculiar feeling" on his forehead. He also claims to be able to hear the thud of a fly landing and that his body rattles with the rumbling of car wheels a mile away. Although his mother has no formal education, she is also very intelligent and has invented many things to increase the convenience and efficiency of her household. Additionally, she has memorized thousands of poems and legends about her homeland. His father, a college graduate, serves as a bishop in the Serbian Orthodox church and is highly regarded for his public speaking abilities.

STUDENT 2, KATIE LIU (ASIAN)

Katie Liu is 6 years old and has just started first grade. She was born in China, and her parents immigrated with Katie and her two brothers to the United States a few years later. Test results put Katie's IQ at 95; however, the test was done in English and Katie and her family hold closely to Chinese traditions and only speak their native language at home to prevent their children from becoming too "Americanized." Therefore, her exposure to the English language has been very limited. Interestingly, Katie lists becoming more like her American classmates as one of her personal goals. In addition to being an avid reader, she has the ability to tell and write very elaborate stories. Katie's parents are very involved in her education and have expressed interest to the school in putting her in science programs that will support *their* goal for her to become a doctor. However, her teachers have expressed concern that Katie's parents are putting too much pressure on her, particularly her mother. Mrs. Liu values music and pushes her daughter in her piano lessons. Consequently, she is also an accomplished piano player, particularly for her age. Additionally, since starting school, her mother has expressed that nothing but A's are acceptable for daughter.

STUDENT 3, LOBSANG THONDUP (ASIAN)

Lobsang is a happy and healthy 6-year-old boy in the first grade who was born to Tibetan immigrant farmers. He has an IQ of 135 and attends a special school for the gifted because his local school could not adequately meet his needs. He learns quickly, is a particularly adept reader, and has very advanced reasoning skills. He has six siblings and his mother and older sister have become his primary caregivers at home. Lobsang spends hours observing the world around him, often noticing details and patterns far beyond the abilities of his peers. He has also been described as a very compassionate boy. His parents recall him helping on the family farm, gathering eggs from the chicken house when he noticed a group of chickens fighting and running to try to help the losing side. Lobsang has talked about traveling to distant places since he was a toddler and would often be found by his parents packing his things into a bag and talking about the exotic locales he wanted to visit.

STUDENT 4, SANTINE BROWN
(AFRICAN AMERICAN)

Santine Brown is 7 years old and in the second grade. His IQ is estimated to be 120 and he has a particular aptitude for mathematics. He is very social and well liked by his teachers and classmates. Santine and his four siblings, of whom he is the youngest, live with their mother in a subsidized housing project. His father has been largely absent most of his life. His mother works multiple jobs and receives public assistance to help make sure that her children are cared for. Concerned about the family's financial situation, Santine can often be seen in his brother's tie, carrying his lunchbox—which he uses as a briefcase—as he sells body lotion and hand-painted rocks door-to-door to help make additional money for the family.

STUDENT 5, NABHA PATEL (INDIAN)

Nabha is 7 years old an in the second grade. Her father has been in and out of jail throughout most of her life due to his radical political beliefs, and her mother suffers from a chronic respiratory disease. She had a younger brother, but he died 2 days after his birth. When her father is at home, it becomes a center of political activity with frequent visitors. Those who visit are activists, often in opposition to the government and frequently incarcerated with her father. Nabha has grown up listening to the political arguments of her father and his friends, and she has developed a general distrust of the government, often eloquently expressing very radical views for a child her age. As a result of her family life, Nabha is frequently absent from school and when she does attend, she has difficulty maintaining normal conversations with her peers.

STUDENT 6, ADA GREEN (AFRICAN AMERICAN)

Originally from Alabama, Ada's family moved to Chicago when she was 3 years old in order to provide her and her older brother and sister with better educational opportunities. Her father is a carpenter and her mother is an elementary school teacher. Now 7, Ada is in the second grade, enjoys school very much, and is known for always having a smile on her face. When she is not in class, Ada can usually be found in the school library. She loves to read about science and is particularly interested in astronomy. Additionally, she loves to dance and has a quick grasp of language. Ada has always had a strong sense of her personal goals. When she was in kindergarten, the students were asked what they wanted to be when they grew up. Ada quickly responded that she was going to be a scientist. When the teacher asked if she wouldn't rather be a nurse, she confidently replied, "I am going to college and I am going to be a scientist."

STUDENT 7, DAVID COLLINS (AFRICAN AMERICAN)

David is 8 years old and in the third grade. David is the middle child and has an older sister and a younger brother. His father, the minister at the neighborhood church, completed college, and his mother, a homemaker, completed high school and has done some postsecondary study. His family is very active in the church and in the neighborhood. Education is very important in the Collins household, and David's parents have high academic standards for all three of their children. Though they are supportive, they are not overprotective. David was expelled from the first grade for being only 5 years old when the minimum age was 6. Although David's exact IQ is unknown, his teachers describe him as a brilliant student, making complex arguments and explaining his thoughts in a manner that is rare for a child of his age. David enjoys swimming, playing the piano, and singing. He is also interested in debate and is concerned with the social injustices that occur in the world.

STUDENT 8, JANICE PHILLIPS (CAUCASIAN)

Janice is 8 years old and in the third grade. Her father is in an engineer in the military and is currently deployed overseas. As a result, their mother and grandmother are raising Janice and her 4-year-old sister. Janice has dreams of one day becoming a writer, like her mother. With an IQ of 125, Janice is a bright girl who is intensely interested in animals and nature. Her family owns many pets that she enjoys spending time with. Her mother supports and encourages her interests and dreams and wants her to succeed. Although she is a good student, her interest in nature often outranks her attention to her schoolwork, hampering her concentration on her studies. However, her teachers report that when she is focused, she's capable of brilliant work.

STUDENT 9, ANGELA BAEZ (HISPANIC)

Angela is 8 years old and in the third grade. She and her younger brother live with their parents in a subsidized housing project where they speak primarily Spanish. Although her mother has completed some postsecondary course work, her father only attended school through the third grade. Both of her parents work full-time, but the family still struggles financially. Angela loves reading, particularly mystery novels, and seems to have an ability to successfully mediate disagreements that arise among her peers. Mrs. Baez places a high value on education and often encourages Angela and her brother to work hard in school. Her teacher last year noted that Angela had one of the strongest work ethics in class. Although she was recently diagnosed with juvenile diabetes, she has not let the illness affect her work at school, and she continues to surpass the expectations for students at her grade level.

STUDENT 10, JAMES WILLIAMS (AFRICAN AMERICAN)

James is 9 years old and entering the fourth grade. James mother married his father, a Baptist minister, when she was 13 years old. The couple was together for 11 years and divorced a year ago. She is currently raising James and his brother on her own, working two to three different jobs to support the family. Although James has stated that he wants to be a doctor, he is currently at the bottom of his class. There is no data on James' IQ, but he is often taunted by his classmates and called a dummy. James has a very explosive temper and is easily provoked, so these taunts have led him at times to violent outbursts. In addition to the occasions when he has tried to hurt his classmates, he has also been know to physically attack his mother when he becomes frustrated at home. In the classroom, James is frequently in trouble and often disrupts class.

STUDENT 11, MARK MATHESON (CAUCASIAN)

At age 9, Mark is entering the fourth grade. When he was younger, he had delayed speech development and was tested and found to have an IQ of 82. He has already been expelled from one school due to frequent emotional outbursts toward teachers and administrators. These outbursts continued at his current school. He is often sick and had to be temporarily removed from school when he was certified as having an emotional breakdown. He does not like the strict rules and rigid structure at his current school and is considered to be unsociable. He can often be found reading alone or escaping into one of his many fantasy worlds. Mark does well only in the subjects he considers interesting, such as mathematics. At home he enjoys working on mathematical puzzles and problems with his parents and uncle, and math is the only class in which he regularly completes his work. His mother loves music and has encouraged him to play the violin and piano. He has a good relationship with his sister and they enjoy building houses of cards together. His parents are once again considering if they should move him to another new school.

STUDENT 12, WILLIAM HORN (CAUCASIAN)

William is 10 years old and entering the fifth grade. He is always well dressed and is known as an organizer and student leader. William is well liked by his teachers and classmates. He has been tested and has an IQ of 159, and his work is frequently what you would expect from an older student. Although he excels in most subjects, he is most interested in mathematics. He is also a very good writer—his work is fluid and demonstrates maturity beyond his years. Outside of the classroom, William is an avid basketball player and spends several hours practicing after school and on weekends. Both of his parents are very supportive of his interests and involved in his education.

STUDENT 13, CALEB RAMSEY (NATIVE AMERICAN)

At the age of 10, Caleb is entering his fifth grade year. Caleb's father suffers from depression and will often go missing for several days on a drinking binge. Consequently, he is unable to hold down a steady job, so Caleb's mother works two jobs to support the family. When Caleb was born, the doctors discovered that he had excess water in the brain, and at the age of 6 months he underwent a brain operation. The doctors held little hope for his survival and told his parents that even if he did survive the surgery, he would be severely brain damaged. Against all odds, he did survive the surgery and by the age of 3 had learned to read. Although his IQ has not been formally evaluated, by the age of 5, Caleb could read and comprehend complete novels. Unfortunately, he suffers from periodic seizures as a result of the surgery. This combined with his advanced academic skills have made him somewhat of a loner at school, and his classmates often make fun of him. Caleb enjoys science and has stated that he wants to be a doctor one day.

CHAPTER **5**

COMPLEMENTING OTHER SERVICES AND PROGRAMS

Cluster grouping coordinates well with other school services, including pull-out programs, the Enrichment Triad Model (Renzulli & Reis, 1994), the Purdue Three Stage Model (Moon, Kolloff, Robinson, Dixon, & Feldhusen, 2009), and even with self-contained programs or special school program options by offering another tier of services for students who may not initially qualify for the self-contained classroom or special school. By offering a variety of services in the school to encourage the development of diverse talents among students, educators increase the odds of reaching and developing strengths among more students. Figure 5.1 contains a list of programs and services that can be implemented in elementary schools.

As depicted in Figure 5.1, a rich variety of services exists to enrich the education of elementary students. General classroom enrichment should focus on that which is interesting to students and targets their strengths. Renzulli suggested the addition of Type I experiences in classrooms to stimulate the interests of all students and the integration of Type II activities that help students use their

Elementary School
General Classroom Enrichment, Talents Unlimited, Junior Great Books
Discovery, Inquiry, Problem-Based Learning
Enrichment Clusters
Differentiation
Curriculum Compacting
Individual and Small-Group Counseling
Social, Emotional, Physical Health
Independent Study in Interest Area
Product/Service in Interest Area
Career Awareness
Within-Class Cluster Grouping
Total School Cluster Grouping
Between-Class Grouping by Skill Level
Nongraded Cluster Grouping
Within and Across Grade Pull-Out by targeted ability, subject and interest areas
Self-Contained Classes (single or multigrade)
Magnet Schools
Integrated Technology
Multicultural/Foreign Language Study
Individual Options: Internships, Apprenticeships, Mentorships, IEP, Dual Exceptionalities
Acceleration Options: Early admission, grade skipping, subject acceleration, dual enrollment in middle school classes
Special Talent Programs: Young Writers, Saturday and Summer Programs, Future Problem Solving, Math Olympiad, Science Olympiad, Math Leagues, Science Fairs, Talent Searches, Odyssey of the Mind, Destination Imagination, Invention Convention, etc.

FIGURE 5.1. PROGRAMS AND SERVICES FOR ELEMENTARY STUDENTS. ADAPTED FROM *SCHOOLS FOR TALENT DEVELOPMENT* (P. 78), BY J. RENZULLI, 1994, WACO, TX: PRUFROCK PRESS. COPYRIGHT 1994 BY PRUFROCK PRESS. ADAPTED WITH PERMISSION.

learning-how-to-learn skills. Some teachers use thematic units to enrich their classrooms. In short, all classrooms in the cluster-grouped school should include enrichment. Discovery, inquiry, and problem-based learning are discussed in Part II, and they add depth to the enrichment.

Enrichment clusters are a schoolwide application of the Enrichment Triad Model designed to bring gifted education services to *all* students and teachers in the school. Thus, they fit well with TSCG and reinforce the use of gifted education pedagogy by all educators with all students, as enrichment clusters place students in their strength and interest areas. Facilitators help students identify products and services in which they use advanced materials and authentic methods to produce their products and services for real-world audiences—much like practicing professionals. Educators using cluster grouping might want to consider adding an enrichment program to their school day, and can learn how to do so by consulting the book *Enrichment Clusters: A Practical Plan for Student-driven, Real-world Learning, 2nd ed.* (Renzulli, Gentry, & Reis, 2014).

Special talent programs provide enriched learning to students in specific areas of interest and are described in Appendix D: Recommended Differentiation and Gifted Education Resources. These programs, with their extracurricular feel, have the potential to elevate academics to the level of sports in the school. Science Olympiad medalists or Odyssey of the Mind team winners can be celebrated alongside the basketball, football, and track stars.

In my work, I have found that "general" educators often borrowed from traditional gifted education materials, strategies, and approaches with their students. As one teacher put it:

> I've learned so much from [Teacher 3A] and I adapt many of the strategies that she uses with her high achievers and use them with my learning disabled and low achievers. I don't think that gifted education is just for gifted students. (Gentry & Owen, 1999, p. 238)

Thus, I encourage educators to view the continuum of services in the context of the distinct possibility that gifted education strategies and programs can benefit the general education program. I also encourage school personnel to consider offering as many *different* options to students with the goal of reaching more students.

PULL-OUT, PUSH-IN, AND SEND-OUT PROGRAMS

In any gifted program that requires a pull-out or send-out component, students who comprise a high-achieving cluster can be sent to the gifted resource teacher and only disrupt a few classrooms. Additionally, gifted education pull-out services are part-time, often as little as an hour a week. Cluster grouping offers full-time services to high-achieving students during the rest of their school experience, and thus complements pull-out services with intensive regular services. This works equally well for any students who receives direct pull-out services for other special needs. For example, a cluster of English as a New Language (ENL) students may receive support services either as a pull-out or from a specialist who comes into the classroom. As a cluster, they can support each other, the teacher who has them in her class can plan around their special services schedule, and a more consistent delivery of services can be maintained. Similar arrangements can be developed by clustering students who receive Title I, Reading Recovery, speech, and/or special education services in designated classrooms. A traditional pull-out application involves many teachers and classrooms, making it difficult to schedule and coordinate and involving varying levels of support and buy-in from different classroom teachers. When the special needs students are pulled out from a clustered classroom on a regular basis, fewer teachers are affected. The teacher of this classroom expects students to leave for services, supports the delivery of these services, and plans for instruction with the rest of the class during the pull-out time.

Similar to pull-out services are push-in services, in which the specialist and education aides work in the classroom alongside the classroom teachers. Cluster grouping facilitates push-in services efficiently by requiring that specialists and educational aides attend fewer classrooms. Thus, their time in the cluster-grouped classroom can be extended. In one of the study schools, each Title I aide spent 5 half-days per week in each of two classrooms, providing quality support to the classroom teacher. Similarly, in another school, the Teacher Consultant for students with learning disabilities was able to attend fewer classrooms for longer periods of time than in previous years by working with students in cluster group. In the push-in approach, students are not seen by other students as those who have to leave class. Moreover, the specialist or aide who works with these students becomes part of the classroom community, helping the targeted students and the classroom teacher and often relating positively to other students in the classroom. Key to the success of this type of cluster is support for the classroom teacher from specialists and teaching aides who assist in addressing these students' special needs.

SELF-CONTAINED CLASSES AND MAGNET SCHOOLS

Some districts implement self-contained classes of gifted and talented students or send identified students to a magnet school setting. Such applications of gifted programming have merit and have been shown in the literature to benefit the gifted students whom they serve academically, socially, and emotionally (Delcourt, Loyd, Cornell, & Goldberg, 1994; Kulik, 2003). However, these programs have a downside, as they can be exclusive and frequently limit the number of students allowed into the program (Renzulli & Reis, 1997). This limitation also often precludes the addition of new students during the program. If a district only offers a program in which a limited number of students can receive services in special classes or special schools, it runs the risk of missing those who could succeed in the program, such as students from impoverished backgrounds and students from cultural groups that continue to experience severe underrepresentation in gifted programs (United States Department of Education, 2000; Miller, 2004; Yoon & Gentry, 2009). In short, programs limited by the number of spaces in a given school or classroom will miss students who would benefit from the services they provide. These programs will also miss students who, after several years in school, catch up and develop into high-achieving students. Fortunately, programs do not have to be limited to a one-size-fits-all approach with only a limited number of options and spaces in the program.

Implementation of TSCG can work in conjunction with magnet schools and self-contained classrooms, thus extending services to more students, involving more teachers, and ultimately developing more talents among students. One might initially think that if students are being identified for a magnet school placement or for a self-contained class, then gifted students won't be available to be identified for placement in the high-achieving cluster classroom. However, we have not found this to be the case. On the contrary, selective magnet schools or self-contained programs, due to their rigid identification protocols, often miss identifying a high-achieving student who will be identified in the cluster program. Further, parents sometimes decline to send their children "away" to the magnet program in order to keep them in the neighborhood school or with their friends, or due to fear of the program being too hard for their children. TSCG offers these kids a safe placement in their home school. Moreover, it offers the opportunity to serve more students and to identify additional students over time. Thus, this model complements existing magnet and self-contained programs that may be in place in a district. Several districts with which I have worked have magnet schools for gifted students *and* TSCG programs in place in their other elementary schools to meet the needs of the many very bright children in these nonmagnet schools. These two services—magnet and cluster grouping—work well in these districts, offering gifted education services in all schools. TSCG offers districts yet another program on a continuum of services that complement each other in the development of student talents.

DEPARTMENTALIZATION IN THE UPPER ELEMENTARY GRADES

Departmentalization involves grade-level teachers each focusing on a content area, and students moving from teacher to teacher for content instruction. For example, one teacher might teach all of the science lessons, another all of the math lessons, and yet another all of the social studies lessons. In a departmentalized grade level, students have a homeroom and then move to the subject area teachers using a mutually agreed upon schedule. In the upper grades, departmentalization is often done to add content expertise to the curriculum as well as to prepare students for middle school, where changing courses and teachers is common practice.

Departmentalization can work with TSCG; however, each content area teacher must agree to further differentiate for the section of students from the homeroom with the cluster of high-achieving students. Such agreement can enhance the reputation and quality of the grade-level teachers, as each of them commits to learn and deliver curriculum to challenge identified high-achieving cluster students. Thus, all teachers develop skills in working with advanced students and create curriculum and curricular extensions to meet these students' needs. These skills can ultimately result in increased expertise and enriched curriculum that benefits all learners at the grade level.

Sometimes, by the time students reach the upper elementary grades, a classroom of high-achieving students exists. In such a case, teachers in a departmentalized arrangement would have one of their classes be comprised of advanced learners. Unfortunately, this arrangement prevents moving students with strengths in only one academic area in and out of the clusters as previously discussed—unless the grade-level team invents some creative scheduling to accommodate individual students.

MULTI-AGE PROGRAMS

Applying TSCG to multi-age or looped settings needs further study. However, in each of these settings, common sense in conjunction with the goals of this model should dictate practice. In a multi-age setting, high achievers from each grade level should form the cluster, and students of other achievement levels should be placed as recommended in Chapter 2. In a looped classroom, in which the teacher moves up a grade level with her students, it might be necessary to add new students during the second year of the loop. This is especially true if the teacher who loops also teaches the high-achieving cluster of students. If more students are identified as high achieving each year, then these students may need to be placed in her classroom in the second year of her loop. If two clusters of high-achieving students are formed, then this may not be necessary.

THE ENRICHMENT TRIAD MODEL AND THE PURDUE THREE STAGE MODEL

The Enrichment Triad Model (Renzulli & Reis, 1994) involves a component in which students revolve into the program for in-depth pursuit of Type III investigations and for intensive training in methodological skills. Although this model employs a revolving door and can involve a variety of students, those students who have been identified as high achieving in the Total School Cluster Grouping Model will likely require services in the Enrichment Triad Model. Further, as discussed in Chapter 3, the Enrichment Triad Model can serve as the basis for schoolwide enrichment and for extending gifted services to students in all classrooms.

Such is the case in the Purdue Three Stage Model (Moon et al., 2009), in which gifted and talented students pursue advanced academics by moving through three stages of more intense study with a final project as an outcome. Stages I and II focus on providing content knowledge and enhancing problem-solving skills. Stage III involves self-directed inquiry and the development of a product for an audience, much like Renzulli's Type III, but focused more closely on an academic area of study. Both of these programs involve a pull-out component that would assist the teachers of the high-achieving cluster students with delivery of advanced services to their students as well as provide these teachers with time to work with the other students in small groups in their classrooms during pull-out time.

Finally, when considering implementing cluster grouping and how it can work with existing or potential services, district personnel should note how this total school model can supplement their existing efforts and bring services to more students, teachers, and schools. Implementing the Total School Cluster Grouping Model should never be used as rationale to eliminate other viable services available or potentially available to students. It is only through a continuum of special services that student talents can be effectively developed. TSCG offers districts a method of placing students in classrooms in a manner that can help teachers better meet their academic needs and help all of their students achieve at higher levels. TSCG done in conjunction with other services simply makes sense.

By grouping students in clusters, classrooms are organized to meet students' individual needs. The strategies teachers use to challenge and meet their students' needs are integral for student growth and fidelity of model implementation. These strategies and supporting resources are the focus of Part II of this book.

CHAPTER 6

COLLABORATIVE EVALUATION FOR PROGRAM MONITORING*

The term *program evaluation* can strike fear and tension in the most confident of individuals. People often equate evaluation with high-stakes decisions about whether or not to cut, or dramatically change, a program. However, there are a variety of reasons why you might conduct a program evaluation, including for the purpose of monitoring the program to ensure that expected outcomes are being achieved and making adjustments if they are not. In this chapter, I describe program evaluation as a way to engage in collaborative inquiry about the operation and outcomes of your TSCG program for the purpose of program improvement.

---

* This chapter was contributed by Kristina Ayers Paul.

PROGRAM EVALUATION FOR RESEARCH-BASED DECISION MAKING

This book advocates for the use of research-based practices. Most of the research cited has emerged from empirical studies of the Total School Cluster Grouping Model (e.g., Gentry & Owen, 1999) and from studies of associated instructional practices (e.g., Brulles et al., 2010, 2012; Pierce et al., 2011). Program evaluation provides another opportunity to make research-based decisions about your TSCG program. Program evaluation is defined by Patton (2008) as "the systematic collection of information about the activities, characteristics, and results of a program to make judgments about the program, improve or further develop program effectiveness, inform decision about future programming, and/or increase understanding" (p. 39). Program evaluators act as applied researchers, asking questions and gathering evidence that will help them answer questions about a program. The main difference between researchers and program evaluators is that researchers aim for developing generalizable knowledge that can be used by anyone, while program evaluators try to generate knowledge about specific programs within a specific context for use by the people involved in the program. However, they use many of the same tools and approaches.

Program evaluation for the purpose of monitoring TSCG operations and outcomes should be an ongoing, collaborative process. It should not be a threatening activity, but rather one that establishes a culture of continuous program improvement through data-driven decision making. Although programs might secure the services of an evaluation specialist to conduct a more formal external evaluation, it is not always feasible or necessary to do so. It is often appropriate to use the resources available within the school district to accomplish the task. Moreover, when programs are in their early stages of development, a formative program evaluation is a more appropriate form of evaluation than a summative approach (Daponte, 2008), which is more often the reason that external evaluators are involved.

CLARIFYING THE PURPOSE

Before beginning an evaluation, it is important to clearly define the purpose. Patton (2008) delineated six types of evaluation, each with a different purpose:
- program development,

- formative improvement and learning,
- monitoring,
- accountability,
- summative judgment, and
- knowledge generating.

These forms of evaluation are described in Table 6.1, and examples of their application for Total School Cluster Grouping are provided. As you will see from the examples, each of these types can be used to evaluate the TSCG Model, but the focus of this chapter will be on formative improvement and learning.

There are a handful of manuals, models, and guidebooks for program evaluation in gifted education, which may be useful for task force members who would like to examine different approaches to evaluating programs for high-achieving students (e.g., Callahan, 2006, 2009a; Callahan & Caldwell, 1997; Renzulli, 1978; Neumeister & Burney, 2012; VanTassel-Baska & Feng, 2004). However, these publications mostly focus on more summative forms of evaluation, treating evaluation more as an event than a continuous process of program monitoring. The following suggestions are focused on infusing evaluation approaches into your TSCG program in ways that promote continuous program monitoring and improvement.

FORMING A TASK FORCE

We suggest that a task force for continuous program improvement be formed to direct the program monitoring activities for your TSCG Model, as research on the most effective program evaluations of gifted programs revealed the critical role of an advisory team in the process (Tomlinson, Bland, Moon, & Callahan, 1994). Task force members should be teachers, administrators, parents, and community members who have a vested interest in the quality of TSCG implementation. It is also constructive to invite more critical members of the school committee to be involved, as their participation in the process may provide a healthy dose of skepticism for an overly optimistic task force, and their involvement may add to the perceived trustworthiness of the results derived from the task force's work. Consider asking members of the committee to serve 2- or 3-year terms before rotating off the committee, thereby providing time for

TABLE 6.1
PATTON'S SIX PURPOSES FOR PROGRAM EVALUATION AS APPLIED TO THE TOTAL SCHOOL CLUSTER GROUPING (TSCG) MODEL

Purpose	General Description	Example Application for TSCG
Program development	Conducted for the purpose of designing new innovations that respond to a changing context.	A task force collects published research and information regarding the TSCG model, hosts focus groups to discuss the plausibility of adopting the model, and develops a 5-year strategic plan for model adoption—along with summarized information from the literature review and focus groups—to present to the school board.
Formative improvement and learning	Used by program leaders, staff, and participants to learn about the success of program implementation and to understand ways that the program can be further improved.	A committee of educators, parents, and students identify a specific issue to explore (e.g., the use of curriculum compacting, students' attitudes regarding the composition of students in their classrooms, and an examination of the program's alignment with the NAGC P–12 Gifted Programming Standards) for the purpose of program improvement.
Monitoring	Low-stakes form of evaluation through which program leaders routinely collect information to ensure that the program is operating as expected and to identify problems as they emerge.	The program coordinator collects survey data from teachers, parents, and students on an annual basis to gather information about satisfaction with the program, as well as an annual review of student achievement data to ensure upward trends, examine patterns, and note anomalies.
Accountability	High-stakes form of evaluation that is used by those at the executive, managerial, legislative, or funding level to confirm that the resources are managed well and the desired results are obtained.	The state department conducts a review of the school district's services for high-ability or gifted students to determine if the school district is in compliance with the state policies regarding gifted and talented students.
Summative judgment	Most often a very high-stakes form of evaluation in which evaluators determine the value and future direction of the program.	An external evaluator is contracted to critically examine the program and determine if the five goals of the TSCG model are being met.
Knowledge generating	Used by researchers, policymakers, and others with a big-picture point of view to develop a general understanding of how certain types of programs operate and to identify general principles about the effectiveness of such programs.	University-based researchers study the effectiveness of the TSCG model across multiple contexts to determine effectiveness of the model in meeting the needs of high-ability students, creating a climate in which differentiation is more feasible, and raising the achievement of all students,

task force members' evaluation knowledge and skills to build over time and with experience.

If there are no members of the staff who have program evaluation expertise, time should be spent developing task force members' knowledge of basic evaluation concepts and approaches among the task force members. Although this chapter will outline some of the basic steps of evaluating programs and can be shared with the task force, it may also be beneficial to have a consultant or program evaluation firm provide a training or workshop focused on introductory evaluation concepts and techniques. Schools might also consider building a reference library of program evaluation books and resources for use by the task force members. Suggested books and resources are provided in Appendix D: Recommended Differentiation and Gifted Education Resources.

EXAMINING PROGRAM THEORY

Every program that is implemented, whether in schools or any other organization, has an underlying program theory, or set of assumptions. The assumptions are that if certain program activities are implemented well, then a set of desired results or goals will be achieved. The goals of the Total School Cluster Grouping Model are listed below.

1. Provide full-time services to high-achieving and high-ability elementary students.
2. Help all students improve their academic achievement and educational self-efficacy.
3. Help teachers more effectively and efficiently meet the diverse needs of their students.
4. Weave gifted education and talent development "know-how" into the fabric of all educational practices in the school.
5. Improve representation of traditionally underserved students identified, over time, as above average and high achieving.

Therefore, the program theory, or logic, of the TSCG Model is that if schools (a) appropriately identify and cluster students within classrooms, (b) assign qualified and willing teachers to teach the high-achieving cluster, and (c) support teachers' development of the knowledge and skill in infusing gifted education instruction in ways that are differentiated to meet the needs of the different student clusters, then the goals listed above will be achieved.

DESIGNING THE PROGRAM MONITORING PLAN

Program monitoring is like going to the dentist regularly to make sure that everything is on track and to find any emerging problems before they become too painful. In the same way, the task force for continuous program improvement should perform regular check-ups and be on the lookout for areas of the TSCG operations that are not working as expected. At times the task force may be performing routine data checks, while at other times it may be necessary to investigate issues or potential problems more deeply to understand them and determine ways to fix them.

Each evaluative effort within the program monitoring plan should be structured around a specific question. Some general, overarching questions are:

- How well does the program adhere to the guidelines described for the program model?
- Is the program operating in the way that is expected?
- Are the expected outcomes being achieved?

More specifically, a monitoring plan for TSCG might include evaluation questions that are directly linked to program goals as previously described. These questions are:

- Are high-achieving and high-ability students receiving full-time services that challenge them to grow? Are the teachers of these classes using appropriately challenging and differentiated instructional strategies?
- Are all students improving their academic achievement and educational self-efficacy?
- Are teachers effectively and efficiently meeting the diverse needs of their students?
- Is gifted education and talent development "know-how" woven into the fabric of all educational practices in the school?
- Is the representation of traditionally underserved populations of students improved in the above-average and high-achieving categories over time?

Evaluation questions bring focus to evaluation efforts and direct the decisions regarding what types of data to collect, whom to collect them from, how to analyze them, and how to present the results in a way that will be most helpful for answering the evaluation question. Evaluation questions should be focused and answerable. Whether designing a continuous monitoring plan that will be repeated regularly or a minievaluation that will probe an emerging problem, it is essential that the efforts be guided by specific, answerable evaluation questions.

IDENTIFY DATA SOURCES RELEVANT TO THE EVALUATION QUESTIONS

These are the different groups of people, or stakeholders, who will need to be considered when determining the data sources to gather. Begin by developing a list of all of the stakeholders for the TSCG program. A starter list of TSCG stakeholders is provided in Table 6.2. Then narrow the list to identify the stakeholders that have a direct relationship to the evaluation question of interest.

As an example, let's consider the evaluation question, *Is gifted education and talent development "know-how" woven into the fabric of all educational practices in the school?* The stakeholders with the most direct relationship to this question are the teachers and administrative staff members who understand "gifted education and talent development 'know-how.'" Now consider the role that parents and students have in helping answer this question. Certainly they have a vested interest in the instructional practices that are used in the school. Might they also be a good source of data in terms of reporting the types of instructional activities that they experience and observe? Once the stakeholder list has been narrowed, think about the types of data that can be collected in relationship to the stakeholders.

Triangulation is an important concept to keep in mind when designing any evaluation. Triangulation is the act of including multiple data types and sources when investigating an evaluation question. It is important that a body of evidence be collected that includes multiple perspectives and multiple types of qualitative and quantitative data, so that results are not based on only one source of data or through the lens of one perspective.

In Chapter 2, we discussed the important role of data collection within the model. These data will serve as the foundation for program evaluation, but there are additional data that should be considered. Table 6.3 contains a starter list of

TABLE 6.2
TSCG STAKEHOLDERS

Students	Classroom Teachers	Administrators
Parents	Special Needs Teachers	Curriculum Heads
	Teaching Aides	School Board Members

TABLE 6.3
POTENTIAL DATA SOURCES AND DATA COLLECTION TOOLS

Student identification records (e.g., student data cards, spreadsheet of students' achievement category assignments throughout elementary school, class lists)
Teacher Observation Form – Revised (see Appendix B)
Documentation (e.g., meeting agendas, professional development schedules, handouts, memos, website descriptions of the program, parent pamphlets)
Student achievement data
Lesson plans
Student products
Classroom assessment tools
Professional development evaluations
Surveys from staff, parents, students, community members
Individual interviews
Focus groups

potential data sources to use for monitoring TSCG programs. Task force members can use this list to help generate ideas for the types of data to collect for each part of the program monitoring plan.

COLLECTING, SUMMARIZING, AND ANALYZING DATA

Different types of data will require different approaches to collecting, summarizing, and analyzing. At a very basic level, you can categorize data into two different types—qualitative and quantitative. Qualitative data are generally those that describe with words, whereas quantitative data are generally those that are counted, calculated, and measured. The W. K. Kellogg Foundation's Evaluation Handbook (1999; available for free from http://www.wkkf.org) provides an excellent overview of the different types of qualitative and quantitative data typically involved in program evaluations, as well as discussions of how to analyze these types of data (see pp. 70–95).

INTERPRETING RESULTS AND ANSWERING EVALUATION QUESTIONS

Once the data have been collected, summarized, and analyzed, the task force will need to interpret the results within the context of the evaluation question. There are several points to remember when interpreting results and answering evaluation questions. First, remember that no matter how well the evaluation approaches are planned or how carefully data are collected, evaluators rarely, if ever, have a 100% accurate and complete picture of an issue. Therefore, interpretations of the results should be balanced according to the degree of comprehensiveness and trustworthiness reflected in the methods used and data collected. Second, the interpretation of evaluation results is an inherently value-laden process. It is one thing, for example, to ask *To what degree do we see upward movement through the achievement categories?* It is quite another thing to ask *To what degree do **we want** to see upward movement through the achievement categories?* Task force members will need to determine how to interpret results in light of the values and expectation of the school community. Finally, it is just as important to draw attention to the good things that are revealed through evaluation as it is to focus on the areas for improvement. It is easy to become hyperfocused on finding problems, because the purpose of program evaluation, in many cases, is to create positive change. However, it is vitally important that program evaluators—especially internal program evaluators—remember to record and report the things that are going well with a program. Critical criticism is received much better when the blow is cushioned by fair praise.

DESIGNING A PROGRAM IMPROVEMENT ACTION PLAN

The results of your monitoring evaluation should lead to assurances that the program is on track and the identification of any emerging problems that need attention. The best investment you can make following the completion of any program evaluation activity is the development of an action plan, particularly in the case of evaluation activities that reveal emerging problems. Action plans should be spelled out with goals, step-by-step actions, timelines, and persons responsible for completing said task. Members of the task force may be responsible for actions and tasks included in the plan, or they may identify other school personnel who should have the primary responsibility for the tasks. A small committee from the task force should be responsible for overseeing progress toward the goals in the action plan. In this way the task force can oversee the cycle of organizational learning—from formative evaluation to program improvement—through to completion.

SHARING RESULTS

You will want to document and disseminate the results of your hard work in ways that are accessible to your stakeholders. The goal should be to document your experience, add transparency to your work, and provide multiple, layered opportunities for your community members to learn about your school's progress toward TSCG goals. Comprehensive evaluation reports are important for documenting your methods, procedures, and results. They are also valuable for adding transparency to your work for school community members who were not part of the process and are interested in knowing how valid and accurate your results may be. However, comprehensive evaluation reports are often not read as comprehensively or frequently as report authors would like. School community members may be interested in the results of your work, but may not have the time to spend reading multiple pages of technical documents. Consider layering your dissemination efforts in ways that provide multiple access points for interested readers. For example, you might provide a brief press release-style article on your school website that links to a one-page executive summary, a more detailed slide show summary with images of data collection tools and products of the evaluation (e.g., a data summary table or chart of student achievement growth), and the full evaluation report. By layering your dissemination products and referencing all of the products within each one, you provide various levels of detail for people to self-select depending on their interest and their need to know.

PART **II**

DIFFERENTIATING IN THE CLUSTER-GROUPED CLASSROOM

CHAPTER 7

DIFFERENTIATION

Demolishing Ceilings*

Much has been said and written about differentiation since the term first began to be used in the 1950s. Often discussed, but seldom practiced (Tomlinson et al., 2003; Archambault et al., 1993), it remains one of the most misunderstood yet powerful tools in a teacher's treasure chest of techniques. On the surface, differentiation sounds like an easy task. After all, how hard can it be to modify the curriculum and instruction for students based on their assessed achievement and individual interests (NAGC, 1994)? In reality, differentiation is an art that can only be developed over time with practice and patience.

In this chapter, I examine the concept of differentiation in depth and explore the intricacies of its practice. Developing a firm foundation grounded in research will allow you to paint a portrait of possibilities for what your classroom could look like in the future. Before you begin, stop and reflect on what differentiation means to you. Write down a short definition and list the differentiation strategies you have used in the past. At the end of this chapter, you will be given the opportunity to revise your definition and set goals for the future.

---

*   This chapter was contributed by Jason McIntosh.

Differentiation is: _____

_____

_____

_____

_____

_____

PART ONE:
THE 2 P'S, THE 2 C'S, AND THE
2 F'S OF DIFFERENTIATION

Some people believe that giving students different tasks is unfair. Imagine two students standing in front of a chalkboard where an assignment has been written. The teacher, in an effort to be fair, removes one student's glasses so that both students are treated equally (Wormeli, 2005). This, of course, seems silly and illogical, but an essentially similar thing happens every day in less obvious ways. Requiring that everyone do the same activity regardless of past learning experiences, readiness levels, abilities, and interests leads to the same results: One student learns something new and one does not. To prevent this from happening, teachers must practice the two P's, two C's, and two F's of differentiation (see Figure 7.1).

THE TWO P'S: PREASSESSMENT AND A PERKY PACE

The first step to remedy this situation is to assess what students already know. This is called preassessment and represents the first of the two P's. Preassessment helps a teacher eliminate unnecessary practice for those who already know the material and identify areas where scaffolding or reteaching is necessary for those who do not. Ausubel (1968) said, "The most important single factor influencing learning is what the learner already knows; ascertain this and teach him accordingly" (p. 36). What students already know is highly correlated to what they will learn in the future (Marzano, 2004). Several easy-to-implement preassessment techniques are listed in Table 7.1.

2 P's	2 C's	2 F's
Preassessment	Choice	Feedback
Perky Pace	Challenge	Flexibility

FIGURE 7.1. THE 2 P'S, 2 C'S, AND 2 F'S.

TABLE 7.1
PREASSESSMENT TECHNIQUES

Pretest / Posttest Design	Give the test you plan to give at the end of the unit (or one similar), at the beginning of the unit.
Curriculum Maps and Markers	At the beginning of the year, ask the students to highlight on the curriculum map document what they already know in green, what they have been exposed to in yellow, and what they have never heard of in red (Stewart, 2010).
Quick Write	Ask students to write everything they know about a topic in 5 minutes or less.
Concept Map	Ask students to create a concept map that includes the "big ideas" related to a topic.
Four Corners	Post one of the following signs in each of the four corners in the classroom: Novice, Apprentice, Practitioner, and Expert. After naming the topic or skill, ask the students to walk to the corner that represents their current level of understanding.
Informal Survey or One-on-One Interview	Ask students what they know about a topic through a survey or an individual discussion.
KWL Chart	Ask students to complete a modified KWL chart (K- what they already know, W- what they want to know, and L- where they learned it).
RAN Chart (Reading and Analyzing Nonfiction)	Create a chart with the following headings: 1) What I think I know, 2) Confirmed, 3) Misconceptions, 4) New Learning, and 5) Wonderings. Students brainstorm what they think they know about a topic and write each fact on a Post-it note. As they read through a text and find confirmation for a fact, they then move its corresponding Post-it to the second column. The process continues as misconceptions are identified and new learning takes place. Finally, students are asked to list what they would still like to learn. (Stead, 2005)

In addition to preassessing content knowledge, it is also important to assess a student's process skills (e.g., problem solving, creative thinking, critical thinking), familiarity with the chosen product he or she will be expected to create in order to show what he or she has learned (e.g., PowerPoint, advertisement, book review), and any affective needs he or she might have (e.g., self-efficacy, motivation, social skills). Affect and intellect are closely connected (Vygotsky, 1986).

How students feel about a given topic will often dramatically affect their level of achievement in the long run.

However, giving a preassessment is a waste of time if you do not analyze the information to identify strengths and weaknesses of individual students. In order to facilitate this process, a preassessment should be given in enough time for the teacher to thoroughly examine it and plan alternative activities before direct instruction begins. If direct instruction is indeed deemed necessary, deliver it with a perky pace, our second P. A perky pace means teaching at a rate that keeps students' attention and does not linger on any point longer than necessary (Archer & Hughes, 2011). Gifted students need only one or two repetitions in order to grasp a concept (Maker, 1986), as compared to the multiple repetitions needed by their typical peers.

THE TWO C'S: CHOICE AND CHALLENGE

Imagine for a moment that a pretest was given to assess the content knowledge of a third-grade student about the solar system. The teacher scores the pretest and determines the student already knows 90% of the material. What should the teacher's next step be? There is no one right answer, but it is safe to say that the teacher should in some way address the two C's of differentiation—choice and challenge. *Choice* refers to allowing the student to participate in decisions regarding how his or her time and energies should be spent, and *challenge* refers to making sure the student engages in an activity that is meaningful and appropriately difficult.

We will first address choice. All humans have three basic needs: the need to feel autonomous, the need to feel competent, and the need to feel connected (Deci & Ryan, 1985). Allowing students to choose the type of replacement activity they engage in will help them feel autonomous because of the opportunity to be self-directed, competent because the teacher has trusted them to make a decision, and connected if the choices offered extend to the ability to decide whether to work alone or with a group. Kanevsky (2011) referred to this as deferential differentiation. She is careful to mention that this does not mean the teacher gives up all control. Deferential differentiation means allowing students to make appropriate choices while retaining the professional obligation to ensure academic standards are met.

Determining the correct level of challenge for each student can be difficult, but the consequences for not doing so are great. Too little challenge results in a low sense of self-worth (Dweck, 1999) and a lack of confidence in one's ability to tackle complex tasks (Gross, 2004). Many times teachers think an activity is appropriately challenging for a student simply because it is more difficult than what others in the class can complete. Although moving in the right direction, this still might not be sufficiently challenging for a gifted student. Instead, make the benchmark for achievement what experts in the specific field might demonstrate (Callahan, 2009b). A student studying geology, for example, could look at the practices geologists in the field use to do their jobs. Delineate for the student what performance at the novice level, apprentice level, practitioner level, and expert level looks like and let him or her work toward the expert level.

A second method for ensuring rigor and challenge is to help students develop into scholars by teaching them Sandra Kaplan's "Habits of a Scholar" (2012). Expert scholars exhibit the following specific traits or habits:

- perseverance,
- goal setting,
- curiosity,
- academic humility,
- intellectual risk-taking,
- multiple perspectives,
- excellence,
- varied resources,
- preparation,
- pondering ideas, and
- saving ideas.

By modeling and reinforcing these habits on a daily basis, students will learn how to learn and develop into expert scholars, capable of self-reflection and independent investigations. Choose one habit each week, define it for students, and give them opportunities to use it on a daily basis. After all, that is how a habit forms. Ask students to set goals for themselves after identifying which habits they find easy and which they need to work on. Students can also look for how people they come in contact with, see on television, or read about in books exemplify these habits and record the details of the scenario in a journal.

THE TWO F'S: FEEDBACK AND FLEXIBILITY

The teacher is not free from all responsibility when students are working independently on topics of personal interest. The biggest impact a teacher can have on student achievement is giving students prompt, individual feedback. Feedback is the first of the two F's. Research has shown that the average student receives only seconds of personal feedback from a teacher on any given day

(Voerman, Meijer, Korthagen, & Simons, 2012). This is hardly enough time to mentor and guide students as they navigate their way through the academic standards, differentiated activities, and personal challenges they face throughout the year. Time must be built into the schedule for conferencing, sharing ideas, and presenting what was learned to authentic audiences. Otherwise, school will turn into something to be tolerated rather than a tool for transformation.

A great way for students to provide feedback to the teacher is through student surveys. One useful tool for third- through eighth-grade students is the My Class Activities (MCA) instrument designed by Gentry and Gable (2001). The MCA is a 31-question survey teachers can use to assess third- through eighth-grade students' perceptions of interest, challenge, choice, and enjoyment of the classroom environment. A slightly longer survey useful for fifth- through 12th-grade students called the Student Perceptions of Classroom Quality (SPOCQ) designed by Gentry and Owen (2004) measures perceptions of appeal, challenge, choice, meaningfulness, and academic self-efficacy. Both the MCA and the SPOCQ can be downloaded at the Gifted Education Resource Institute's website (http://www.geri.education.purdue.edu).

The second of the two F's is flexibility. The teacher of a differentiated classroom must be willing to make use of flexible groups based on accurate and up-to-date student data. Relying on assumptions based on labels or preconceptions is bound to lead to problems down the road. No predetermined or fixed ends should be put into place for students (Kaplan, 2007). In short, all ceilings standing in the way of student growth should be demolished. This will ensure that everyone has an equal opportunity to participate in tasks that will meet their needs. Once again, preassessment is an invaluable tool for accomplishing this. It is crucial that all differentiation be defensible (Borland, 2009). Teachers should not reserve certain tasks or skills for gifted students if others are capable of learning them as well. All differentiated tasks should be respectful of the learner regardless of their ability level (Tomlinson, 1999). This goes both ways. Students working on lower level tasks should not be forced to complete endless worksheets while advanced students create lavish projects and use interesting technological tools.

Designing respectful tasks includes making sure tasks are sensitive to culture, race, and gender. Quality differentiation is multicultural and not color-blind. One way for ensuring curriculum for students is responsive to the needs of culturally, linguistically, and ethnically diverse students is through the use of the Bloom-Banks Model of multicultural education created by Ford and Harris (2010). This model consists of a matrix that combines Bloom's taxonomy with

Banks' classification system for multicultural lessons. In Banks' view, a lesson meant to be multicultural will fall into one of four categories: contributions (e.g., food, events, people), additive (i.e., cultural concepts and themes), transformation (multiple perspectives), and social action (steps taken to create change). The goal should be to design lessons which could be categorized as transformative and embody social action as often as possible. A copy of the matrix can be found at Donna Ford's website (http://www.drdonnayford.com).

Remember the 2 P's, the 2 C's, and the 2 F's as we move into a more in-depth discussion of specific strategies and techniques for differentiating instruction. We will also discuss common mistakes teachers make and how to avoid them. It is important to remember, however, that differentiation is not simply a collection of strategies, but a mindset (Heacox, 2002)—one that values the needs of students above all else to ensure that learning takes place (Wormeli, 2011).

PART TWO:
SPECIFIC DIFFERENTIATION STRATEGIES

Differentiated lessons for gifted students typically fall into one of two domains: enrichment or acceleration. An enrichment activity is one in which the student stays with the current topic, but explores it more deeply than required by the standards. An accelerated activity involves skipping a topic altogether due to a student's previous knowledge or moving at a faster pace so that the student can advance to the next topic or skill as quickly as possible once mastery has been demonstrated. One is not better than the other, and each comes with its own challenges. The National Association for Gifted Children (NAGC) cautioned teachers in their 1994 Position Paper on Differentiation of Curriculum and Instruction not to rely on one or the other, but advocated using both enrichment and acceleration based on the needs of the child. Table 7.2 lists many of the most widely used differentiation techniques in classrooms today. I will describe each strategy, as well as suggestions for implementation. Most differentiation techniques can be applied to multiple subject areas and adapted for use with any age. Exceptions to this statement are noted in the descriptions that follow.

ENRICHMENT TECHNIQUES

Choice Menus. A choice menu is a list of activities that students can choose from based on their interests, learning preferences, or skill level. Choice menus

TABLE 7.2
DIFFERENTIATION TECHNIQUES

Enrichment	Acceleration
1. Choice Menus	1. Curriculum Compacting
2. Kaplan Depth and Complexity Model	2. Subject Acceleration
3. Problem-Based Learning	3. Grade Skipping
4. Passion Project or Independent Study	4. Independent Study + Check Points
5. Tiered Instruction	5. Expert Mentors
6. Enrichment Triad Model	

come in many forms and can be developed to accommodate the needs of all students. An example choice menu is shown below in Figure 7.2. A second example can be found in Chapter 8: Curriculum Compacting. Choice menus serve as great anchor activities that students can turn to whenever they finish an assignment early or need an extra challenge. Be specific with students about how and when you intend the choice menu to be used. Details to consider include the number of activities students are to complete, if set due dates are to be enforced, and how the completed activities will be evaluated. Whenever possible, involve the students in the creation of the choice menu, include activities at the upper end of Bloom's taxonomy, and ensure several, if not all, multiple intelligences have been addressed.

Kaplan Depth and Complexity Model. The Kaplan Depth and Complexity Model (Kaplan, 2009) is an instructional tool that teachers can use to add rigor to content and foster higher level thinking among students of all ages. The model uses 11 icons or pictures that serve as prompts for students to analyze a topic in a meaningful way. The 11 icons are:

- ethics,
- multiple perspectives,
- change over time,
- big ideas,
- rules,
- across the disciplines,
- trends,
- patterns,
- language of the discipline,
- unanswered questions, and
- details.

Take a poll among the students in your class to determine how many have had chickenpox or the flu. Create a bar graph to show what you discover.	Draw a diagram or create a flow chart displaying how the influenza virus attacks a human cell, eventually making the body sick.	Research online the qualifications someone interested in becoming an epidemiologist would need to fulfill. Which universities offer such training programs?
Visit the website http://www.microbeworld. org/. Click the "Video" tab at the top and watch one of the videos. Create a newscast dramatizing the event as if it were happening now.	YOUR CHOICE *(Talk with your teacher about an idea you have!)*	Bacteria can divide very quickly. If you start with two E. coli bacteria, how many would you have after four hours? Make a guess then watch the video below: http://www. cellsalive.com/ecoli.htm
Create a user's manual or online tutorial explaining how to use a microscope.	Find an epidemiologist you admire or would like to learn about. What about this person makes him or her special? How will you introduce him or her to your classmates?	All bacteria can be categorized into three groups. Conduct research to find out what these three groups are and what makes them unique. Present your findings in a creative way.

FIGURE 7.2. EPIDEMIOLOGY CHOICE MENU.

The first step is to teach students the meaning of each icon. Introducing one or two each week is a good way to begin with younger students. Next, provide opportunities for students to apply the icons to a topic of study together as a class. An example practice lesson is shown in Table 7.3 on the next page. Once students have been exposed to each icon and had sufficient guided practice, they will begin to spontaneously or with limited prompting create rich dialogue and deep understanding about whatever is being investigated. Prompting may come in the form of pointing to the icons displayed on the wall or giving students a graphic organizer to complete. A copy of the icons can be found in the book cited as a reference above.

Problem-Based Learning. Problem-based learning (PBL) is an instructional technique that was first used in the medical field to train aspiring doctors and nurses (Wirkala & Kuhn, 2011). PBL is now widely used in many fields and has been integrated into numerous gifted education programs and models. One well-known example is VanTassel-Baska's integrated curriculum model (Van Tassel-Baska & Little, 2011). The idea is a simple one. Students are presented with an open-ended or "messy" problem and asked to work together to come up with a solution. Before the problem is introduced, the students need to have been

TABLE 7.3
EXAMPLE PRACTICE LESSON USING THE KAPLAN MODEL

Lesson Plan Procedures:

1. Read "The Three Little Pigs" as a class.

2. Choose four icons students have already gone over. (e.g., ethics, multiple perspectives, patterns, and unanswered questions)

3. Ask the students to discuss in small groups how the icons you chose can be applied to the story.

4. Ask the students to write down on a chart, graphic organizer, or journal their ideas.

5. Give each group an opportunity to share with the class.

Example Responses for the Four Icons in this Lesson Plan:

Ethics	Multiple Perspectives
1. The wolf destroyed the pigs' houses.	1. The mother of the wolf might either be proud of her son's violent tendencies or very disappointed.
2. The author of this story seems to have a bias against wolves.	2. An alien from space reading this story might get the idea that animals on Earth can talk and build houses.
3. The moral of the story is that working hard will lead to good things.	
4. It is natural for a wolf to hunt small animals. He should not be punished for this.	

Patterns	Unanswered Questions
1. The number three and the phrase "Not by the hair of my chinny-chin-chin" repeats often in the story.	1. What would have happened if the wolf were a vegetarian?
2. Fairy tales usually begin with "Once upon a time…", have a happy ending, and involve talking animals.	2. Who originally created this fairy tale?
	3. Where did the third pig learn to build houses out of bricks?

taught the steps in the PBL method. This framework consists of identifying the facts within the problem, brainstorming possible solutions, determining what information is needed, applying the new information, and evaluating whether the solution was effective (Hmelo-Silver, 2004). Research has shown that PBL is better than traditional instruction at increasing long-term information retention, conceptual understanding, and self-directed learning (S. Gallagher, 1997). An example PBL activity is shown in Table 7.4.

Passion Projects or Independent Study. Independent study can come in many forms, but three requirements must be met if it is to be successful:

1. students need to have a say in what they are studying,

2. sufficient time must be dedicated for exploring the topic, and

3. specific research skills must be taught.

TABLE 7.4
EXAMPLE PBL ACTIVITY

The Scenario	You receive a birthday card in the mail containing a new crisp $20 bill. You want to thank the person who sent it, but there is no name on the return address or signature on the card. The envelope was sent from a P.O. Box at the zip code 92154. You know the letter was sent three days before your birthday because of the date stamped over the top of the postage stamp in the upper right-hand corner. The postage stamp displays a picture of an endangered sea turtle and there are three balloons and the words "Happy Birthday" on the front of the card. A short message written inside says, "I hope this card gets to you on time. Don't spend all the money in one place!"
What is the main problem?	*List the problem (e.g., We need to identify who sent the card.).*
What do we know?	*List the facts (e.g., We know when the card was sent and from which post office.).*
How can we solve the problem?	*Brainstorm (e.g., Look up the location of the zip code 92154, talk to relatives and ask if anyone in the family loves sea turtles, check your email or Facebook page to see if the person sent a message asking if you received the card.).*
Which idea or ideas will you use?	*Make a decision (e.g., Research the zip code and check email.).*
Were you successful?	*Evaluate the results.*

One of my personal favorite independent study methods is the Passion Project (Cash, 2011). First, ask the students what they would like to learn more about or what they find fascinating. A good way to phrase the question is to say, "If you could teach the class or spend your time learning about anything you wish, what would it be?" Next, develop a plan collaboratively with the student that delineates in writing how the student will explore the topic, when the student can work on his or her project, and how he or she will share the final product with the rest of the class. The Passion Project form and a rubric for evaluating it can be found in Figure 7.3.

Tiered Instruction. Many times teachers think differentiation means creating an individualized lesson plan for each student. Tiered instruction is a great way to use the same objective for all students, but with varying degrees of scaffolding or teacher support. The first step is to determine what the objective or standard you plan to address will be. Next, assess students to determine their readiness level for that material. After carefully analyzing the preassessment, place students into groups (usually two to four) and teach them accordingly.

A teacher can tier by readiness, challenge, interest, content, product, process, resources used, and more. Let's tier a lesson on multiplication facts as an

GUIDELINES FOR CREATING A PASSION PROJECT

1. Passions are those things you love, greatly enjoy doing, and have a good storehouse of knowledge about. Clearly explain your passion and why others would want to know about this topic:

2. Meet with the teacher to find an appropriate unit project that can be replaced by your passion project.

    Teacher meeting date:

    Unit project to be replaced by the passion project:

    Due date for the passion project:

    Signature of teacher:

    Signature of student:

3. Construct your passion project for presentation to the class.
   - Think of an interesting way to present your passion project (PowerPoint, speech, role play, charts/posters, etc.).
   - In your presentation, tell the class:
     - how you became involved with the topic
     - how you came to know your topic
     - why you enjoy your topic
     - what makes your topic interesting

   - Provide the class with information that could stimulate them to investigate this topic.
   - Offer the class a list of resources, websites, books, or other materials that could get other students started on your topic.

4. Your passion project will be graded based on the rubric attached. Your grade on the passion project will replace the grade on the unit project.

continued ➜

FIGURE 7.3. GUIDELINES FOR CREATING A PASSION PROJECT. EXCERPTED FROM *ADVANCING DIFFERENTIATION: THINKING AND LEARNING FOR THE 21ST CENTURY* BY RICHARD M. CASH, ED.D., COPYRIGHT © 2011. USED WITH PERMISSION OF FREE SPIRIT PUBLISHING INC., MINNEAPOLIS, MN; 800-735-7323; HTTP://WWW.FREESPIRIT.COM. ALL RIGHTS RESERVED.

RUBRIC FOR PASSION PROJECT

CATEGORY	4	3	2	1
Preparedness	Student is completely prepared and has obviously rehearsed.	Student seems fairly prepared but might have needed a couple more rehearsals.	Student is somewhat prepared, but it is clear that rehearsal was lacking.	Student does not seem prepared to present.
Enthusiasm	Student's facial expressions and body language generate a strong interest and enthusiasm about the topic in the audience.	Student's facial expressions and body language sometimes generate a strong interest and enthusiasm about the topic in the audience.	Student's facial expressions and body language are used to try to generate enthusiasm, but seem somewhat faked.	Student makes very little use of facial expressions or body language and does not generate much interest in the topic in the audience.
Content	Student shows a full understanding of the topic.	Student shows a good understanding of the topic.	Student shows a good understanding of parts of the topic.	Student does not seem to understand the topic very well.
Resources	Student provides a wide range of resources (at least 10) including websites, text, and artifacts.	Student provides a range of resources (at least 8) including websites, text, and artifacts.	Student provides some resources (at least 5) including websites and text.	Student provides few resources (less than 5), which include websites and text.
Connection to Content	Student makes exceptional connections to content including math, science, social studies, language arts, the arts, physical education, and/or other areas of study.	Student makes some connections to content including math, science, social studies, language arts, the arts, physical education, and/or other areas of study.	Student makes few connections to content including math, science, social studies, language arts, the arts, physical education, and/or other areas of study.	Student makes no connections to content.

FIGURE 7.3. CONTINUED.

example. After giving a pretest, it is determined that students in tier one have not mastered their basic multiplication facts. Their task will be to count by 2's, 3's, 4's, etc. and use manipulatives to solve simple multiplication problems. Tier two students solve multiplication problems correctly 75% of the time, but need a little more practice. Their task will be to play a multiplication game with a partner and then create multiplication word problems for their partner to solve. Tier three students have mastered their basic facts and have moved on to division. Their task will be to solve three-digit by two-digit multiplication problems and then create a learning center that the rest of the class can use for additional practice. Each group is working on multiplication facts, but with varying degrees of difficulty.

Enrichment Triad Model. The Enrichment Triad Model (Renzulli, 1976) is designed to develop interest and expertise in students by providing the opportunity to participate in three types of activities. Type I activities are general exploratory activities intended to expose students to a wide variety of topics, people, hobbies, and events. It is impossible for students to know if they have interest or talent in something if they have never experienced it before.

Type II activities involve individual and small-group lessons that teach a specific thinking skill, research skill, or domain-specific method of study. The initial curiosity resulting from the Type I activity can be nurtured through Type II activities by giving students the tools they need to apply, create, analyze, or evaluate the topic in a systematic way.

If a student continues to show interest and desires to become an expert, they may self-select to pursue a Type III activity. Type III activities are individual or small-group investigations of real-world problems in which students use advanced content and authentic methods to create a product of service for a real audience. At this point, the student will identify a problem related to the a topic of interest, conduct research, and develop a proposed solution. The Enrichment Triad Model is just one component of the Schoolwide Enrichment Model (Renzulli & Reis, 1994), a well-researched, highly effective method for developing talent in students.

ACCELERATION TECHNIQUES

Curriculum Compacting. Curriculum compacting is a technique for eliminating the portions of the curriculum students already know and replacing it with either new material or time to explore topics of interest to the student (Reis, Burns, & Renzulli, 1992). Depending on how the technique is used, curriculum compacting could be listed under both enrichment and acceleration. See Chapter 8: Curriculum Compacting.

Subject Acceleration. All acceleration methods can be divided into two categories: content-based acceleration and grade-based acceleration (NAGC, IRPA, & CSDPG, 2009). Content-based acceleration involves exposing students to content before the typical time a student would encounter it during their academic career (Colangelo, Assouline, & Gross, 2004). Subject acceleration may involve curriculum compacting (see above), sending the student to the next grade level for instruction in that area, Advanced Placement (AP) classes, or even dual enrollment in high school and college.

Regardless of the method of acceleration used, it is crucial that teachers ensure students do not end up with significant gaps in content knowledge. It is not enough to assume a student has mastered a skill simply because he or she is gifted. Teachers need to collect and analyze both formal and informal assessment data to make sure foundational skills have been acquired first. Otherwise, this may cause stress and frustration for the students you are trying to help. Collecting this data on all students, instead of just those identified for gifted programs, will help to ensure everyone has an equal opportunity to participate regardless of gender, race, and socioeconomic status. Relying on general impressions and subjective measures of achievement alone will result in some students falling through the cracks.

Grade Skipping. Grade skipping is one of the most well-known forms of grade-based acceleration. It involves moving a child who chronologically belongs in one grade to a higher grade due to advanced ability. This form of acceleration is often met with skepticism and concern by parents and teachers. Researchers who have studied grade skipping, however, have found no reason for concern. The groundbreaking report *A Nation Deceived* (Colangelo et al., 2004) concluded that grade-accelerated students generally outperform their new classmates even though they are a year or more younger. The researchers also found no differences in socioemotional development between the two groups.

The National Work Group on Acceleration offers several suggestions for ensuring the process of grade skipping is conducted properly (NAGC et al., 2009). The number one point made by this report is that the best interest of the student should always be kept the center of attention. This can be accomplished through making sure that the decision to accelerate a student is made by a child study team and not one individual, that a written acceleration plan is created, that a monitored transition period is observed, and that open and honest communication between all parties is maintained. One tool often used to help in the decision-making process is the Iowa Acceleration Scale (Assouline, Colangelo, Lupowski-Shoplik, Lipscomb, & Forstadt, 2009). It helps parents and teachers objectively look at students and consider carefully each of the important factors necessary to make an informed decision.

Independent Study + Check Points. You will notice that independent study is listed both under enrichment and acceleration. Independent study can be effectively used as a method for accelerating a student in a content area if check points, or time with the teacher, are built into the process. Take math as an example. Imagine that you have an eighth-grade student who is advanced in math. This student is ready for geometry, but it is not possible to transport her to the high school for math class. One possible solution would be to create an independent study plan that involves the student using the free online math videos provided by Khan Academy (http://www.khanacademy.org) to study geometry in combination with a 15-minute meeting with the teacher twice a week to answer questions and monitor progress. The student is able to self-pace, and the teacher provides support and extra practice when it is needed. Other forms of technology could be used as well to allow the student to participate in an online class or video conference with students of similar ability. The same technique using different resources would also work with language arts, social studies, and science topics.

Expert Mentors. As mentioned earlier in this chapter, it is important to use experts in the disciplines as the standard for achievement and not simply a student's peers. A great way to ensure this takes place is through helping to facilitate a relationship between a student and an actual expert. This can be accomplished through reaching out to the local university, turning to an "ask the expert" website, or even making a phone call or writing a letter the old-fashioned way to someone of note. You may be surprised at what could develop. If things do not fall into place, however, suggest that the student identify an expert that he or she would like to learn from and research the expert's work online or in the library. Doing this will allow the student to learn indirectly from the expert and the contributions he or she has made to society.

PART THREE:
COMMON MISTAKES AND HOW TO AVOID THEM

Effective teachers must be well versed in the content areas they are responsible for teaching as well as all relevant pedagogical principles that apply to it (Ellis, Lieberman, & LeRoux, 2009). Tomlinson (2000) wrote that "It is not as difficult for teachers to understand ideas from staff development opportunities as to translate them into consistent classroom practice. Calling for transfer asks teachers to shed comfortable classroom functioning for less predictable ways of working" (p. 28). Becoming competent in differentiated instruction requires being willing to take risks and make mistakes. A few of the most common mistakes include simply requiring more work, teaching skills out of context, thinking of gifted students collectively instead of individually, forgetting to teach students how to handle a situation where differentiation is not possible, and assuming gifted students do not need direct instruction or the teacher's time and attention.

COMMON MISTAKE ONE: THE MORE WORK TRAP

Probably the easiest trap to fall into when differentiating is to require students to solve more of the same type of problem or cover more of the same level of material (NAGC, 1994). This is not differentiation, nor is giving students additional work that is only different because it is not included in the required curriculum. Students often view this as a punishment for being smart. In some cases, this can lead to underachievement.

Instead of more work, the focus should be on providing different work. Change the content, the process, or the product to meet the needs of the student using one of the strategies discussed in part two of this chapter. Let's say a student finishes writing an essay on her favorite book well before others in the class. Instead of asking the student to write a second essay, give her a choice menu or allow her to work on her Passion Project. A third option would be to teach the student a more advanced writing technique the next time an essay is assigned or allow her to move on to a different genre altogether.

COMMON MISTAKE TWO: TEACHING SKILLS IN ISOLATION

A second common mistake is to teach critical thinking skills in isolation from the curriculum (NAGC, 1994). Students will not always make the connection between the skill and when it is to be used without a teacher's guidance. Knowing the steps in the Creative Problem Solving Process, for example, without ever being asked to solve an authentic problem leads the students to ask the question, "So what?" The skill becomes irrelevant and the information is not retained.

Let's use the Kaplan Depth and Complexity Model introductory lesson I presented in this chapter to illustrate this point. If all we did was talk about the icons in relation to "The Three Little Pigs" and never took the next step, the students would not see the usefulness of the icons and how they can be applied to real life. The next step might be to ask the students to read a newspaper article or watch the news and apply the same four icons to what they read or hear. See Table 7.5 for what this might look like.

COMMON MISTAKE THREE: THINKING ALL GIFTED STUDENTS ARE THE SAME

A third common mistake is to put all the gifted students in one group without changing what is taught or how the students are to show what they have learned (NAGC, 1994). Gifted students are not all the same, and an effective teacher will seek out their differences and attempt to address them appropriately (Tomlinson, 1999). Flexible grouping is useful, but only if it is accompanied by a change in the curriculum or instructional technique. It is also important to recognize that many teachers believe that gifted students prefer to work alone. Although true for some, a recent study showed that gifted students often enjoy working in groups as long as their learning goals are being met and mutual respect is maintained (French, Walker, & Shore, 2011).

Teachers can foster positive group dynamics by following a few simple strategies. One of the most important is to remember that the difference between the abilities of the students in any one group should not be too extreme (Robinson, 1991). Otherwise, the gifted student ends up doing most of the work, especially if a group grade is assigned. This also leaves the lower ability student feeling as if he or she is not able to contribute. Instead, assign roles to each student and evaluate their performance separately.

COMMON MISTAKE FOUR: FORGETTING TO EXPLAIN HOW TO HANDLE A NONDIFFERENTIATED TASK

The next mistake is more of an oversight. Many times teachers forget to discuss with students how to deal with assignments or tasks that are not or cannot be differentiated for them (Wormeli, 2005). An undifferentiated assignment may come in the form of a high-stakes test or a task given to students by a teacher who is not familiar with differentiation. In these circumstances, students

TABLE 7.5
EXAMPLE QUESTIONS FOR A NEWSPAPER ARTICLE OR LIVE NEWS COVERAGE

Ethics	Multiple Perspectives
◆ What are the positive and negative effects of this event taking place?	◆ Did the writer or news anchor present all perspectives of the story?
Patterns	**Unanswered Questions**
◆ Did this event remind you of something that happened in the past?	◆ What questions would you ask a witness to the event that the reporter did not ask?

need to know how to respectfully advocate for themselves or, in the case of state testing, take a deep breath and just get through it. The best way to approach this is through meaningful dialogue. Have a conversation with your students and explain the constraints teachers are operating under. Role play with students how they can approach a teacher unwilling to make accommodations and coach them on what or what not to say.

It is important to remind ourselves that differentiation and state standards are not mutually exclusive (Hertberg, 2009). There is a difference between standards and standardization (Tomlinson, 2000). The current accountability movement and a reliance on standardized testing should not be an excuse for sticking to the teacher's manual for those students ready for more. Remove the artificial ceilings holding them back by determining what they know, teaching them what they do not, and providing an opportunity for students to invest the remainder of their time in a meaningfully enriched or accelerated activity.

COMMON MISTAKE FIVE: THINKING "GIFTED STUDENTS DON'T NEED MY HELP!"

The last mistake we will discuss is one of the most pervasive myths teachers hold regarding gifted students. Many teachers believe that gifted students will do well on their own and do not need any help from the teacher (Cleaver, 2008). This is not the case. They need attention, supervision, and, yes, direct instruction as well. It is not acceptable to send gifted students to the back table to work alone for hours at a time or to the library to read on their own.

Consider using a Response to Intervention (RtI) approach with your gifted students. RtI for the gifted is used in almost the same way as it is with students who have learning difficulties. Students' needs are assessed, strategies to meet those needs are implemented, and the results are monitored to see how effective they were over time. Imagine you have a student who is gifted in science but seems bored in class. After talking with the student, you realize she hasn't learned anything this quarter because she spent all summer studying biology for fun at home. An RtI approach would involve sitting with the student to devise an intervention plan using research-based practices to address the boredom issue (e.g., curriculum compacting, independent study, subject acceleration), followed by monitoring her motivation and level of engagement daily over the next few weeks. A great resource for learning more about RtI for the gifted is the book *The New RtI: Response to Intelligence* (Choice & Walker, 2010).

CONCLUSION

Differentiation has been shown to positively affect student achievement and attitudes toward learning (Brighton, Hertberg, Callahan, Tomlinson, & Moon, 2005). Nothing worthwhile comes easily. Patience and perseverance over time will enable you to acquire the skills and mindset necessary to become an expert. Jacobs (2010) described change as being trendy and superficial. What we should aim for instead is growth that is both positive and deep. Revisit your responses to the questions at the beginning of this chapter. Use the lines below to modify your definition of differentiation, if necessary, and create two or three goals for the future.

Differentiation is: _____

_____

_____

_____

_____

In the words of Tomlinson (2004), "A readiness match maximizes the chance of appropriate challenge and growth. An interest match heightens motivation. A learning profile match increases efficiency of learning" (p. 188). Use the checklist in Figure 7.4 to remind you of the principles discussed in this chapter and create meaningful learning experiences that your students will take with them for a lifetime.

Is the differentiated activity:		
Deferential?	☐ Yes	☐ No
Defensible?	☐ Yes	☐ No
Respectful?	☐ Yes	☐ No
Multi-cultural?	☐ Yes	☐ No
Appropriately challenging?	☐ Yes	☐ No
Connected to the curriculum?	☐ Yes	☐ No
Different work NOT more work?	☐ Yes	☐ No

FIGURE 7.4. DIFFERENTIATION CHECKLIST.

CHAPTER 8

CURRICULUM COMPACTING

Organized Common Sense[*]

Before reading this chapter, please take the following pretest.

CURRICULUM COMPACTING PRETEST

1. How would you rate your current level of knowledge regarding curriculum compacting?

    NOVICE   PROFICIENT   ADVANCED   EXPERT

2. Please complete this statement: The purpose of curriculum compacting is to . . .

    _____

    _____

    _____

---

[*]   This chapter was contributed by Jason McIntosh.

3. What are the two prerequisites for implementing curriculum compacting?

     _____

     _____

     _____

4. If a student compacts out of a concept, I should require that student to work on a skill he/she is having difficulty with.

     ❏ TRUE   ❏ FALSE

5. Who decides what the replacement activities should be?

     _____

     _____

     _____

6. How would you compact for a gifted student who is underachieving in all subjects?

     _____

     _____

     _____

"When once the child has learned that four and two are six, a thousand repetitions will give him no new information, and it is a waste of time to keep him employed in that manner" (Greenwood, 1887, p. 138). Although written more than 100 years ago, this statement illustrates the fact that the ultimate goal of curriculum compacting is to eliminate unnecessary repetition and replace it with meaningful and rigorous learning experiences tailored to the needs of advanced learners (see Figure 8.1). As Sally Reis and Joseph Renzulli (1992) have said, curriculum compacting is best understood as "organized common sense" (p. 51). In today's age of high-stakes testing, standards-based curriculum, and large class sizes, teachers simply cannot afford to waste a minute of valuable instructional time. Curriculum compacting is one way to efficiently use the limited time and resources available to meet the needs of individual students and ensure that everyone learns something new each and every day.

What is curriculum compacting?

"A procedure used to streamline the regular curriculum for students who are capable of mastering it at a faster pace."
(Reis, Burns, & Renzulli, 1992, p.5)

FIGURE 8.1. CURRICULUM COMPACTING DEFINITION.

Too often, gifted students feel that they are forced to "learn" anew the concepts or skills they have already mastered (J. Gallagher, 1997). Think for a moment what it would be like if you attended a daylong teachers' conference and discovered that every keynote and breakout session addressed the same three main points. It may have been interesting the first time, but by the end of the day you would probably ask for your money back. Chances are you probably would leave after lunch. What if you were not allowed to leave and you found out the conference lasted a week? Imagine experiencing this day after day, month after month, for years. Many gifted children experience this phenomenon on a regular basis.

A study conducted by Reis and Purcell concluded that, in many cases, 40%–50% of the regular curriculum could be replaced for gifted learners (1993). Teaching to the middle is no longer acceptable. "It is important that all teachers recognize that working to meet the needs of bright students is not an option, but a responsibility" (Starko, 1986, p. 33). It is our job to remove the artificial ceilings holding students back and begin thinking outside the age/grade box.

Much has been said and written about Vygotsky's "Zone of Proximal Development" (Vygotsky & Cole, 1978). This theory explains the difference between what a student can do with help from a more capable learner versus what they can do alone. If this zone can be identified, instruction can be designed to ensure that the level of challenge and scaffolding provided is at an appropriate level for each individual learner. If the level of challenge is too high or the amount of scaffolding is too low, students experience frustration and anxiety. If the level of challenge is too low or the amount of scaffolding is too high, students experience boredom and do not learn anything new. It can be difficult to determine the level of challenge and support needed by each student, but curriculum compacting is one tool for accomplishing this.

AN OVERVIEW OF THE PROCESS

You may have wondered why you were asked to take a pretest before reading this chapter. Assessing previous knowledge is one of the three important steps in compacting curriculum. In this case, you are seeing the process from the learner's perspective. It may appear to you that this was the first step. Determining what the learner already knows is actually step number two. The first step was covertly executed during the writing of this chapter. As the "teacher," I had to conduct a literature review, carefully analyze the research on the topic in order to determine the salient points I wanted to communicate to you, and then create a preassessment to measure your prior knowledge.

The third and final step to compacting curriculum involves creating replacement activities for learners who have already mastered the concept as determined by the preassessment. These replacement activities are best created collaboratively with the students and can fall into two broad categories. A replacement activity can be used to accelerate the learner to new concepts or to enrich the original concept by adding depth or breadth. Using this chapter as an example, if I chose to focus on acceleration, I might ask anyone who scored an 85% or higher on the pretest to skip the remainder of this chapter and proceed directly to the next chapter. If I chose to enrich the topic instead, I might ask those who scored 85% or higher to locate and read two research articles on curriculum compacting and then share what they learn with a colleague.

There are many facets to curriculum compacting and numerous considerations to ponder. The remainder of this chapter will elaborate on the compacting process, offer suggestions, and answer frequently asked questions in order to maximize the likelihood that you will be able to successfully implement curriculum compacting with the students in your classroom. I will also examine how the process can be adapted to meet the needs of different types of gifted learners. Four student archetypes will be used to facilitate this discussion: a *high-achieving* gifted student I will call Amy, an *underachieving* gifted student I will call George, a student gifted in only *one specific area* I will call Juan, and a student from a *low socioeconomic background* I will call Alisha.

Steps in Curriculum Compacting

1. Define the goals and outcomes for the unit.
2. Identify the students who have already mastered the objectives.
3. Decide on replacement activities.

(Reis & Renzulli, 1992, pp. 53–55)

FIGURE 8.2. CURRICULUM COMPACTING STEPS.

STEP ONE:
DEFINE THE GOALS AND OUTCOMES

As mentioned in Figure 8.2, the first step in the compacting process is to define the goals and outcomes of the unit. This entails having a thorough understanding of both the content and standards embedded within the lesson or lessons. It is the teacher's responsibility to have a strong grasp of what the students are expected to know, understand, and do (Tomlinson, 2001) before proceeding to the next step in the process. No two students are the same, but this is true of teachers as well. One of the wonderful characteristics of curriculum compacting is that it can accommodate any teaching style, as long as the individual has a thorough knowledge of the content to be studied and is capable of carefully analyzing student data (Sisk, 1988).

There are two ways of looking at step one. A teacher may choose to define the goals and outcomes of a topic *or* a time period (Renzulli, Smith, & Reis, 1982). For example, during a unit on the solar system, Teacher A may closely examine each major topic covered during the unit (planets, comets, constellations, other galaxies, etc.) to decide what students need to know about each one. Teacher B, however, may decide to break the unit down into weeks and examine what needs to be covered holistically during week one (gravity and the sun), week two (planets and the asteroid belt), and so on. How you approach this step will have implications for step three. I will discuss this in more detail later in the chapter.

Step one would not look significantly different for Amy, George, Juan, or Alisha. The characteristics of each learner will, however, help to inform the decision as to what to compact for each student and when.

STEP TWO:
PREASSESS STUDENT KNOWLEDGE

The second step in the compacting process is to identify the students who have already mastered the objectives of the unit or are capable of progressing at a much faster pace than their peers. It is important to recognize that students from low socioeconomic backgrounds, like Alisha, may not have been exposed to certain concepts but can master them quickly when given the chance. They may not look like candidates for compacting at first glance, but they should be afforded the same opportunities as those with plenty of social capital and a wealth of experiences.

The most common method of assessing prior knowledge is through a pretest, such as an end-of-unit assessment or a quarterly benchmark test. Other frequently used, nontest preassessments include past grades, discussions with a student's prior teacher, achievement test scores, and student demonstrations of proficiency (Reis, Kulikovich, Callard, Hébert, Plucker, Purcell, Rogers, & Smist, 1993). One simple method involves giving the students 10 minutes at the beginning of a unit to write down everything they know about the upcoming unit or topic. Their responses can easily be analyzed for detail and accuracy. I incorporated this technique into an instrument I created called the General Preassessment of Students (GPS). It was designed to assess both motivation to learn and prior knowledge of content for students in grades 3–12 and requires minimal preparation by the teacher. It can be found on pages 128–130.

Whichever method of preassessment you decide to use, make sure you have clear and convincing evidence that the student is ready to move on. It is not sufficient to assume that because a child is gifted in a particular subject he or she must already have prior content knowledge and be able to accurately demonstrate whatever the given subject-specific skills might be. Situations like the one illustrated in the note in Figure 8.3 can result when teachers do not use data to guide their decision making. This is an actual note from a fifth-grade student.

Now, let's look at how step two might look different for Amy, George, Juan, and Alisha. Amy is a high-achieving, intrinsically motivated gifted student. There are few concepts she has difficulty mastering. The first step in choosing the best plan of action for Amy is to take a careful look at her preassessment to determine what she already knows. Due to the fact that she is a quick learner and highly motivated, I might not only accelerate or enrich the aspects of the topic she already knows, but compact for time the components of the unit she

Dear Teacher,
I don't quite get division. I well…don't know how. EEEP! But, please don't tell my grandma cause then she won't be proud of me. So maybe could you please help me? Please! I'm desperate. Really desperate!
                                                                        Your Student

FIGURE 8.3. NOTE FROM STUDENT.

does not know. Knowing it will take Amy only one or two repetitions to master the material she is unfamiliar with, I will allow her to judge how long it will be necessary for her to participate in whole-group instruction on those topics. Once she feels confident that any holes have been filled, she can proceed to the next gap or to an enrichment activity requiring her to apply her newfound knowledge.

George presents a different scenario. Underachievement can have several sources. It will be necessary to discover why George is underachieving before deciding what the next steps should be. If George has an undiagnosed learning disability, it would be necessary to proceed quite differently than if he is simply bored in class due to unchallenging assignments or has had previous bad experiences with well-meaning, but inflexible, unsympathetic teachers. Typically, students compact due to their ability to demonstrate upcoming objectives before they are taught. In George's situation, it might be a good idea to find out what his interests are and compact a subject he is unmotivated to learn, at least temporarily, in order to afford him the time to pursue a passion of his own. This might very well contribute to a complete turnaround in his attitude and motivation toward school for the remainder of the year.

The approach to Juan, a gifted mathematician but struggling reader, will be altogether different than the approach to Amy and George. One thing is certain: Juan would definitely benefit from a compacted math curriculum. We will examine what this might look like in step three. As a rule, it is important to remember that when students buy back time through compacting, they should not be required to spend their extra time remediating a weakness. In this example, I would not tell Juan he has to practice phonics while the rest of the class works on the math skills he has already mastered.

The best strategy for meeting the needs of students from low socioeconomic backgrounds like Alisha would be to follow the same steps as those used with Amy, our high-achieving gifted student, except with additional monitoring and scaffolding from the teacher. The keys here are communication, feedback, and possibly, additional opportunities for formative assessment. If evidence of underachievement or a learning disability are demonstrated as time goes on, the same techniques used with George would apply.

GPS PREASSESSMENT

Name _____ Date _____

Please answer the 10 questions below based on the information in the box provided to you by your teacher.

Unit or Topic: _____

Major objectives of the unit:

- _____
- _____
- _____

1. Pretend your brain is like a gas tank. Shade in on the gas gauge how full you feel your tank would be if it were filled with everything you know about this topic.

2. Write a few sentences telling me what you already know about this topic.

_____

_____

_____

_____

_____

3. List two "big ideas" and four vocabulary words that go along with this topic.

Big Idea #1	Vocabulary Words	
	1.	2.
Big Idea #2	**Vocabulary Words**	
	3.	4.

4. If you could ask an expert on this topic one question, what would it be?

_____

_____

_____

_____

_____

5. Describe the event, concept, object, or term shown in the box.

_____

_____

_____

6. Where did most of your knowledge come from? (Circle ALL that apply)
   a. Parents
   b. Teachers
   c. Television
   d. Books
   e. Other

7. How interested are you in learning more about this topic? (Circle ONE answer)
   a. Not at all.
   b. If I have to.
   c. Sure, why not?
   d. I can't wait!

8. How important do you think this topic is for you to learn? (Circle ONE answer)
   a. I'll never use it.
   b. I'm not sure.
   c. My teacher says it's important.
   d. I think it will be important for me.

9. What do you think your grade will be on the test over this topic?

   _____

   _____

10. Write a goal for yourself related to learning this topic.

    _____

    _____

    _____

    _____

    _____

STEP THREE:
CHOOSE REPLACEMENT ACTIVITIES

The third step in the compacting process has traditionally proven to be the most difficult for teachers (Reis & Purcell, 1993). Many teachers feel that they do not have the time or expertise to plan appropriate replacement activities. The most important point to remember is that students should not simply be given more work, but altogether different work. "If we are to expect them to work harder and faster to prove mastery of basic skills, it is unreasonable to expect them to do so when the reward is more of the same" (Starko, 1986, p. 29).

The most frequently used method of replacing previously mastered material is through enrichment (Reis & Purcell, 1993). To review, enrichment means to add depth or breadth to the content being studied. This could take the form of learning games, commercially created units of study, extension activities found in the teacher's guide you seldom have time to try, making use of Sandra Kaplan's Depth and Complexity Model (Kaplan & Gould, 2005), problem-based learning, or any number of projects. High-achieving Amy might benefit from being provided a choice menu. Figure 8.4 shows a possible choice menu that might be used during a science unit on invasive plants.

A wonderful option for underachieving George is to have him engage in an independent study project within an area of interest to him. Involving students in the process of selecting and developing their own replacement activities is the most powerful way to create meaningful and relevant learning experiences for them. Through their own involvement, they are also more likely to be invested and committed to the project, thus producing high-level work. This may take the form of a Passion Project (Cash, 2011), Type III enrichment (Renzulli & Reis, 1997), or the development of individual excellence goals (Gagne, 1999). A description of a Passion Project and Type III enrichment can be found in Chapter 7: Differentiation. Individual excellence goals are goals students create for themselves targeting something they would like to develop expertise in. A framework I developed for accomplishing this with third through 12th-grade students can be found on pages 134–137.

Juan, our gifted mathematician, might enjoy creating a learning center on a mathematics concept being taught in the near future that the other students would benefit from. He might also enjoy solving logic problems, playing math-related online games, or learning about the stock market and graphing its

Invasive Plants Choice Menu		
Choose an invasive plant found in our area. Give it human characteristics and create a "wanted" poster.	Pretend you are an invasive plant. Write a letter to a town asking permission to grow there. Be persuasive!	Invent your own invasive plant. What native species will it displace? What positive or negative side effects will it have on the environment?
Create a television commercial to run on ABC during your favorite program that uses the slogan, "Don't Plant a Pest!"	**Student Choice** (Negotiate With Teacher)	Identify the plants in the works of art your teacher will show you using a reference book. Create your own work of art that includes at least one invasive plant species.
Pretend the governor of your state has asked you to join a panel of citizens charged with designing a plan for combating invasive plants. What would you recommend and why?	Choose an invasive plant found in our area. Research how it was introduced, why it is a problem, and what can be done about it. Create a PowerPoint presentation to share.	Imagine waking up to find ALL the plants in your neighborhood are invasive. Create a skit with a partner about the plants you discover. Make sure to mention where each plant originates from.

FIGURE 8.4. INVASIVE PLANTS CHOICE MENU.

daily changes. Possibly, a more appropriate educational intervention would be to use acceleration instead of enrichment.

Mathematics provides an easy platform for subject acceleration. After identifying Juan's weaknesses using an end-of-unit assessment, a teacher could then work with him to fill any gaps and then have him move on to the next chapter. The process would repeat and he could potentially finish all grade-level work by the end of the second quarter. The next question you might ask is, "Then what do I do?" Once again, you have options. You might acquire the next grade-level textbook for him and continue on, or you could use free online resources such as Khan Academy (http://www.khanacademy.org). A third option might be to partner with the next grade level's math teacher and have Juan go to his or her class during math time.

Teachers often feel the effects of the "Don't Steal My Thunder Syndrome" (Sebring & Tussey, 1992, p. 4) from their colleagues. Some districts even have formal policies forbidding teachers from accelerating beyond the present grade level. It is important to remind ourselves as educators that our job is to do what is best for the students, not what is convenient for us. Will accelerating Juan in math create more work for you and possibly others? Yes, but Juan will benefit greatly from this accommodation. Work as a team with Juan, your principal, and his parents to ensure that no artificial ceilings hold him back.

According to the Templeton Report, a national report on acceleration in the United States otherwise known as *A Nation Deceived* (Colangelo et al., 2004), acceleration can be broken into two categories: grade-based and subject-based. Grade-based acceleration is equivalent to grade skipping, whereas subject-based acceleration refers to giving students access to advanced content in one or more subject areas before they traditionally would encounter it. The authors of the Templeton Report reviewed more than 380 studies and concluded that almost all types of acceleration result in achievement gains for students. Just remember that acceleration should not cause undue stress on the students (Renzulli et al., 1982). Monitor their progress as you would any students' and provide "reassurance of support, insight, and occasional direction" (Menke, 1993, p. 39).

The learning opportunities offered to Alisha could quite possibly resemble those offered to Amy, George, or Juan. Once again, the important considerations for teachers are that she may need a little more support and additional feedback. It might be a good idea to have Alisha work with Amy or one of the other students in a small group. Her fellow students would be able to quickly provide any needed background information, enabling her to move through the curriculum at a pace appropriate for her rate of learning.

INDIVIDUAL EXCELLENCE GOALS
(3rd–12th Grade)

Student Name: _____

Teacher's Name: _____

Grade: _____ School: _____ Date: _____

1. Please fill in the table by listing three or more strengths, interests, and challenges that you have. (To be filled in by student)

STRENGTHS • *What am I good at?* • *You may use a Multiple Intelligences survey to help you.*	
INTERESTS • *What would I like to know more about or be able to do? Be specific!* • *You may use an interest survey to help you.*	
CHALLENGES • *What gets in your way or is hard for you?*	

2. Think about the interests you listed above. Choose one or two interests that relate to language arts, math, science, social studies, or the arts that you would like to become an expert in this year.

First Choice	
Second Choice	

3. How would you rank your current level of expertise in that area? (Circle one)

   Novice   *Proficient*   *Advanced*   *Expert*

4. How much time are you willing to commit to becoming an expert in that topic? Remember, the higher the goal, the more effort you will need to achieve your goal. Make sure you consider your strengths and challenges as well. (Circle one)

   Little Time   *Some Time*   *A Lot of Time*

   Caution: If you are not willing to spend time exploring the topic or are already an expert in that area, choose a different interest.

5. List in the table below any materials or resources you will need in order to explore your first choice.

6. Your teacher will give you opportunities throughout the year to buy back some of your time so you can explore your area of interest. The regular curriculum will be differentiated for you in the following ways: (To be completed by the teacher)

    _____

    _____

    _____

    _____

    _____

    _____

    _____

    _____

7. In order for this to happen, you must promise to do several things. Read through the list and sign your name saying you agree to abide by these conditions.

I will not bother anyone or call attention to the fact I am doing different work than others.	I will stay on task at all times when exploring my chosen topic.	I will keep a daily log of my progress.
I will participate in whole-class activities as the teacher indicates without arguing.	I will not interrupt the teacher while he or she is teaching.	I will share what I have learned with the class at the end of the year.

I agree to these conditions: _____

(Student signature)

8. How will you show what you have learned?

First Choice	
Second Choice	

(Examples: PowerPoint, skit, learning center, video, collage, song, teaching a lesson, pamphlet, essay, model, journal, exhibit, experiment, speech, invention, magazine, scrapbook, etc.)

9. At the end of each quarter, you and your teacher will evaluate your progress using the chart below. You will be compared only to yourself. (Your personal best!)

Quarter	Date	Student Self-Evaluation				Teacher Evaluation			
1		1	2	3	4	1	2	3	4
2		1	2	3	4	1	2	3	4
3		1	2	3	4	1	2	3	4
4		1	2	3	4	1	2	3	4

Key: 1–Still a Novice   2–Proficient   3–Advanced   4–Expert

10. Set a completion target date! I plan to complete my goal by: _____

GETTING STARTED

The easiest way to begin compacting is to start with the subject you feel most comfortable teaching, or by implementing compacting with one or two students who are talented in that particular domain. Once your confidence increases, you can then branch out into other subjects or increase the number of students involved. It can be helpful to think of curriculum compacting in terms of a student being absent from school (Starko, 1986). When the student returns the following day, chances are you do not ask him or her to complete every activity that he or she missed. You consider his or her current level of performance and the value of each activity to ultimately select the most relevant activities for the student to make up. In short, you compact the previous days' learning experiences for an individual student.

Group compacting is another option for getting your feet wet. This involves choosing a small group of students, for example the top group in reading, and having those students work as an entity at a faster pace than the rest of the class (Starko, 1986). It can also be helpful to analyze student data and plan differentiated activities with a team of teachers instead of trying to do it all alone. Do not forget to consult with your district's gifted coordinator if you have one. The gifted coordinator can be a great source of guidance along the way.

Many elementary teachers choose to begin by compacting spelling. The pretest is given at the beginning of the week and one of two things typically happens: a more rigorous word list is given to the students who have already mastered those words, or alternate assignments are given that require the students to use those words at an ever-increasing level of difficulty (Starko, 1986). A different way to compact spelling is to give the students the words prior to the pretest, possibly the Friday before. This will allow more students to participate in compacting besides just the innately good spellers. You will also be rewarding the motivated spellers who need only a few days to study. Eventually, you might be able to replace a large portion of the in-class time dedicated to teaching spelling with more important content.

Math is the subject most often compacted (Reis & Purcell, 1993) due to its linear nature. Just as with Juan, the end-of-unit test is given at the beginning of the unit, the results are analyzed, and the students who have mastered the concepts covered can either go on to the next skill in math or participate in an independent study project or enrichment activity.

You might have noticed that I have not used the word "gifted" at all in this section of the chapter. Curriculum compacting is something from which many students can benefit. James Borland (2009) addressed this notion in his antimodel of gifted education by introducing the concept of "defensible differentiated curriculum" (p. 105). If all students can benefit from learning a particular skill or strategy, why shouldn't they be given access to it? From this perspective, introducing curriculum compacting to the entire class would be imperative. In the beginning, have all students take the pretest, but with the understanding that it will cover concepts they have not yet been taught. You might be surprised at who does unexpectedly well. Continued failure on the pretest, however, can demoralize students. A choice to opt out after a certain time period is appropriate.

I have always posted a sign in my classroom that reads, "Fair is not everyone getting the same thing. Fair is everyone getting what they need to be successful." Reinforcing this message throughout the year helps students understand your intentions and alleviates most, if not all, possible concerns voiced by parents, students, and administrators.

Documenting the process is very important. If a parent comes to you and says, "How are you differentiating for my child?", you can simply go to your filing cabinet and pull out the evidence. The most widely used instrument for collecting this information is The Individual Educational Programming Guide (Reis, Burns, & Renzulli, 1992), shown on page 141. Supporting documentation such as copies of preassessments, the student's daily log, and documentation of the final project can be attached directly to this form.

When teachers who do not consistently use compacting were asked why, multiple reasons were given. Lack of teacher preparation to initiate preassessment and differentiation, limited time to create replacement activities, and a lack of money to purchase the supplies necessary to conduct certain types of enrichment activities (Reis, Westberg, Kulikowich, & Purcell, 1998) were at the top of the list. One major concern voiced by many teachers is fear related to lower test scores. You can put your mind at ease, however. Multiple studies have shown that students who experience curriculum compacting do as well or better on standardized tests than those who do not (Reis et. al., 1998; Rogers & Kimpston, 1992; Schultz, 1991). Of course, there is more to student achievement than test scores. Engaging students in challenging work increases cognition, which then increases overall achievement as well. Increased motivation to learn due to opportunities for autonomy and the elimination of the boredom factor is something not to be forgotten as well.

A new concern has recently been raised. How do the Common Core State Standards fit into this equation? These standards are internationally benchmarked and therefore more rigorous and challenging for most students. This does not mean, however, that they are sufficient to meet the needs of gifted learners. In fact, the following statement is written right into the standards themselves: "The Standards do not define the nature of advanced work for students who meet the Standards prior to the end of high school" (English Language Arts Standards, p. 6).

Differentiation is still critical. Because the Common Core State Standards are new, it will be even more important to take considerable time with step one in the compacting process. Make sure to closely analyze each standard in order to determine exactly what it is asking your students to understand or be able to do. The National Association for Gifted Children has created an online document that discusses in great detail how the Common Core State Standards directly affect gifted students. It can be accessed at http://www.nagc.org/ CommonCoreStateStandards.aspx.

CONCLUSION

In true pretest/posttest fashion, take the test from the beginning of the chapter once again in order to assess how much you have learned. Just remember, the point of compacting is to ensure there is no cap on achievement in your classroom (Stiles, 1994). Removing previously learned material with the eyes and careful hands of a surgeon will help to remove the weight of an unchallenging curriculum from the backs of your students (Renzulli, 1995). Who knows? You might actually eliminate the dreaded phrase "I'm bored" from the mouths of your students once and for all.

INDIVIDUAL EDUCATION PROGRAMMING GUIDE
THE COMPACTOR

Prepared by: Joseph S. Renzulli and Linda M. Smith

Name _____   Age _____   Teacher(s) _____   Individual Conference Dates and Persons Participating in Planning of IEP

School _____   Grade _____   Parent(s) _____

Curriculum Areas to be Considered for Compacting Provide a brief description of basic material to be covered during this marking period and the assessment information or evidence that suggests the need for compacting.	Procedures for Compacting Basic Material Describe activities that will be used to guarantee proficiency in basic curricular areas.	Acceleration and/or Enrichment Activities Describe activities that will be used to provide advanced-level learning experiences in each area of the regular classroom.

☐ Check here if additional information is recorded on the reverse side.

FREQUENTLY ASKED QUESTIONS ABOUT COMPACTING

Question 1: How do I grade a student who has compacted out of the regular curriculum?

Answer: In most cases, students who are compacting have already demonstrated mastery of the regular curriculum. For that reason, give them an "A" for meeting the standards. That being said, compacting students will still benefit from receiving feedback. Consider using a rubric or more qualitative approaches to accomplish this.

Question 2: What percentage should I use to determine mastery on the preassessment?

Answer: The most commonly used standard is 85% (Reis & Purcell, 1993); however, you can set your standard at whatever level you choose. Also, remember that the information you use to determine if a student has already mastered the objectives of the lesson or unit does not have to be in the form of a formal written pretest.

Question 3: How should I explain compacting to my students?

Answer: Begin by explaining the concept of differentiation to students using this example. When we go to the doctor, he or she examines us to decide what we need and then gives us the prescribed treatment for that ailment. The doctor does not say, "Well, I'm only treating broken arms today, so I'm going to put a cast on your arm. I hope it helps with your headache." That would be silly. For that reason, there will be several groups working in the classroom because we all learn differently. Draw a flow chart on the board illustrating the steps in the compacting process (Sutton, 2000) and explain that this is one way you will implement differentiation in your classroom. Encourage the students to ask questions.

Question 4: How do I support the students working independently while I am teaching the regular lesson?

Answer: One great idea is to provide students with a form to complete at the end of each work session (Sutton, 2000). The form has three items:

- We need our teachers to answer these questions:
- We will bring the following supplies tomorrow:
- We need our teacher to supply these things:

It is important to set the ground rules for the students who are compacting. Make sure they know not to brag about their opportunity to participate, to use "6-inch voices" if working with a partner, to stay on task, and not to disturb the rest of the class.

Question 5: What other traits should I consider when deciding if a student should compact or not?

Answer: Their capacity to learn at a faster rate, their task commitment, and their maturity level (Reiss & Follo, 1993) are three major characteristics. Do not forget to consider the unique needs of underachieving or twice-exceptional students.

Question 6: If I am a coordinator of a gifted program, how do I encourage classroom teachers to implement curriculum compacting?

Answer: Research has shown that the single greatest factor in determining a teacher's willingness and ability to compact is the quality of the training and support they receive (Starko, 1986). Remember to be patient, for as teachers begin to see the benefits of compacting they will be more committed to applying it on a daily basis (Reis et al., 1993). If you happen to encounter a teacher who is unwilling to compact despite offers of help and support, the answer is quite simple: do not place a gifted student in their classroom in the future (Starko, 1986).

CHAPTER 9

IDENTIFYING AND SERVING TWICE-EXCEPTIONAL STUDENTS IN A TSCG CLASSROOM*

In recent years, more consideration has been placed on identifying and serving twice-exceptional students—those who are gifted but also have co-occurring learning and/or behavioral differences. (I believe that learning and behavior disabilities should be seen not as deficiencies but as "learning differences" by educators. If teachers differentiate instruction in a way that honors learner interests and learning and production preferences, all students will continue to grow. And after all, isn't this the purpose of education?)

---

* This chapter was contributed by C. Matthew Fugate.

For many teachers and administrators, twice exceptionality can seem like an oxymoron. How could Johnny be gifted but also read below grade level? Rachel is always acting out and interrupting others; therefore, she couldn't possibly be gifted, could she? The challenge for teachers in recognizing these students, and the reason that this population of gifted students has been overlooked for so long, is due to a phenomenon known as masking—the students' gifts mask their differences and/or their differences mask their gifts. The end result for many of these students is that neither of their needs is met and they may be seen as "just an average student" (Foley-Nicpon, Assouline, & Colangelo, 2013).

The question we must then ask ourselves as educators is, are these differences necessarily a bad thing? Many of the traits that differentiate these twice-exceptional students in our classrooms are those that ultimately may hold the most value as these students leave school and enter the workforce (Robbins, 2011). Until educators begin to recognize the potential of this special group of students, many of our best and brightest might continue to be overlooked as just average or unexceptional, resulting in a potential loss to us all. This loss may be avoided through the implementation of a research-based program such as Total School Cluster Grouping.

WHO ARE THEY?

To fully understand who these students are, it is first important to establish the definitions that delineate their unique qualities. The U.S. Department of Education (USDOE) has defined giftedness as:

> Children and youth with outstanding talent perform or show the potential for performing at remarkably high levels of accomplishment when compared with others of their age, experience, or environment. These children and youth exhibit high capability in intellectual, creative, and/or artistic areas, possess an unusual leadership capacity, or excel in specific academic fields. They require services or activities not ordinarily provided by the schools. Outstanding talents are present in children and youth from all cultural groups, across all economic strata, and in all areas of human endeavor (O'Connell-Ross, 1993, p. 26).

The Individuals with Disabilities Act (IDEA; 2006) and the USDOE define students with learning disabilities as:

> The child does not achieve adequately for the child's age or to meet State-approved grade-level standards in one or more of the following areas, when provided with learning experiences and instruction appropriate for the child's age or State-approved grade-level standards: oral expression; listening comprehension; written expression; basic reading skills; reading fluency skills; reading comprehension; mathematics calculation; mathematics problem solving. The child does not make sufficient progress to meet age or State-approved grade-level standards in one or more of the areas identified . . . when using a process based on the child's response to scientific, research-based intervention; or the child exhibits a pattern of strengths and weaknesses in performance, achievement, or both, relative to age . . . (http://www. idea.ed.gov).

Baum (2010a) noted the definition for twice exceptionality proposed by a joint commission consisting of representatives from the Nationals Research Center on the Gifted and Talented (NRC G/T), the Association for the Education of Gifted Underachieving Students (AEGUS), and the Bridges Academy:

> Twice-exceptional learners are students who give evidence of the potential for high achievement capability in areas such as specific academics; general intellectual ability; creativity; leadership; AND/OR visual, spatial, or performing arts AND also give evidence of one or more disabilities as defined by federal or state eligibility criteria such as specific learning disabilities; speech and language disorders; emotional/behavioral disorders; physical disabilities; autism spectrum; or other health impairments, such as ADHD (para. 4).

Gifted children need experiences that that are outside the realm of the traditional school environment. Further, in this age of high-stakes testing, limited budgets, and limited time, states and individual school districts have been allowed to determine the criteria they use in identifying gifted students (McCoach, Kehle,

Bray, & Siegle, 2001), often ignoring all other areas of giftedness beyond traditional intellect (Baum & Olenchak, 2002). This can cause problems in the identification of gifted students with learning differences.

Due to the nature of twice exceptionality and the masking effect that often results, it is difficult to precisely state exactly how many students would fall into this category. However, it is estimated that there are currently more than 360,000 twice-exceptional students in schools across the United States (Kalbfleisch, 2013). The problem for these students is that many teachers, gifted coordinators, special education professionals, and administrators fail to recognize the potential of this group of students, and if they are recognized at all, it is sometimes their perceived weaknesses, and not their strengths, that become the focus for learning in the classroom.

CHARACTERISTICS OF TWICE-EXCEPTIONAL LEARNERS

Often, twice-exceptional students struggle with fundamental skills due to difficulties with cognitive processing, requiring them to develop compensation strategies to help them acquire basic skills and information. However, Baum and Owen (1988) conducted a study with 112 gifted and/or learning different students and discovered that although twice-exceptional students had a tendency to achieve at lower levels than their peers and/or misbehave in the classroom, these same students possessed higher levels of creativity, a finding supported by other researchers (e.g., Cramond, 1994; Fugate, Zentall, & Gentry, 2013; Kalbfleisch & Iguchi, 2008; White & Shah, 2006, 2011).

Frequently, twice-exceptional students have reading difficulties due to cognitive processing deficits that make it difficult for them to master necessary skills (e.g., automaticity, fluency, perceptual scanning; Baum & Owen, 2004). Additionally, although twice-exceptional students can have high verbal abilities, they often have difficulties with written expression and may use language inappropriately. Finally, these students may have keen observation skills yet have poor working memory, the ability to hold information in mind. However, despite these issues, once these students have had the opportunity to effectively decode the material presented to them, their ability to comprehend and synthesize that material exceeds that of their typical peers (Baum & Owen, 2004).

Often, when disruptive behaviors do occur in the classroom, it can be an outward sign of the students' feelings of inadequacy and low self-esteem. Dabrowski and Piechowski (1977) found that these students displayed emotional intensity and experienced extreme depression and frustration that led to a general lack of motivation. All too often, these students perceive their work in school to be either too difficult or too easy. As a result, they feel that they have no control over their academic achievement and often blame others when they are faced with an academic failure (Baum & Owen, 2004).

Characteristics of students with specific differences can be very distinct. For instance, the characteristics of students diagnosed with ADHD are frequently similar to the characteristics commonly associated with giftedness (Baum & Olenchak, 2002). In fact, Gates (2009) found that inventories used to identify giftedness and ADHD shared 82% of the same traits. Similarly, students with high-functioning autism are often associated with twice exceptionality and have been found to share similar traits with giftedness, such as visual-spatial ability, single-minded focus, profound knowledge in areas of interest, and exceptional memory (Kabfleish, 2013). Despite these strengths, the inability of students with autism to recognize basic social cues can inhibit their ability to build peer relationships (Kalbfleish & Iguchi, 2008). Finally, twice-exceptional students with dyslexia may have heightened visual-spatial abilities, as well as a heightened ability to process information through the integration of sight, sound, and other senses (Kalbfleish, 2013). Regardless, one common characteristic of twice-exceptional learners is their ability to develop compensation strategies for their area(s) of difference (Neilsen, 2002). Table 9.1 compares some of the characteristics associated with giftedness, learning differences, and those typical of twice-exceptional students.

ASSESSMENT AND IDENTIFICATION

All too often, twice-exceptional children go unrecognized in schools, often due to the use of a single-score criterion when identifying giftedness. Therefore, in order to appropriately address the identification of twice-exceptional students for inclusion in high-ability clustered classrooms, multiple criteria must be used (Slade, 2012). Nielsen (2002) provided a multiphased approach to assessing and identifying this population of students. A key feature in this approach is the development of a multidisciplinary task force that includes general, special, and

TABLE 9.1
DIFFERENCES IN CHARACTERISTICS AMONG GIFTED, LEARNING DIFFERENT, AND TWICE-EXCEPTIONAL STUDENTS

Gifted Students	Learning Different Students	Twice-Exceptional Students
Advanced vocabulary	Frustration with school	Feelings of inferiority
High creativity	Low self-esteem masked by disruptive behaviors	General lack of self-confidence
High problem-solving ability	Impulsive	Frustration at knowing the answer but unable to effectively communicate that knowledge
Talents and interests outside the traditional school curriculum	Highly distractible	Intense emotions
Keen sense of humor	Uneven academic abilities	Poor social skills, often seen as antisocial behaviors
Good memory	Processing deficits	Failure to complete tasks
Spatial ability	General apathy for tasks	Lack of motivation
Task commitment	Poor organizational skills	Highly distractible

gifted education teachers and diagnosticians. The goals of this task force would include raising awareness and advocacy for twice-exceptional children through professional development, establishing and implementing identification processes, and implementing a program of services.

Further evaluation for giftedness should then be conducted for all students identified through this examination process. Nielsen (2002) emphasized the importance of maintaining flexible identification criteria for giftedness, as a rigid adherence to IQ scores may prove to be inappropriate. Rather, she recommended examining the individual subtest scores in addition to general performance, making note of an extreme scatter of 7 scale-point differences or more between the lowest and highest subtests. In addition, tests of auditory and visual processing should be conducted to identify specific processing weaknesses.

Finally, reliance on testing alone is not enough to appropriately identify twice-exceptional learners. Therefore, Nielsen encouraged the use of multiple data sources to identify strength areas, including the use of rating scales such as the Scales for Rating the Behavioral Characteristics of Superior Students-Revised (Renzulli et al., 2010) and the Checklist of Creative Positives (Torrance, 1997; Torrance, Goff, & Satterfield, 1998). By developing a well-planned process of identification, more students with special needs will be recognized for their gifts, leading to appropriate placements in high-ability cluster classrooms that will emphasize their strengths and celebrate their learning differences.

PROGRAM OF SERVICES

Assessing and identifying twice-exceptional students is only half the battle. Meeting the needs of these students requires a continuum of services and interventions. All too often, when services are provided, they only address the students' areas of weakness and not their gifts, or conversely, the students are placed in a gifted program without recognition of their need for intervention. In either situation, students quickly become frustrated with school. In order to become successful learners, twice-exceptional students must be allowed to develop compensation strategies (Baum & Olenchak, 2002; McCoach et al., 2001; Reis & Ruban, 2005). Within the TSCG model, gifted students with learning disabilities are placed in the high-achieving cluster classroom that allows them to develop their potential by focusing on their strengths while developing their compensation strategies.

When working with twice-exceptional students in their areas of challenge, it is important that educators avoid what is referred to as "educational enabling"—the tendency for teachers to make learning tasks easier in an attempt to boost the learner's self-esteem (Schunk, Pintrich, & Meece, 2008). However, the opposite effect occurs as students feel they are unable to do grade-level work. True self-esteem is bolstered when students are given challenging tasks that address their areas of strength and when teachers work to find appropriate ways for these students to learn using near grade-level or grade-level tasks when addressing their weaknesses (Baum & Olenchak, 2002). In order for a program to be successful, it must be overarching, providing a range of services for gifted and learning disabled (LD) learners in the general classroom, with support from both special education and gifted education professionals (Nielsen & Higgins, 2005).

TSCG provides a flexible framework for educators to provide these services that meet the unique academic and social-emotional needs of gifted students with learning differences. Baum (2010b) specified Ten Commandments for addressing these needs that can be easily implemented into a high-achieving cluster classroom within the TSCG model.

1. **Provide a challenging curriculum that is contextual, meaningful, and in-depth.** First and foremost, twice-exceptional students are

gifted. Therefore, teachers should address theses students' areas of strength before remediating their weaknesses. When teaching content in a TSCG classroom, the use of global concepts encourages students to utilize their gifts when considering complex issues. For the twice-exceptional student, this means that skills training becomes a secondary process, allows the student to find meaning and purpose in their use (Nielsen, 2002; Nielsen & Higgins, 2005; Reis & Ruban, 2005; Weinfeld, Barnes-Robinson, Jeweler, & Shevitz, 2005), and ultimately reinforces those basic skills (Baum & Owen, 1988). Additionally, when students are provided with challenging, in-depth instruction, they can develop higher order problem solving and information processing skills, which may then lead to greater self-esteem and increased academic performance (Reis, McGuire, & Neu, 2000).

2. **Provide access to the curriculum by using a variety of entry points and resources.** Provide students with activities that help them to better understand and accept their gifts, as well as their learning differences, and help them use these gifts to compensate for their challenges (Nielsen & Higgins, 2005). Zentall, Moon, Hall, and Grskovic (2001) found that twice-exceptional students in classrooms with traditionally gifted peers often struggled if accommodations were not made to meet their specific needs. TSCG lends itself to this finding by allowing students opportunities to focus first on their strengths while providing the flexibility for teachers to also work on their skill-specific needs. This can be accomplished through the use of, but not limited to, targeted interest centers, field trips, extracurricular opportunities, music, DVDs, and a variety of print materials (Baum, 2010a; Nielsen & Higgins, 2005). In the cluster-grouped classroom, the strengths of the twice-exceptional student are emphasized, allowing for compensatory strategies to be developed in areas of weakness. When this occurs, the student's efficacy is increased and allows for more opportunities for success (Olenchak & Reis, 2002).

3. **Provide vehicles for communication.** Twice-exceptional students should be provided with a variety of ways in which they can express what they have learned that permits them to focus on their strengths. Not only will this help to build up self-efficacy and reduce frustration within this population, but it will also provide them with an opportunity to develop their own creative productivity (Olenchak & Reis, 2002). Table 9.2 provides a listing of some possible product options

TABLE 9.2
SOME OPTIONS FOR INCREASING CREATIVE PRODUCTIVITY

◆ Independent study projects	◆ Problem-based learning
◆ Architecture	◆ Game development
◆ Experiments	◆ Jounaling
◆ Self-directed learning	◆ Learning contracts
◆ Student-created interest centers	◆ Mentor-guided investigations
◆ Reader's theater	◆ Student-created films
◆ Debates	◆ Blogs
◆ Website development	◆ Painting/Drawing
◆ Interactive bulletin boards	◆ Multimedia presentations
◆ Comic strips	◆ Mock trials

that can be used in the classroom. This is by no means an exhaustive list, and many other options are also available.

4. **Use engaging instructional strategies.** Educators must teach the way that their students learn, and for many twice-exceptional students, that means incorporating more visual and tactile-kinesthetic methods into instruction. Varying types of classroom instruction—whole-group, small-group, and individual—not only provide unique learning situations, but also allow the student time to move about. Other strategies include the integration of drama, art, music, the use of a variety of technological tools (e.g., computer programs, voice recorders, MP3 players, spell checkers, e-books), scaffolding, visual and graphic organizers, simulations, curriculum compacting, acceleration, and Socratic seminar (Baum, 2010; Baum & Olenchak, 2002; Moon & Reis, 2004; Nielsen, 2002; Nielsen & Higgins, 2005; Reis & Ruban, 2005; Renzulli, 2002; Weinfeld et al., 2005).

5. **Incorporate movement into activities.** Give students the chance to get up and move. Often students with learning differences find that their "behaviors are at odds with the typical demands of school classrooms in which movements typically are restricted, openness of exploration may be discouraged, and instruction and curricula are seldom other than predetermined by some imagined group need" (Baum & Olenchak, 2002, p. 80). When working with twice-exceptional learners, it is important to immerse all of their senses in the learning process. Movement can become a valuable teaching tool once educators come to realize that this is in fact a learning style for many children. Paul and Gail Dennison (2010) have created a program called Brain Gym International. The Dennisons found that through simple movements

incorporated into classroom instruction, students were able to increase focus, comprehension, and allowed them to "harmonize emotion with rational thought."

6. **Be creative with classroom space, lighting, and furniture.** Nielsen and Higgins (2005) noted that because twice-exceptional learners may have difficulty finding success in traditional classroom settings, a different environment should be created with separate spaces that take into consideration the need for diverse works areas as well as space for self-reflection and recentering. This coupled with comfortable furniture, varied lighting, plants, and soft music can be beneficial for students who are uncomfortable with totally quiet spaces and need a chance to move around or to work in a relaxed posture (Nielsen & Higgins, 2005).

7. **Provide a reading corner.** A cozy reading corner with pillows, beanbag chairs, and ambient lighting will provide a quiet place for students to read and reflect on their thoughts (Baum, 2010a). Because reading is one of the most dominant challenges facing twice-exceptional students, the comfortable environment of the reading corner will provide a secure space for developing readers to explore a variety of texts at their own pace. Include headphones and audiobooks in this corner. For those students with behavioral differences, the reading corner becomes a peaceful place for them to retreat and refocus when they are feeling anxious or stressed.

8. **Provide grouping arrangements.** Create separate spaces for whole-group direct instruction, small-group work, and one-on-one interaction between students or a student and the teacher (Nielsen & Higgins, 2005). Additionally, teachers should be flexible in their grouping strategies, providing twice-exceptional students opportunities to participate in groups that highlight their abilities while ensuring that they are appropriately placed in groups that will help them develop in challenge areas.

9. **Provide social and emotional support like teaching stress and time management strategies.** Twice-exceptional learners have unique social-emotional needs that must be addressed. Nielsen and Higgins (2005) stated that "an empathetic understanding of this population leads to a global focus on four components: competence, choice, connections, and compassion" (p. 10). TSCG allows educators the time to teach twice-exceptional students a variety of organizational strategies including using notebooks color-coded by subject area, providing

textbooks for both school and home, and using planning calendars to keep track of homework and due dates. Direct instruction in anger management, self-regulation, and social thinking may be in order for some twice-exceptional students, particularly those with ADHD who may have difficulties sustaining peer relationships (Zentall et al., 2001). Additionally, providing opportunities for choice in their social behaviors allows students to utilize their strengths and develops their self-esteem (Nielsen & Higgins, 2005). For instance, for those students with high-functioning autism or other nonverbal learning differences, choices may focus on:

1. How you look (hygiene, dress);
2. What you say (choice of words); and
3. What you do (nonverbal cues, tone, physical proximity, pitch and volume; Neihart, 2000; Nielsen & Higgins, 2005).

Finally, to combat feelings of isolation, allow time for twice-exceptional students to work in peer groups. These students may often feel that because of their disability, they are unable to relate to other gifted students. However, they also are often unable to relate to nongifted learning different students, who don't understand their humor, creativity, or superior vocabulary (Baum & Olenchak, 2001; Nielsen & Higgins, 2005; Reis & Ruban, 2005). Time spent working with other twice-exceptional students will help give them a sense of belonging (Nielsen & Higgins, 2005).

10. **Empower students through talent development.** Moon and Reis (2004) stated, "Personal talent development is important for all gifted students, but essential for twice-exceptional children, because these twice-exceptional individuals must be resilient in order to overcome their handicaps and fulfill their potential" (p. 117). Research shows that when teachers focus on twice-exceptional students' gifts rather than their weaknesses, these students will develop a positive sense of themselves and their self-efficacy, build intrinsic motivation, and become more successful in school (Baum, 2010; Baum & Olenchak, 2002; Moon & Reis, 2004; Nielsen, 2002; Nielsen & Higgins, 2005; Reis & Ruban, 2005; Renzulli, 2002; Siegle & McCoach, 2005; Weinfeld et al., 2005). There are several opportunities for talent development available that can be implemented in the TSCG classroom and that allow teachers and students to focus on strengths rather than

weaknesses, including curriculum compacting, acceleration, independent study, mentoring, and competitions (Baum, 2010a; Baum, 2010b; Baum & Olenchak, 2002; McCoach et al., 2001; Moon & Reis, 2004; Nielsen, 2002; Nielsen & Higgins, 2005; Reis & McCoach, 2002; Reis & Ruban, 2005; Renzulli, 2002; Siegle & McCoach, 2005; Weinfeld et al., 2005; Yssel, Margison, Cross, & Merbler, 2005). Additionally, Renzulli's (2002) Schoolwide Enrichment Model is built upon the idea of the Three Ring Conception of Giftedness. In this model, gifted behaviors are manifested when there is a convergence of above-average ability, creativity, and task commitment. This convergence can happen in any child, in any place, and at any time. As part of this model, provide students with the opportunity for in-depth exploration and to gain a working knowledge of their area of interest.

In his TED Talk, Robinson (2010) called for an end to all discussion of school reform, calling reform merely an evolution to try to improve a broken system. Instead, he called for a revolution in education to put an end to the "crisis of human resources." To do this, educators need to recognize the talents of the students in their classrooms, in spite of the differences they may also possess. Total School Cluster Grouping provides teachers with a comprehensive and well-thought-out framework that will put the gifts of the twice-exceptional student first and foremost while also addressing his or her academic skill development and social and emotional needs. In this setting, these students will have the opportunity to grow socially, emotionally, and academically (Olenchak & Reis, 2002).

CHAPTER 10

DEVELOPING RESILIENCE AMONG HIGH-ABILITY LEARNERS

What We Should Know and What We Can Do*

A decade ago, Robinson wrote in a collaborative literature review (Neihart, Reis, Robinson, Moon, & National Association for Gifted Children, 2002) that "There is no research evidence to suggest that gifted and talented children are any less emotionally hardy than their age peers" (p. xiv). However, because of characteristics associated with giftedness, such as various sensitivities and intensities, needs of gifted students and how they experience social and emotional development might be qualitatively different from those of their less-able age peers (Peterson, 2003). A few of the emotional issues mentioned by clinicians who worked regularly with gifted learners are anxiety and depression, underachievement, perfectionism, and relationships (Mendaglio & Peterson, 2007). It

---

* This chapter was contributed by Enyi Jen.

is important to emphasize that these concerns do not mean that gifted students are more vulnerable to mental health problems than regular students. In fact, the social and emotional development of gifted students, just as with regular students, is a result of an interaction between environment and personal characteristics. Additionally, giftedness is an asset that can serve as a protective factor for gifted learners in adverse environments. For instance, previous studies have indicated that resilience is a characteristic of gifted learners (e.g., Bland & Sowa, 1994; Dole, 2000; Hébert, 2011; Peterson, 1997, 2012). Researchers found that the early development in their cognitive system may help gifted students cope with stressors. Moreover, if gifted learners have support from their environment and learn skills that enable them to make efficient use of their abilities, they may overcome challenges and develop well. There are three goals of this chapter: to help practitioners understand the social and emotional development of gifted learners, to help them understand the concept of resilience, and to describe strategies for educators to help students develop positive social and emotional skills in school.

SOCIAL AND EMOTIONAL DEVELOPMENT OF GIFTED LEARNERS

DIFFERING PERSPECTIVES

Many teachers have shared their experiences of working with high-ability learners, and often these experiences vary in how they begin. One kind of story usually begins with a statement like "I once taught a gifted kid who was smart and thoughtful and more mature than peers." The second kind of story might begin with "I taught a gifted kid who was smart, but had a really hard time dealing with others—very sensitive. I needed to pay a lot of attention to this child's emotions." These stories usually convey vivid memories. We value these personal experiences with high-ability students because they help us build connections between theory and practice in the real classroom quickly. However, we should be careful not to allow these personal experiences to become biases that feed common stereotypes related to giftedness. As teachers, we need to remember that no two children or adolescents are the same. This principle is also true when we work with gifted students. Before we discuss research findings, we need to discuss the long-standing controversy about research in the area of social and emotional development of gifted students. One reason for attending to differences of perspective is that, although gifted youth share similar personality characteristics, their development may vary due to their economic and cultural contexts, services they received, and personal choices they have made. A second reason is that the "gifted" populations various researchers have studied are also not the same (Neihart, 2002a). A researcher who studies students who have been identified for, and served in, gifted programs might draw conclusions that differ from those of scholars who have focused on gifted underachievers. With these realities in mind, we can now start to think about what social and emotional development of gifted students entails.

It cannot be overemphasized that, according to available studies, highly able students are neither more nor less well adjusted than their typical age peers are, and they face the same developmental tasks as anyone their age does. Not all gifted children and teens are at risk for problems related to social and emotional development. However, because of their *asynchronous development* (Silverman, 2002), with potentially great differences especially between emotional and cognitive development, they have additional challenges related to specific aspects of giftedness. Silverman used asynchronous development to describe the phenomenon of differing levels of development between mental age (intellectual ability) and chronological age (physical abilities) of gifted learners. For instance, a third-grade gifted child may be advanced in math, working at the fifth-grade level. However, at the same time, this child experiences developmental challenges similar to those of any other third grader, such as developing and maintaining friendships. Because of this discrepancy, gifted students must spend more time focusing on balancing themselves. The discrepancy also influences how others interact with them. Therefore, how they experience developmental challenges is likely to be qualitatively different from how age peers experience them (Neihart, 2002a; Peterson, 2003).

Research findings have reflected several common social and emotional traits in gifted students that affect how they react to various environments. Hébert (2011) summarized eight social and emotional traits of gifted learners:
- high expectation of self and others, associated with perfectionism;
- internal motivation and locus of control;
- emotional sensitivity, intensity, and depth;
- empathy;
- advanced levels of moral maturity with consistency between values and actions;
- strong need for self-actualization;

- a highly developed sense of humor; and
- resilience.

For most practitioners in education, these characteristics are familiar. However, it is important to understand these characteristics and how they affect a gifted child's interaction with various contexts. Additionally, Peterson (2007a) pointed out that when discussing characteristics, viewing them dichotomously is not appropriate—that is, as "having" or "not having" them. Instead, characteristics vary in degree. Moreover, a characteristic related to giftedness may affect life positively or negatively. A gifted student who behaves maturely may deal with others easily and demonstrate thoughtfulness in many situations. However, when they face transitions (e.g., death of someone close, parents' divorce, or relocation), they may be overwhelmed by feelings of loss and by feeling responsible for taking care of others.

Perfectionism is among characteristics mentioned most often as a problem for gifted children and teens. In general, *perfectionistic* can describe individuals who have high standards or expectations for performance (Peterson, 2007a). In general, gifted students seem to be more perfectionistic than average-ability peers (Schuler, 2002). However, the tendency toward perfectionism influences gifted students in various ways and may contribute to a variety of issues. For some gifted students, their perfectionism can be a positive force for high achievement. When working with this type of gifted student, educators might be able to help them to lessen the pressure they put on themselves. Some gifted students might be unwilling to try new behaviors or strategies or might find it difficult even to begin a project because they fear they may not be able to develop it to a high level, thus affecting their image as a stellar performer. Educators might focus on creating a safe environment for these students, helping them develop strategies for coping with extreme expectations and fear of failure and avoiding extreme self-criticism. Moreover, when working with underachievers, educators can consider that the fear-of-failure aspect of perfectionism in some students with high potential might at least partially explain why they do not exert effort. Underachievement should always be viewed as complex and idiosyncratic, with potentially multiple contributing factors, including difficulty with one or more developmental tasks.

Many gifted students have high levels of intensity and sensitivity, and it is noticeable that this sensitivity is related to cognition (Mendaglio & Peterson, 2007; O'Conner, 2002). Dabrowski (1972) used *overexcitability* to describe sensitivity, which is an inner tendency of surplus of energy characteristic of gifted and creative people. He defined overexcitability as "a factor predisposing toward physical self-mutilation and emotional self-torment" (Piechowski & Chucker, 2011, p. 202). Dabrowski's theory of overexcitabilities calls attention to five areas of responses to environmental stimuli: psychomotor, sensual, intellectual, imaginational, and emotional. Table 10.1 lists a description of each of the five areas. Scholars have found that gifted and nongifted individuals can be differentiated in three of those areas: emotional, intellectual, and imaginational (Hébert, 2011; O'Conner, 2002). People with overexcitability in one of these areas respond to the stimuli in the area in a different and more complex way. Their reaction may exceed the stimulus, last longer than average, and is often not related to the stimulus. Additionally, their emotional experience is promptly relayed to the sympathetic nervous system (Piechowski & Chucker, 2011). Since these responses may be different from those of regular students in type and degree, gifted students sometimes are misunderstood as "odd kids" or "difficult kids." In turn, attitudes of school personnel about them may contribute to additional emotional tension.

Educators need to understand the qualitative differences in social and emotional development between gifted children and adolescents and those not identified as gifted. Additionally, educators need to ask themselves how their knowledge about social and emotional development of gifted students shapes their behaviors and attitudes when interacting with gifted students. Furthermore, the more essential question is what educators can do to make the school environment appropriate and friendlier for gifted students.

BASIC CONCEPTS OF RESILIENCE

The concept of resilience has a long history in positive psychology, with pertinent literature appearing in the 1970s. Resilience is identified as the process that a human develops positively while experiencing adverse conditions (Masten, 2001). Researchers have found that although many individuals encounter challenges and threats in their lives (e.g., psychopathology, problems in development), some of them not only prevail through the difficulties but also seem to develop more positively than do their age peers who face the same adverse environment. Researchers have claimed that resilience produces different results (Brooks & Goldstein, 2008; Kitano & Lewis, 2005; Luthar, 1991; Masten, 2001; Neihart, 2002b; Werner & Smith, 1992). Some researchers tried to investigate what factors could be identified as protective factors and enhance students' resilience,

TABLE 10.1
EXPRESSION OF OVEREXCITABILITIES

Forms	Expression
psychomotor	Surplus of energy; psychomotor expression of emotional tension (e.g., compulsive talking, nervous habits)
sensual	Enhanced sensory and aesthetic pleasure; sensual expression of emotional tension
intellectual	Intensified activity of the mind; penchant for probing questions and problem solving, reflective thought
imaginational	Free play of the imagination; capacity for living in a world of fantasy; spontaneous imagery as an expression of emotional tension; low tolerance for boredom
emotional	Feelings and emotionally intensified, strong somatic expressions; strong affective expressions; capacity for strong attachments and deep relationships; and well-differentiated feelings toward self

Note. Adapted from *Understanding the social and emotional lives of gifted students* by T. P. Hébert, 2011, pp. 18–19. Copyright 2011 by Prufrock Press.

especially students who are from disadvantaged backgrounds (e.g., Alvord & Grados, 2005; Werner & Smith, 1992). Some researchers, based on the understanding of resilience, promoted a strength-based counseling approach which focused more on what is right instead of what is wrong and helps students build strength and assets (Erford, 2010).

The concept of resilience is pertinent here. Educators may not be able to change students' families or life challenges, but protective factors in their environment can make positive outcomes possible for 50%–80% of high-risk populations (Werner & Smith, 1992). When interacting with gifted children and adolescents, educators can call attention to factors of resilience they have observed in children living in adverse circumstances, or these professionals can attempt to enhance or develop such factors in these students.

Researchers have identified four important aspects of resilience (Alvord & Grados, 2005; Brooks & Goldstein; 2008; Kitano & Lewis, 2005, Masten, 2001; Neihart, 2002b; Reis, Colbert, & Hébert, 2004; Werner & Smith, 1992). First, resilience is a common, complex phenomenon in the human adaptive process, rather than being just a characteristic. It develops through dynamic interactions of individuals within their ecological systems (e.g., family, school, community). Brooks and Goldstein (2008) asserted that resilience is a complex ecological phenomenon. The ecosystem includes adults in school systems such as teachers, administrators, and school counselors, all of whom play vital roles in the adaptive process and potentially influence how students develop.

Second, resilience and protective factors are complementary. Werner and Smith (1992), based on their 30-year longitudinal Kauai study, defined resilience and protective factors as positive counterparts to vulnerability, an individual's susceptibility to disorders or risk factors, these being psychosocial or biological hazards that increased the likelihood of negative developmental outcomes. When people faced challenges in life or were born into adverse circumstances, development was influenced negatively. However, some components in life were protective factors that mitigated the influence of risk factors. These researchers concluded that individuals develop better when they have more protective and fewer risk factors in their life.

Third, resilient children can also be those traditionally identified as "at risk." Although resilient children may not remain resilient over time, the tendency of maintaining resilience exists. Thus, it is important to help gifted children in adverse situations to identify their own strengths. For instance, Peterson (1997), through interviews with 11 high-ability middle school students from low-functioning families, found that although these bright children came from difficult and sometimes dangerous family circumstances and were not doing well academically, they had developed self-reliance and resilience.

Fourth, proactive parenting, positive and meaningful school experiences, and caring adults can foster resilience. In a 3-year longitudinal study of an urban high school, researchers attempted to determine why some high-ability students from disadvantaged backgrounds became high achievers and others become underachievers. Reis et al. (2004) found that protective factors for the high achievers were a belief in self, personal characteristics (e.g., motivation and inner will, independence, and realistic aspirations), support systems (honors classes, a network for high-achieving students, family support, supportive adults), participation in special programs, extracurricular activities, summer enrichment programs, and appropriately challenging advanced classes. These researchers found that the underachievers failed because of lack of appreciation of the curriculum, absence of positive peer support (peers who achieved in school), lack of study habits established in the early school years, unrealistic future plans, and poor time management. Comparing the reports of high achievers with those of underachievers, the results indicated that a lack of protective factors was itself a risk factor. It is also noteworthy that Bland and Sowa (1994) found that not all gifted children were resilient children.

Descriptors of resilient children may also describe gifted students. Neihart (2002b) listed several of these: intelligence, curiosity, self-efficacy, a high moral regard, a positive explanatory style, a keen sense of humor, and problem-solving ability. As mentioned earlier, some of these protective factors are personal traits and some are external environmental factors. With resilience, protective factors, and social and emotional development in mind, educators can consider how they themselves can become a protective factor in individual gifted students' personal ecosystems, help them develop internal positive characteristics, and help to reduce pressing issues, especially for those from adverse environments.

WHAT EDUCATORS CAN DO TO FOSTER POSITIVE SOCIAL AND EMOTIONAL DEVELOPMENT IN GIFTED STUDENTS

When considering how to help gifted students achieve positive social and emotional outcomes, it is important to think about all education professionals in the school system, no matter what roles they play. Whether they are teachers, school counselors, or administrators, they all can contribute to a positive school climate. All can address the social and emotional needs of gifted learners in school. With this perspective in mind, three approaches are discussed here: strategies that increase school protective factors, guidance curriculum that helps gifted students understand themselves, and small groups that allow gifted students to normalize and validate their feelings and concerns.

STRATEGIES THAT INCREASE SCHOOL PROTECTIVE FACTORS

Benard (1995) identified three critical school protective factors: caring relationships between students and adults in school, high expectations for students' behaviors and performance, and opportunities for meaningful participation. Other scholars have noted that the presence of at least one caring adult is an important protective factor for children at risk (Benard, 1995; Dole, 2000; Downey, 2008; Masten, Herbers, Cutuli, & Lafavor, 2008; Peterson, 1997; Reis et al., 2004; Werner & Smith, 1992). Teachers who interact daily with gifted students and school counselors who counsel gifted students individually can be such a caring adult. The process of building a healthy and supportive relationship between teachers or school counselors and students can help the students feel cared about, promote a positive self-concept, and help them achieve academic success (Wang, Haertel, & Walberg, 1994). In Benard and Slade's (2009) study, when students were asked what they expected teachers to do, the students said they wanted adults in school to be there for them, guide them, and establish a connection with them. These researchers explained that students judged whether a teacher cared about them based on simple acts, such as asking them "How was your weekend?" and taking time to say hello to them. Additionally, the students said that caring teachers used positive words to express their reasonably high expectations for them. The students viewed these expectations as encouragement and as teachers' belief in them. A caring relationship is a foundation for other school protective factors as well. Students feel they are not alone and are connected to their environment. Furthermore, when students are surrounded with nurturing, caring relationships in school, they develop a sense of security and self-respect. Successful experiences and positive outcomes contribute to resilience (Erford, 2010).

Students can have high rates of school success when they hear the message that they are capable of learning and when they receive support for achieving their goals (Benard, 1995; Benard & Slade, 2009; Wang et al., 1994). Therefore, it is important for school administrators and teachers to set high and reasonable expectations for all students and help them meet these expectations. What *high* and *reasonable* mean differs from individual to individual, and goal setting should be based on students' abilities. School administrators and teachers need to provide a challenging curriculum that addresses the learning needs of gifted students and clarifies expectations about positive behavior so that students know how to behave appropriately (Downey, 2008). Moreover, Morrison and Allen (2007) pointed out that providing challenging, interesting, and culturally relevant educational programs can enhance students' academic self-concept. Opportunities for meaningful participation in school fit naturally with high expectations in school (Benard, 1995). Extracurricular activities also help students enjoy school and establish positive habits, such as scheduling and efficiently using their time in meaningful activities during unstructured time (Benard & Slade, 2009; Reis, et al., 2004). Meaningful participation helps students see themselves as valued members of the school community and also helps them establish positive relationships with others (Werner & Smith, 1992).

In summary, resilience-based interventions emphasize strengthening assets and protective factors. These strategies focus on what students have and what they can do (Alvord & Grados, 2005). When educators consider interventions to foster resilience, they need to intervene before existing problems spread (Masten et al., 2008; Werner & Smith, 1992). Each educator is therefore part of the intervention plan and may choose to focus on one or more specific protective factors. For instance, to make sure students have an opportunity to participate meaningfully in a challenging curriculum and enjoy positive teacher-student relationships in school, school administrators can implement specific educational models—for example, Total School Cluster Grouping, an out-of-school enrichment program, or the Schoolwide Enrichment Model (Renzulli & Reis, 1997). They can also design and conduct professional development programs for teachers to help them understand social and emotional characteristics of gifted students so that they can build positive relationships with students. Teachers can implement curriculum compacting and differentiated lesson plans in their classroom to reflect appropriate, high expectations for all students. School counselors can teach students problem-solving skills, time management skills, and encourage them to join extracurricular activities. The idea of caring relationships can also be expanded to the creation of a schoolwide caring system, which not only includes positive, nurturing teacher-to-student relationships, but also caring student-to-student, teacher-to-teacher, and teacher-to-parent relationships (Benard, 1995; Masten et al., 2008; Reis et al., 2004). School counselors can serve as a conflict mediator and an advocate for individual students or groups to help build a positive school climate (Erford, 2010). When all educational professionals embrace the notion that they themselves can be protective factors, and if all work together to help students fulfill their potential, they can enhance student development.

GUIDANCE CURRICULUM

Some people use the term *affective curriculum* to refer to components in a program that focus on the social and emotional development. Here, this term and *guidance* will be interchangeable—for several reasons. First, the educational philosophies of guidance and affective curriculum are similar. They are offered for all students, not just for students with difficulties. Second, the goals of guidance and affective curriculum are similar. They both address academic, personal/social, and career development. Third, the format for guidance and affective curriculum are similar. For instance, they both can include exploratory or hands-on activities, panels, and the use of biographies.

Guidance curriculum is usually geared to large groups. Gifted students are part of the "all students" that school counselors are to serve, and they benefit from a guidance curriculum, especially if curriculum developers can incorporate the needs of gifted students into the goals of the curriculum. As VanTassel-Baska (2009) pointed out, guidance curriculum can support gifted students' cognitive characteristics (e.g., motivation to achieve), leading to the development of specific talents. Guidance curriculum is a part of a compressive developmental counseling program in schools. In elementary school, counselors are expected to spend approximately 35%–45% of their time providing guidance curriculum. Middle school counselors usually spend less time, approximately 25%–35%, delivering guidance curriculum. Topics can vary, but should accommodate various levels of cognitive ability within stages of development. Delivery of guidance curriculum is flexible, not stable, addressing developmental needs at various age levels (Erford, 2010).

School counselors are not the only educational professionals who can work with guidance curriculum. After some training, classroom teachers and gifted education teachers can also do this (Peterson, 2009). Other education professionals can work together as well to help gifted students. For example, school personnel can design and coteach schoolwide units because guidance curriculum is expected to link to the school's core curriculum. Teachers in self-contained gifted programs can include affective curriculum in their classrooms. It is important to note that affective curriculum does not need to reference the concept of giftedness specifically. Gifted students simply benefit from discussing developmental issues with their intellectual peers (Peterson, 2003). Another potential benefit of implementing affective curriculum is that gifted students' special needs may be revealed, and educators can then provide appropriate interventions.

A guidance curriculum is not just a series of suitable activities and units. Instead, it is essentially a lesson plan for the school's core curriculum, with objectives, implementing procedures, and outcomes clarified. Guidance curriculum also should address developmental tasks at each age level. Therefore, educators might design units based on observed student needs in particular school contexts. When educators develop an affective curriculum, they should have a clear rationale for it and be creative with the design components. Examples of guidance curriculum appropriate for use at the elementary school level to serve gifted students are listed in Table 10.2 (Erford, 2010; Hébert, 2011; Peterson, 2009; VanTassel-Baska, 2009).

TABLE 10.2
EXAMPLE TYPES OF GUIDANCE CURRICULUM

Type of activities	Example
Exploratory activities	Career exploration helps to increase students' understanding of "career," particularly important in the primary grades, because gifted children, lacking tolerance for ambiguity, may prematurely foreclose on career choice. One concern of gifted students is that if they are good in some areas (e.g., math), adults may say they should pursue a career associated with that area (e.g., engineer) even though the gifted students are better suited for other areas because of personality, needs, or values.
Hands-on activities	To help them identify talents and weaknesses, primary-level children often learn effectively with visual assistance. For instance, using figures to represent Gardner's multiple intelligences and encouraging students to identify areas of strength and limitation can be both interesting and helpful for them. Children can also draw what they would prefer to do in these areas. Gifted students, particularly those struggling with perfectionism, benefit from understanding that they have both exceptional talents and relatively weaker areas.
Panels	Panels with older gifted students or adults can help gifted students anticipate transitions, which they may experience qualitatively differently from how their peers experience them. Educators can arrange to have gifted sixth graders talk with gifted middle school students in an environment that feels safe for gifted students to express their concerns about middle school, thereby relieving anxieties and learning that their concerns are not unusual.
Use of biographies	Through reading biographies, gifted students consider life challenges that highly successful people faced. Gifted students without advantages can connect these challenges to their own. Helping students create autobiographies that highlight where and what they are currently can also be effective. Storing these, for later rereading, allows students to see how they have changed.

SMALL GROUP

Semistructured, topic-oriented small groups are an especially effective mode for helping gifted students with social and emotional development (Peterson, 2009; Peterson, Betts, & Bradley, 2009). Regardless of the kinds of gifted education programs offered and even if no formal gifted education program is in place, educators can implement small discussion groups to address needs related to social and emotional development. Based on the belief that students often learn best from each other, small group settings with same-age peers are ideal for conducting proactive, prevention-oriented discussions (Erford, 2010). Gifted students in small groups learn that they have more in common than previously assumed. They feel heard as they discuss topics they usually do not have a chance to talk about (Peterson, 2008). Gifted education teachers can learn basic listening and responding skills to help them facilitate the groups, in a training format or through detailed written guidance (Peterson, 2008). Peterson and Lorimer (2012) found that when gifted education teachers served as facilitators, their confidence for leading small groups increased over time and their perceptions of needs related to social and emotional development of gifted students changed. The school climate was also positively affected by the small groups. Unlike traditional therapy groups, the proactive small groups described here focus on fairly universal developmental challenges, not on pathology or crises. If distress is noted, however, noncounselor group facilitators can refer them to a school counselor, who might refer a gifted child or teen to other counseling professionals if warranted.

Designing a successful small group for gifted students requires that educators understand how to form a group, how to arrange time and location for the group, what to expect in evolutionary group dynamics, and how to facilitate discussions. At the outset, the logistical aspects may be challenging, but once one or more groups are established, the meetings establish a rhythm in the school schedule. A basic model for forming a small group includes the following sequential steps (Erford, 2011; Peterson, 2007b; 2009):

1. *Starting a small group.* Although group size should vary according to age level (e.g., three in grade 3, four at grade 4), Peterson (2008) suggested no more than eight students in small groups regardless of age. Meanwhile, when working with gifted students, she also argued for placing students in groups by age, regardless of grade acceleration, because students within a narrow age range face similar developmental tasks. She also emphasized that achievers and underachievers should be mixed, whenever possible, given their similar developmental challenges. When designing a small group, it is effective when there is an appropriate location allowing students to meet regularly. A small room with few visual distractions is better than a classroom, although sitting at a table in one area of a no-traffic classroom can be sufficient. Having at least six to eight sessions is best because students need time to build relationships in the group. The length of the group meeting may be 20–60 minutes, depending on time available, age level, and collective attention span. Sometimes a few minutes can be borrowed from the beginning or end of a classroom to extend a group meeting.

2. *Establishing goals and objectives.* It is important for educators to have goals in mind when implementing any educational service. The goals of small groups include helping gifted students learn expressive vocabulary,

connect with peers, normalizing feelings, and experience validation of feelings. When parents have concerns about the purposes of development-oriented discussion groups, educators should be able to articulate these. Proactive small groups, focused simply on "growing up," are for *all* gifted students.

3. *Selecting topics.* Materials developed by researchers and practitioners specifically for working with gifted students are available (e.g., Peterson, 2007b; Peterson et al., 2009), but gifted education teachers can design group curriculum themselves, based on what they learn through interactions with gifted students. Having a focus for each meeting and some structure is important because it helps to rein in dominators, helps to engage shy group members, and helps facilitators avoid wandering into inappropriate territory—that is, content that cannot be defended to parents or administrators. Some topics are appropriate across grade levels, altered as needed (e.g., peer relationships, anger, fear, worries, loss, and transitions); some topics are appropriate only at older or younger age levels. Format can be dialogue, hands-on activities, activity sheets to prompt discussion, or catalytic abstract concepts or a combination of these (Peterson, 2009). Facilitators should probably prepare two topics for each meeting, with the second topic used only if students do not respond well to one topic. Most available group curriculum offers guidance for sustaining topics (e.g., Peterson, 2007b).

4. *Facilitating groups.* Discussions inevitably provoke thought about personal issues. Therefore, facilitators should explain at the outset that the facilitator will keep shared information confidential (and be genuine about that promise), but with caveats related to suspected danger of self-harm or harm to others, abuse, and neglect. In group work, confidentiality cannot be guaranteed in the same way for members. However, serious discussion, at the outset, about how quickly trust can vanish in "their group" usually establishes a culture of respect for privacy. Nevertheless, facilitators should remind the group about confidentiality when sensitive information is shared. It is also important to remember that facilitators should be nonjudgmental. The function of the adult is to facilitate group discussion, allowing students to learn from each other and learn skills. Therefore, facilitators should not self-disclose or dominate the conversation and should refrain from giving advice. Some strategies for effective facilitation are asking open-ended questions (without implicit direction), providing short statements of validation,

using active listening skills, and encouraging students to respond to each other.

5. *Evaluating the groups.* It is important to use sentence prompts or other types of surveys or questionnaires to evaluate groups, with feedback helping to improve group components in the future. Since small groups are proactive, an appropriate evaluation objective is to understand how group members perceive their experiences in groups and how they view their own changes. Facilitators can also self-evaluate the process and decide what needs to be changed for the future.

CONCLUSION

As discussed in this chapter, researchers have not concluded that gifted students as a group are particularly vulnerable or especially strong. However, myths about their academic and emotional needs still exist (Moon, 2009; Peterson, 2009). As Moon asserted, one reason educators ignore the needs of gifted students is that if there appears to be no special need, they assume that no special services are needed. Additionally, positive behaviors and high performance can mask distress, and positive stereotypes of gifted students may prevent adults from giving attention to concerns (Peterson, 2009). However, gifted students might experience various areas of development qualitatively differently from how age peers experience them, and affective curriculum can provide opportunities for gifted youth to discuss developmental challenges. Educators who work with gifted youth can play important roles in these children's and adolescents' lives. Invested adults can provide crucial support and be a protective factor for them. Many strategies can potentially be helpful, and most of these cost little if anything. The best strategy might be to support small steps toward healthy and effective social and emotional functioning with one or more types of affective curriculum.

CHAPTER **11**

STUDENT-FOCUSED DIFFERENTIATION

Differentiation centers on providing quality education to students based on their various educational needs, which include their strengths, weaknesses, readiness, skill levels, interests, and learning preferences (Roberts & Inman, 2007; Tomlinson, 1999). School mission statements frequently reflect the duty of schools to prepare youth for the future and to contribute to the maximum educational growth of individual children—goals best achieved through effective differentiation practices. Most schools have mission statements similar to the following:

> It is the mission of Happy Elementary School to educate each individual child to help him or her reach his or her fullest potential for lifelong learning in a diverse democracy.

These mission statements contain quality ideas. Yet often school practices that deliver lockstep content based on one-size-fits-all standards run contrary to this mission. Quite simply, we must consider whether children are the same as or different from one another. By acknowledging their differences, we can begin to use cluster grouping and differentiated practices to address their individual learning needs.

Rather than emphasizing and measuring how students achieve when compared to other students, we ought to focus on how much they individually improve. What has each child learned during the school year based on where he or she began in the fall? Children start school in different places, with different levels of readiness and experiences and with different beliefs about their ability to succeed on the tasks being asked of them in school. When test scores are used to compare one group of students to another without regard to where they began, educators are, in effect, held accountable for factors out of their control. How often or whether parents read to their children, the developmental readiness of the child, the child's past failures or successes, how much the child lost or gained over the summer, and whether the family values education all affect students' achievement in school. However, by paying attention to where the child begins, we can assess how much he or she learns during the school year. We can adjust the curriculum and instruction to a level that encourages learning and success for the child. And we can become accountable for individual gains.

As discussed in Part I, when we cluster-group children, we do so to increase the teachers' ability to address the varied individual needs of her students. Clustering reduces the range of achievement levels in each teacher's classroom and provides teachers with groups of students who achieve at or near the same level. The initial grouping offers a beginning point for differentiation; however, without differentiation, no reason exists to cluster students.

In addition to teacher-directed efforts toward differentiation, what we call "student-discovery" strategies offer teachers a means of increasing student motivation, creativity, and ownership in their learning. In effect, the student-focused strategies offer a different approach to more traditional curricular differentiation discussed in Chapters 6 and 7. This menu does not represent a one-size-fits-all list of things that teachers must do, but rather a collection of effective practices borrowed from great teachers around the country, from the teachers in our research, and from our own experiences. Specifically, these student-focused practices are designed to help teachers turn the learning back over to the students and to help students take responsibility for their own learning. Thus, they provide teachers a quick start to differentiation because they often require less work and planning on the part of the teacher. Moreover, these strategies engage students in individualized rigor, depth, and complexity based on genuine interest, and in doing so, they develop creativity, buy-in, work ethic, and engage students (Kaplan, 2009; Kaplan & Cannon, 2001). In the following paragraphs, we outline 26 strategies. Take some ideas, try them, and adjust them to your own strengths, needs, and styles. Most importantly, use these strategies to help your students take charge of their learning in a meaningful manner. When used frequently, these strategies can help teachers create learning environments in which the students consider being smart cool!

MENU OF STUDENT-FOCUSED STRATEGIES

1. **Offer students the opportunity to do fewer, but more difficult, problems.** This simple approach can be highly motivating to students of all achievement levels, and it works across the curriculum. In language arts, students can answer a dozen comprehension questions about the reading, or they could respond to two questions (that require comprehension) that ask them to go in depth using higher order thinking skills into more abstract literary components such as theme, voice, or characterization. In mathematics, students might choose to complete three story problems or 20 computation problems, or they might create their own problems and an answer key. Offer this option often enough, and students will actually begin to ask if they can have fewer but harder problems!

2. **Share yourself and encourage the same from your students.** Students who know each other and who know the teacher provide the foundation for a responsive classroom (Rimm-Kaufmann & Sawyer, 2004). When kids know and understand each other and when respect for individual differences is encouraged, they are less likely to bully or be bullied, and they develop a rapport in the classroom that is supportive of their peers (Peterson, 2003; Peterson & Ray, 2006a; Peterson & Ray, 2006b). In a supportive environment, students feel safe to take risks—an essential element of academic growth and creativity—and students can make mistakes without fear of ridicule and thus learn from those mistakes (Rimm-Kaufmann & Sawyer, 2004). Finally, when students know each other's interests, those interests can be effectively integrated into the educational content.

3. **Ask the students what will work.** As a teacher, I often encountered situations in which what I was trying to do with the kids failed miserably. As a beginning teacher, I found these instances extremely frustrating. Despite my best efforts to prepare an engaging lesson, the students seemed to find the lesson dull, boring, and uneventful. And I had just put hours into planning! During one of these disappointing lessons on photosynthesis, I finally, out of desperation, asked the students, "What do you think would work to teach this concept to you guys?" I was astounded when I received about a half-dozen really great suggestions. I had given the students the terms, a diagram, and (what I considered to be) thought-provoking questions. They suggested that we become the water, sunlight, carbon dioxide, glucose, and oxygen. So we did, and they learned the content. In fact, fourth graders were able to balance the photosynthetic equation. They did so by becoming molecules of water, complete with two hydrogen atoms duct-taped to an oxygen atom. Since then, asking the students what would work has provided me with more free time, as well as let loose my creative energies as I listen to and respond to their ideas. I believe that encouraging their voices in the classroom leads to greater ownership by students of the learning activities.

4. **Laugh, care, and appreciate energy, creativity, and humor.** Like strategy 2, this strategy holds the promise of creating an inviting and safe learning environment. Laughter and humor can carry students and teachers through even the most difficult of days. Humor is a sign of creativity and can add enjoyment to the classroom. Overexcitabilities (Dabrowski, 1972) in gifted children, including psychomotor, sensual, imaginational, emotional, and intellectual have been discussed (Piechowski, 1985). These intensities can be misunderstood and mistaken for weaknesses rather than signs of talent among young children. For example, sometimes adults consider a child to be hyperactive when in fact she is simply delightfully energetic and in need of physical and mental stimulation. Similarly, what may appear to be a deficit in attention might really be an indication of a child who is mentally very busy. Sometimes bright students will have "different" senses of humor, and seeing their humor as an asset rather than a liability can lead to recognition of talent among these students. Research and practice have shown that there is an increase in misdiagnosis of disorders such as ADHD based on a misunderstanding of behaviors (Eide & Eide, 2006; Webb

et al, 2005). Gates (2007) found, in her study of the co-occurrence of giftedness with ADHD and the potential misdiagnosis of giftedness as ADHD, that some rating scales for ADHD and giftedness have as much as an 80% overlap of items. Thus, it depends on whether one is viewing the gift or the liability (Webb, 2000; Webb et al., 2005). Fugate, Zentall, & Gentry (2013) found that gifted students with characteristics of ADHD were more creative than gifted students without ADHD, despite having poorer working memory. ADHD in a gifted student may just be a gift.

5. **Assess, incorporate, and develop student interests.** Chapter 5 has a section describing the importance of learning about your students and their interests. As we learn about students' interests, these interests can be incorporated into the curriculum and serve as the basis for further independent investigations or extensions. Equally important to assessing and incorporating interests is developing them. Renzulli and Reis (1997) discussed using Type I activities to develop student interests. School should be a place where students learn and develop. Putting into place a plan to expose students to concepts and ideas with which they may not be familiar helps develop new interests. This exposure is especially important for elementary students and for children who live in poverty, as their knowledge of and exposure to the world may be more limited than that of older students or students from higher socioeconomic backgrounds. Mrs. Rogers has a speaker come in to her fourth-grade classroom each week to share careers with her students. Mr. Smith selects a science show each month to stimulate students' interest about research in science and schedules field trips to nearby areas of educational interest.

6. **Be interesting in your teaching.** One surefire way to hold the interest of students is to keep them guessing. Some teachers tell stories, something Phenix (1964) referred to as artistic modification. Others dress up in character, while still others put learning to music. Whatever it is that sets you apart from other teachers, that connects you with your students, and that brings your lessons to life—do that. We can all remember an interesting teacher, a teacher to whom we listened and from whom we learned. Many of us actually connect a specific content area to the teacher who taught it. This connection is strong evidence concerning the power of a teacher to bring content to life.

7. **Share your interests.** Mr. Cohen is interested in theater; he also coaches soccer and raises Boston Terriers. His shares his interests with his students, who eagerly await news of a new litter of puppies, try out for a part in the school musical, and enjoy watching him in a community play or seeing him on the sidelines of the recreational soccer league. By sharing his interests with his students he serves as a model for the power of interests to enrich one's life. He also connects with the other theater types, dog lovers, and soccer players in his class. He appreciates them, and they appreciate him. He is more than a teacher; he is a whole person to his students.

8. **Choose controversy.** Nothing can incite learning more than emotion. Most areas of study have controversial issues related to them. Controversy provides powerful learning opportunities because, by its very nature, it is multifaceted, open-ended, and fuels high-level debate. Should wolves be taken off the endangered species list? Should farmers be allowed to use genetically modified animals in breeding? Should America provide resources to countries that violate the international moratorium on whaling? Can eating french fries cause cancer? When kids are still arguing at the end of the day about a controversial topic addressed before lunch, you have their attention. Often these kinds of topics afford opportunities to teach the finer skills of debate.

9. **Remember that students can produce knowledge.** Of all the strategies for differentiation, this one is probably used the least. In school, we teach children stuff, ask them to learn it, and occasionally, we even ask them to apply it. Rarely do we ask them to answer a previously unknown question—to produce knowledge. Yet, they are capable of doing that very thing, from writing an original story or poem to conducting a research project to which the answer is unknown. For example, Hunter Scott investigated, through original survey research, the circumstances surrounding the sinking of the SS Indianapolis in World War II (Nielson, 2002). Based on the accounts of remaining survivors, he testified before Congress and posthumously reversed the court marshal of the ship's captain. New knowledge. A fifth grader investigated the quality of the drinking fountain water in the school and five other public places. New knowledge. A group of second graders found out how much paper the school wasted in a day and developed a plan for recycling and reusing paper in the school. New knowledge. A sixth grader posed a question about whether freezing a tadpole would

kill it (it won't; they have antifreeze in their cells). New knowledge. Students investigated truth in advertising and found that there weren't a thousand chocolate chips in every bag of chocolate chip cookies as advertised. New knowledge. Think about helping students learn to ask questions and find answers. What new knowledge might your students produce during the school year?

10. **Provide depth and complexity based on student questions and interests.** This strategy represents the opposite of teaching to the objective; rather, it focuses on seizing the teachable moment and using student questions and interests as a basis for providing the depth. For example, Joshua stomped into the classroom one morning shortly after Hurricane Katrina had made landfall. "They shouldn't have messed with the Mississippi!" he exclaimed when Mr. Neville asked him what was on his mind. There was a look of confusion on the faces of many of Joshua's fellow fourth graders. Mr. Neville looked at the class and asked, "How might things have been different during Hurricane Katrina if people hadn't 'messed with the Mississippi'?" Mr. Neville planned to teach a wetlands unit in the spring, but his plans just changed. Joshua's passion about the impact of Hurricane Katrina developed into a problem-based learning activity. The students explored the effect that the levees and floodwalls had on the protective wetlands. They compared the Gulf Coast coastal wetlands to the New England inland wetlands. Mr. Neville was amazed at the extent of the knowledge his students gained during their exploration. Joshua's outburst resulted in an investigation that far exceeded the grade-level expectations for the wetlands unit.

11. **Take the time, jump in over your head, and start with a big-picture problem that students don't have all the skills or knowledge to solve.** Students often look to the teacher to know all the answers, especially in the elementary grades. However, equally powerful as knowing all the answers is helping students learn to find answers to complex problems. As discussed in Chapter 7: Differentiation, the development of knowledge and skills in problem-based learning results from the need to acquire them to solve an urgent problem. Thus, jumping in the deep end, but with a flotation device that can help you navigate those waters, can be an effective way to facilitate learning. It requires little preparation, an open mind, and the ability to see where the journey leads. Student and teacher can learn together. For example, an elementary student was very interested in equity, and she worried that a classmate who was

wheelchair bound could not access the playground equipment. Clearly, neither she nor her teacher had the knowledge necessary to design, propose, raise funds, and build a new playground. They started small—just with an idea—worked with experts, and gained the knowledge and skills during the course of the project. The student's work resulted in the construction of a new, wheelchair-accessible playground.

12. **Whenever possible, provide open-ended assignments; be ambiguous.** Students often want to know what, exactly, they need to do and what, exactly, is expected of them. They seek the one right answer to the closed problems and assignments that dominate schoolwork and testing. Moreover, some high achievers keep school exciting by seeing how quickly they can arrive at these right answers and finish their assignments. Unfortunately, closed, one-right-answer problems do very little to develop the intellectual dispositions of children, "where risk-taking, exploration, uncertainty and speculation are what it's about" (Eisner, 2001, p. 368). On the other hand, by providing fewer details, less structure, and questions or problems that have multiple solutions, you encourage students to think and to struggle, cornerstones of intellectual development.

One of my favorite examples of a totally ambiguous assignment involved a teacher who taught fossilization to her students. As a culminating project at the end of the unit, she told her students to "bring something in that demonstrates your understanding of fossilization." To up the ante, she also awarded extra credit to students who added new content to their project. Tom brought in an ice cube tray full of frozen tadpoles and suggested that he be given 20 extra credit points because, although they had learned about fossilization in sediment, in amber, and through petrification, no mention had been made of fossilization in ice. He went on to discuss ice mummification, antifreeze in frogs, and how preservation of remains has been of interest to humans for as long as there have been humans. Had this teacher assigned a poster with specific criteria, this student would not have been forced to engage his thinking and creativity and to explore uncharted areas of the content that they had studied. Ambiguity often leads to much more than we could assign, and it also leads to a rich diversity in student responses. Finally, ambiguity takes less planning on the part of the teacher, saving valuable time for other tasks.

13. **Use challenge problems daily, weekly, monthly, and on tests and assignments.** These provide a low-risk way to elevate the level of advanced content, challenge students willing to attempt them, and create a classroom environment that supports intellectual risks and accomplishments. Teach above the standard. Tell students that the hard content will be on the test or assignment only as extra credit. Then encourage all students to attempt the challenging extra credit problems. These problems will motivate some of the students who may not consistently achieve at high levels but who welcome a challenging problem. I have found that using challenge problems on tests that frustrate even the highest achieving students raises the bar for these students and provides a means of checking who understands the advanced concepts. This strategy is low-risk to students because they have nothing to lose, but they can gain extra points for their efforts in solving these challenge problems. We have even seen students begin to bring in challenge problems for the teachers to use or try to solve, reinforcing that being smart in this classroom is desirable.

14. **Begin at the back of the book.** Every elementary math book begins with number sense, place value, adding, subtracting, multiplying, and dividing whole number, then decimals, then fractions. Turn to the end of the math book and find the chapter on probability, which integrates all of the basic concepts in a much more interesting and relevant format. Additionally, find the chapter on geometry, which might excite some of the more concrete and spatial learners and which also uses basic operations. These last two chapters often go untouched or end up relegated to the very end of the school year. Try them first. Likewise, language arts curricula typically deal with parts of speech, grammar, punctuation, sentence, and then paragraph structure. Turn to the last chapters in the text and find exploration of different forms of writing and voice, followed by various purposes for writing. Each of these topics integrates the basic content found in the first chapters, but in a more engaging and authentic manner. Try these chapters first, or at the very least, pretest in the content areas to avoid the massive unengaging repetition that occurs each year. Start with that which is interesting to the students whether they have the requisite skills or not, then build the skills through engaging them in the more interesting and relevant content.

15. **Ensure access to advanced content for all students.** Advanced content—the what, the why, the controversy, the unanswered questions, and

the "what is new" about a topic—can be extremely interesting. Typically, textbooks, educators, and curricula reserve the advanced content (if it is offered at all) for high-achieving students, while focusing more on core content and basic skills with other students. However, like beginning at the back of the book, the advanced content can provide students with context, meaning, and relevance for the basic knowledge. Not all students will engage in high-level projects based on the advanced content, but most students, even nonreaders or those who always seem to be behind in their work, will find the advanced content interesting and be able to comprehend it. For many students, the interest stimulated by advanced content can play a role in increased motivation and offer a medium in which to deliver the basic knowledge and skills. Just because teachers introduce advanced content doesn't mean that they have to hold all students accountable for it. Rather, introduce it and let students learn what they can about it—learn for the sake of learning, because it is interesting. Put questions about the advanced content on a test or quiz, but only for extra credit points. Make it cool to be smart and earn extra points by understanding the hard concepts. Teach difficult content to a level that ensures no students correctly answer all the extra credit points. This provides a safe challenge (it is extra) and removes the ceiling for students who always get everything right, a practice that can lead to underachievement, lack of resilience, and inability to fail, recover, and work hard (Neihart et al., 2002; Peterson, 2003).

What effects does genetically modified corn have on the Monarch butterfly population (in conjunction with the life-cycle unit)? Why didn't Emily Dickenson publish any of her poetry (in conjunction with the poetry unit)? How did J. K. Rowling develop her characters in *Harry Potter* (in conjunction with a writing unit)? How did Krakatoa differ from Mount St. Helens (in conjunction with a geology unit)? Which countries still engage in whaling and what reasons do they have for doing so (in conjunction with the study of endangered species)?

16. **Let students choose content.** This simple strategy builds ownership and, thus, quality into assignments and projects by students. Mrs. Wellman "let" students choose an animal on which to develop a report. They were studying oceans, and each student had to make a case concerning why he or she should be allowed to report on an animal of his or her choice. In allowing choice in the content area of study and by having students explain why they should be allowed to have their chosen

animal, she increased both interest and motivation prior to the assignment. One third grader was overheard explaining to her parents, "I got the Orca. Can you believe it? I get to do my ocean animal on the Orca. I can hardly wait." Similarly, a Native American student, when given the opportunity to choose which president about whom to develop a biography, picked Andrew Jackson. He developed a biographical account of the influence of Jackson from the perspective of the Navajo people whom he had persecuted. This project was original, passionate, and resonated with the voice of the child who chose this president. Choice of content is a simple strategy that holds great potential for engaging students by putting them in charge of their projects and assignments.

17. **Offer students opportunities to choose products, audiences, and ways of presenting what they know.** Similar to allowing students choice of content, offering them choices concerning the types of products, the audiences with which they share their work, and how they share their work can be equally motivating to students. Roger, a student who in fifth grade had not yet learned to read, had been given a social studies assignment by his teacher. Fortunately for Roger, his teacher allowed students to show their understanding of the content in a variety of ways. His teacher posed three questions and asked the students to create something that demonstrated that they understood the answers to the questions. Roger created a drawing in which he placed three sailing ships. He explained to his teacher that he "drew the ships chained together because they represented our three branches of government. None could sail in waters if the others would not let them." He further explained that "the banks of the river represented the United States Constitution—the boundaries of the waters in which the ships could sail." Roger went on to point out the sails and "how the wind that blew them and moved the ships represented the will of the people who put the government into office." Finally, he described how "the river in which the ships sailed, as it connected to the ocean, represented the interconnectedness of our country with the rest of the world." Clearly, Roger understood. Yet, if he had been required to write answers to the three questions, his responses, due to his learning disability, would have revealed quite a different understanding than the one he conveyed using his art and metaphorical thinking. We do not intend to minimize the importance of reading and writing. Rather, we suggest that if teachers

want to know whether students understand, then students ought to have a variety of ways available to them to express their understanding.

Likewise, students can participate in selecting outlets and audiences for their work. Students in an elementary school in Michigan created a poetry booklet, and through a simple brainstorming session concerning who should receive a copy of their publication, they thought well outside of the four walls of the classroom. They suggested that each child whose poem was published should receive a book as well as each classroom teacher and the school library. Students then thought they could donate one to the community library and some to doctor and dentist office waiting rooms in the community. Another student suggested that poems be displayed in local restaurants in the plastic "table tents" that restaurants usually use to advertise desserts and specials. (The restaurants provided free kids' meals to each child whose work they displayed.) Finally, some students suggested a grand opening at a local coffee shop in which their work would be read. Having an authentic audience helped to elevate the quality of their work. This work was made available for the community and interested audience members—a much more authentic audience than classroom teacher or parents. One teacher went so far as to create bulletin boards on which students kept track of all the different products and audiences that they created and touched during the school year. The bulletin board then served as a menu of sorts for students who needed inspiration when choosing how to show what they learned.

18. **Provide choice concerning whether to work alone or together.** Elementary schools today often seat children at tables and focus on group work or cooperative learning. Group work provides students with the opportunity to learn collaborative skills and can also make schoolwork more enjoyable. But sometimes students view cooperative learning unfavorably, especially when group grades are attached or when groups are assigned by ability levels without clear roles in which each student can make a meaningful contribution (Kagan, 1992; Robinson, 1990). Some students would simply rather work alone. If the goal of the activity is to enhance students' collaborative skills, then group work is warranted. However, if the goal is for students to understand content, then teachers should consider students' learning preferences and offer them choices of whether to work alone or together. A student who would rather work alone and who does better work alone should often

have the option to work alone. In some classrooms these children are rarely given the option to work alone, and thus are denied a mode for learning that best meets their educational needs.

When teachers seat students at tables, they force them to interact whether they work together or not. Sam picks on Sally, moves into her space, whispers put-downs, and quietly invades her thinking and learning area. Sally uses Suzie's stuff, and Suzie simply doesn't like Sally. The personality dynamics invade the learning space, and behavior management takes center stage in the classroom as the teacher is forced to deal with tattling, spats, territorial battles, and stolen items. If students must be seated at tables, they need to have the option to go somewhere else to work, or, as Mrs. Scanlon called it, "set up an office" using a barrier of cardboard to provide privacy and space at the "table spot." After 5 years in school working at tables with other kids, one 9-year-old girl who would rather work alone wrote the following entry in her daily journal:

> If I could change one thing about my life it would be to have my own desk. If I had my own desk in school it would be great in lots of ways. I would have more room to move around. It would get me away from other students who tempt me to talk. I wouldn't have people putting their stuff in my space. Having my own space would give me room to concentrate without being bothered by Kevin. The best part would be having room for my items and my thinking. That is why I want my own desk.

19. **Offer students choices concerning due dates.** Providing students with choices for project due dates or order of presentations can not only help students learn self-regulation and time management, but it also offers them some control over their learning, which can lead to a sense of greater responsibility for their learning. For example, Mahera has soccer practice on Monday and Tuesday, with games every Saturday. If she had a project due on a Tuesday, it might be difficult for her to complete it. If she were allowed the opportunity to select the day to turn in her project, she might look at her schedule and choose a Friday, allowing herself more time to do a good job on the work. Consider this example: Mrs. Lee assigned reports each quarter to her second and

third graders with the same due date for all students. Then over the next several weeks she would have each student read his or her report. By the time some students had a turn to read, they had forgotten what they had written. Had she chosen to have two students each day bring and read their reports, some students would have continued to work on and polish their reports right up until the day they elected to present their finished work.

When a teacher creates a due date, then takes points for one day late and awards no points for 2 or more days late, smart underachievers know that they only need to wait until after the due date to avoid doing the assignment at all. Better to demand that they do the work, while at the same time ensuring that the work is worth doing. I have always viewed a due date like a pregnancy. It might be early, it might be on the due date, or it might be late, but it will happen. With this approach, students must do the work. Setting a window of time for them to turn in a large project and allowing them to choose the date during that window will lead to more projects turned in "on time." If students fail to finish by their due date, then it is their fault—not the teacher's fault—that their work isn't done. They own it.

20. **Help students consider and evaluate the importance of their work by posing questions such as "So what?" "Who cares?" "Who might care?" and "How might we have a greater effect?"** These questions provide powerful opportunities for students and their teachers to consider whether what they are studying is important. If it seems unimportant (i.e., nobody would care about it and no one can figure out why someone would care about it), then consider spending less time on this content in favor of content that has greater meaning. Once determining that content is worth caring about, students and teachers can begin to consider what effects it might have on the classroom, school, community, or larger audience. For example, students in a small Michigan town wrote letters to the editor concerning a landfill in their community that had been proposed by an out-of-town developer. After sending their letters, they researched the wetlands protection act and attended township meetings. Their interest, knowledge of the situation, and tenacity resulted in denial of a permit for the landfill. These students learned about law, the environment, and how to effect change in their community by using communication and political action. Likewise, students in Kenosha, Wisconsin, interviewed senior citizens and created a

photojournalistic display for the local history museum on the influence of immigration on Kenosha. In doing this project, students refined their written and oral communication skills, learned local history, and developed artistic displays that enriched their community.

21. **Connect schoolwork to the real world deliberately and often by engaging in community involvement, service learning, mentorships, and apprenticeships.** Connecting students with the community and professionals in their areas of interest links them to our democracy and sets them up as future productive members of society. Schools often have as a goal to increase community involvement, and having community members to share their knowledge or work with interested students provides an authentic experience for the community members and students alike.

    Trinity started a newspaper in his enrichment class and wrote columns about topics of local interests. His teacher sent one of his columns to the local paper, and the editor found his voice so fresh that she "hired" him to write a column a week. He was in the fifth grade at the time. Trinity continued to contribute to his local paper throughout middle school and high school, eventually as a paid employee. His journalism interests followed him to college!

    Students in Victoria's school adopted a courtyard that they transformed into a bird and butterfly sanctuary. They worked with a local Department of Natural Resources officer and with a landscape architect in planning the courtyard. They used math, science, economics, and artistic design in this endeavor as they calculated how much mulch they needed, learned about which plants attracted which birds and butterflies and about the life cycles and needs of these animals, planned fundraising activities to help pay for the renovation, and designed the plantings and hardscape for the space. Eventually, they developed a courtyard brochure that described the specific flora and fauna they had brought to the school.

22. **Provide opportunities for deep involvement.** Jacky came to school crazy about horses. She read all of the Marguerite Henry and Walter Farley books in the library before fourth grade. Any assignment in which she was given a choice, she related to horses. She did reports on horse breeds, made a bridle rack in wood shop, drew horses in art, read horse books (both fiction and nonfiction) in language arts, explained the geologic time eras through the evolution of *Eohippus*, and calculated

the speed of muddy and dry tracks for both Standardbreds (trotters and pacers) and Thoroughbreds. She even did a language report on all the common sayings used in the English language that come from horses (e.g., don't look a gift horse in the mouth; getting a little long in the tooth; champing at the bit; rode hard and put away wet; you can lead a horse to water, but you can't make him drink). Rather than forbidding her to use horses in her educational projects, her teachers encouraged her to learn more about a topic that clearly excited her. One science teacher helped her learn genetics through studying the inherited patterns of coat colors, a concept that she found much more interesting than studying Mendel's peas. Her teachers helped her explore her passion about horses from a variety of angles. The amount of work and the quality of work that Jacky produced when she could connect it to horses was simply outstanding.

23. **Tell students to come see you if they have a better idea for an assignment, discussion, anything.** This strategy involves low creativity on the part of the teacher and the opportunity to be creative on the part of the student. As one second grader put it, "Teachers should ask the students because we often have great ideas about how to make school interesting." When giving students an assignment, simply offer them the option of "any other teacher-approved project." Students in a sixth-grade unit on simple machines found the lab activities both tedious and boring. They were not excited about dragging a weight up an inclined plane and calculating work, nor were they interested in how a pulley could reduce work. Their teacher was at her wits' end. Student behavior was terrible, and their engagement was low. Finally she said to the students, "If someone has a better idea of how we might learn this unit I'd like to hear it." Two students suggested that it would be fun (and educational) if they could build complex machines out of the simple machines. Thus, a Rube Goldberg activity was implemented in this teacher's classroom. From this beginning, she offered students the chance to "improve" on her assignments, and often they suggested quality alternative activities. This approach not only allows for engagement and ownership by the students, but also provides the teacher with a variety of interesting and quality student responses to her content assignments. Just imagine what Jacky from strategy 23 might suggest related to horses and simple machines!

24. **Explicitly discuss process to encourage metacognition.** Understanding how students think, helping them to understand their own thinking, and recognizing that students think differently from each other provides a solid foundation for cognitive growth and student achievement. By talking with kids about how they solved a problem and helping them understand their thinking processes, we help them solve future problems. Did you write from an outline, or did you do the outline last? Neither is correct, and each reflects a particular style, one linear and the other holistic. Yet in some schools an outline is required, leaving the holistic learners thinking they write or think poorly. Leah came home at the beginning of her second-grade year distressed, explaining how the teacher was making her call a ten a one. She had been given the problem of adding 29 and 34. The teacher told her to add the nine and the four and carry the one. She asked why she would call it a one when it was really a 10. She would have solved the problem by adding 20 and 30 to get 50, then adding nine and four to get 13, then adding 50 and 13 to get 63. Renaming a 10 as a one rightly confused her. There are many ways to understand and to solve problems, and if we are to develop a generation of students who can think, then we need to encourage thinking and thinking about thinking. The best way to do that is to discuss how and what is involved in thinking.

25. **Throw away the rubric and provide minimum requirements instead.** Rubrics are great tools for helping students understand what is expected of them. They provide guidelines concerning what is substandard, standard, and exemplary on a variety of criteria. Put simply, rubrics provide students (and their parents) recipes for successfully completing assignments and for earning high grades. Even at the university level, students seek rubrics so that they will know exactly what they have to do (and no more) to obtain an A on a project. I believe that rubrics should be used in moderation and on basic-skill types of assignments. If you want to know if a student can write a good paragraph, then provide an exemplar and criteria to guide that good paragraph. It is doubtful, however, that J. K. Rowling had a rubric for her *Harry Potter* series, or that Van Gogh had a rubric for "Starry Night."

    If the assignment is important, then provide students with a floor of minimum requirements rather than with a ceiling of exemplars. By providing exemplary criteria, we tell the students what is exemplary before they ever begin to engage in thinking about how they might develop a high-quality response to our assignment. In short, they follow our recipe. Rarely do they go beyond what we have already defined as exemplary. In effect, we put a lid on the assignment before the students ever begin work. It is like the difference between a cook who follows a recipe and a chief who creates the recipe. If we want to develop students who can think, solve problems, define problems, and who are capable of original thought, then we need to encourage such actions on a regular basis.

By providing them with minimum criteria, we give students a starting place. They know what has to be done to earn a C. They can then decide whether they want to exceed the minimum and apply themselves to define and develop an exemplary response to the task. If they choose the C, don't criticize their choice. Perhaps they don't view the assignment as particularly interesting or important, or perhaps they have other priorities. Whatever the case, they are learning to make decisions about their learning and we should support this developing autonomy. Many students will, however, seek an A. Some will be upset and demand to know exactly what is required for an A. A good answer to such queries is "More than the minimum requirements," or "What will it take for you to develop an exemplary project?" Both responses will frustrate and challenge the students, a first step to engaging them in generating quality work in response to the assignment.

The simple machine unit that we discussed in Strategy 24 involved using minimum criteria. The teachers simply told the students that they "had to build it, demonstrate it, and that they had to use and be able to identify at least three simple machines." For the final minimum criteria the teacher explained, "Each machine had to have a purpose and do something." If students met these minimum criteria, they would earn the grade of C. This ambiguity drove the A-getting, teacher-pleasing students crazy. How could their teacher be so vague? When they demanded more structure, their teacher smiled and encouraged them to apply themselves to the task, to prove to her that they could produce creative, exemplary work. Basically, she set no limits, and the students responded by producing excellent and different machines. The variety and originality in their responses provided interest, learning, and enjoyment to their peers and to their teachers. These results are the antithesis of 25 very similar projects developed in response to a common rubric.

One student, Megan, built a toothpaste dispenser out of a series of levers and inclined planes with a pulley for good measure, but when the hammer dispensed the toothpaste, it did so with such force that it shot the toothpaste to the classroom wall. The students that year had agreed that to earn an A the machine must also "work." After the toothpaste hit the wall, a heated discussion ensued concerning whether or not the machine had worked. The naysayers argued that the toothpaste should have been dispensed onto the toothbrush, whereas the supporters said that the machine had after all dispensed the toothpaste. In the middle of the fray, Megan simply took the toothbrush out of the machine and taped it to the wall. Problem solved—creatively. Students in this teacher's class began to ask for more open-ended criteria in their assignments and less structure as they became comfortable with their creative selves.

REFERENCES

A+E Television Networks (2013, September, 4). Bio. True Story. Retrieved from http://www.biography.com

American Academy of Achievement. (2013, September, 4). American Academy of Achievement. Retrieved from http://www.achievement.org/

Alvord, M. K., & Grados, J. J. (2005). Enhancing resilience in children: A proactive approach. *Professional Psychology: Research and Practice, 36*, 238–245. doi: 10.1037/0735-7028.36.3.238

Archambault, F., Westberg, K., Brown, S., Hallmark, B., Emmons, C., & Zhang, W. (1993). *Regular classroom practices with gifted students: Results of a national survey of classroom teachers.* Storrs, CT: University of Connecticut.

Archer, A., & Hughes, C. (2011). *Explicit instruction: Effective and efficient teaching.* New York, NY: The Guilford Press.

Assouline, S., Colangelo, N., Lupowski-Shoplik, A., Lipscomb, J., & Forstadt, L. (2009). *Iowa acceleration scale manual: A guide for whole grade acceleration K–8.* Tucson, AZ: Great Potential Press, Inc.

Ausubel, D. (1968). *Educational psychology.* New York, NY: Hold, Rinehart & Winston.

Balzer, C., & Siewert, B. (Eds.). (1990, July). *Identification: A suggested procedure for the identification of talented and gifted students K-12. Technical Assistance Paper 1* (revised). Salem, OR: Oregon State Department of Education, Division of Special Student Services. (ED 330 146)

Baum, S. E. (2010a, May 16). What's in a name? Defining and reifying twice-exceptional education. *The 2e Education Blog*. Retrieved from http://twice-exceptional.com/2012/05/16/whats-in-a-name-defining-and-reifying-twice-exceptional-education/

Baum, S. E. (2010b). *The Enigma of the 2E Learner: Practical Strategies for Meeting Their Needs* (PowerPoint slides). Retrieved from http://confratute.ning.com.

Baum, S. E. & Olenchak, F. R. (2002). The Alphabet children: GT, ADHD, and more. *Exceptionality, 10*, 77–91.

Baum, S., & Owen, S. (1988). High-ability/learning-disabled students: How are they different? *Gifted Child Quarterly, 32*, 321–326.

Baum, S., & Owen, S. (2004). *To be gifted and learning disabled.* Waco, TX: Prufrock Press.

Bear, C. S. (1998). *An evaluation of the effects of cluster grouping on the academic achievement of elementary students in the regular classroom.* (Order No. 9911919, Saint Louis University). *ProQuest Dissertations and Theses.* Retrieved from http://search.proquest.com/docview/304452884?accountid=13360. (304452884).

Benard, B. (1995). *Fostering resilience in children.* Urbana, IL: ERIC Clearinghouse on Elementary and Early Childhood Education. (ERIC Document Reproduction Service No. ED386327)

Benard, B., & Slade, S. (2009). Listening to students: Moving from resilience research to youth development practice and school connectedness. In R. Gilman, E. Huebner, M. J. Furlong, R. Gilman, E. Huebner, M. J. Furlong (Eds.), *Handbook of positive psychology in schools* (pp. 353–369). New York, NY: Routledge.

Bland, L. C., & Sowa, C. J. (1994). An overview of resilience in gifted children. *Roeper Review, 17*, 77.

Borland, J. (2009). Gifted education without gifted programs or gifted students: An anti-model. In J. Renzulli (Ed.), *Systems and models for developing programs for the gifted and talented.* Waco, TX: Prufrock Press.

Brighton, C., Hertberg, H., Callahan, C., Tomlinson, C., & Moon, T. (2005). *The feasibility of high end learning in academically diverse middle schools.* Storrs, CT: National Research Center on Gifted and Talented.

Brooks, R., & Goldstein, S. (2008). The mindset of teachers capable of fostering resilience in students. *Canadian Journal of School Psychology, 23*, 114–126.

Brown, S. B., Archambault, F. X., Zhang, W., & Westberg, K. (1994, April). *The impact of gifted students on the classroom practices of teachers.* Paper presented at the annual conference of the American Educational Research Association, New Orleans, LA.

Brulles, D. (2005). *An examination and critical analysis of cluster grouping gifted students in an elementary school district.* (Doctoral dissertation, Arizona State University). Available from ProQuest Dissertations and Theses database. (UMI No. 3194889)

Brulles, D., Peters, S. J., & Saunders, R. (2012). Schoolwide mathematics achievement within the gifted cluster grouping model. *Journal of Advanced Academics, 23,* 200–216.

Brulles, D., Saunders, R., & Cohn, S. (2010). Improving performance for gifted students in a cluster grouping model. *Journal for the Education of the Gifted, 34,* 327–352.

Bryant, M. A. (1987). Meeting the needs of gifted first grade children in a heterogeneous classroom. *Roeper Review, 9,* 214–216.

Callahan, C. M. (2006). Developing a plan for evaluating a program in gifted education. In J. H. Purcell & R. D. Eckert (Eds.), *Designing services and programs for high-ability learners: A guidebook for gifted education* (pp. 195–206). Thousand Oaks, CA: Corwin Press.

Callahan, C. M. (2009a). Evaluating for decision-making: The practitioner's guide to program evaluation. In J. S. Renzulli, E. J. Gubbins, K. S. McMillen, R. D. Eckert, & C. A. Little (Eds.), *Systems and models for developing programs for the gifted and talented* (2nd ed). Waco, TX: Prufrock Press.

Callahan, C. M. (2009b). Making the grade or achieving the goal. In K. Beans (Ed.), *Methods and Materials for Teaching the Gifted.* Waco, TX: Prufrock Press.

Callahan, C. M., & Caldwell, M. S. (1997). *A practitioner's guide to evaluating programs for the gifted.* Washington, DC: National Association of Gifted Children.

Cash, R. (2011). *Advancing differentiation: Thinking and learning for the 21st century.* Minneapolis, MN: Free Spirit.

Choice, P., & Walker S. (2010). *The new RtI: Response to intelligence.* Marion, IL: Pieces of Learning.

Cleaver, S. (2008). Smart and bored: Are we failing our high achievers? *Instructor, 117*(5).

Colangelo, N., Assouline, S., & Gross, M. U. M. (Eds.). (2004). *A nation deceived: How schools hold back America's brightest students.* Iowa City, IA: University of Iowa, The Connie Belin & Jacqueline N. Blank International Center for Gifted Education and Talent Development.

Coleman, M. R. (1995). The importance of cluster grouping. *Gifted Child Today, 18,* 38–40.

Coleman, L. J., & Cross, T. L. (2005). *Being gifted in school: An introduction to development, guidance, and teaching* (2nd ed.). Waco, TX: Prufrock Press.

Cramond, B. (1994, April). *The relationship between attention-deficit hyperactivity disorder and creativity.* Paper presented at the American Educational Research Association Annual Meeting, New Orleans, LA.

Dabrowski, K. (1972). *Psychoneurosis is not an illness.* London: Gryf Publications.

Dabrowski, K., & Piechowski, M. M. (1977). *Theory of levels of emotional development* (Vols. 1 & 2). Oceanside, NY: Dabor Science.

Daponte, B., O., (2008). Evaluation essentials: Methods for conducting sound research. San Francisco, CA: Jossey-Bass.

Darling-Hammond, L., Wei, R. C., Andree, A., Richardson, N., & Orphanos, S. (2009). *Professional learning in the learning profession: A status report on teacher development in the United States and abroad.* Dallas, TX: National Staff Development Council.

Davis, G. A., & Rimm, S. W. (2004). *Education of the gifted and talented* (5th ed.). Englewood Cliffs, NJ: Prentice-Hall.

Deci, E. L., & Ryan, R. M. (1985). *Intrinsic motivation and self-determination in human behavior.* New York, NY: Plenum.

Delcourt, M. A. B., & Evans, K. (1994). *Qualitative extension of the learning outcomes study.* Storrs, CT: The National Research Center on the Gifted and Talented.

Delcourt, M. A. B., Loyd, B. H., Cornell, D. G., & Goldberg, M. D. (1994). *Evaluation of the effects of programming arrangements on student learning outcomes.* Storrs, CT: The National Research Center on the Gifted and Talented.

Dennison, P. E., & Dennison, G. (2010). *Brain gym international.* Retrieved from http://www.braingym.com

Dole, S. (2000). The implications of the risk and resilience literature for gifted students with learning disabilities. *Roeper Review, 23,* 91–96.

Downey, J. A. (2008). Recommendations for fostering educational resilience in the classroom. *Preventing School Failure, 53,* 56–64.

Dweck, C. (1999). *Self-theories: Their role in motivation, personality, and development.* Lillington, NC: Psychology Press.

Easton, L. B. (Ed.). (2008). *Powerful designs for professional learning.* Oxford, OH: National Staff Development Council.

Eide, B., & Eide, F. (2006). *The mislabeled child.* New York, NY: Hyperion.

Eisner, E. (2001). What does it mean to say a school is doing well? *Phi Delta Kappan, 82*, 367–372.

Ellis, K., Lieberman, L., & LeRoux, D. (2009). Using differentiated instruction in physical education. *Palaestra, 24*(4), 19–23.

Encyclopedia of World Biography. (2013, September, 4). Encyclopedia of World Biography. Retrieved from http://www.notablebiographies.com

Erford, B. T. (2010). *Transforming the School Counseling Profession* (3rd ed.). Upper Saddle River, NJ: Merrill/Prentice Hall.

Finerman, S. T. (Producer) & Starkey, S. (Director). (1994). *Forrest Gump* [Motion picture]. United States: Paramount Pictures.

Foley-Nicpon, M., Assouline, S. G., & Colangelo, N. (2013). Twice-exceptional learners: Who needs to know what? *Gifted Child Quarterly, 57*, 169–180.

Ford, D., & Harris, J. (2010). A framework for infusing multicultural curriculum into gifted education. *Roeper Review, 23*, 4–10.

French, L., Walker, C., & Shore, B. (2011). Do gifted students really prefer to work alone? *Roeper Review, 33*(3), 145–159.

Fugate, C. M., Zentall, S. S., & Gentry, M. (2013). Creativity and working memory in gifted students with and without characteristics of attention deficit hyperactive disorder: Lifting the mask. *Gifted Child Quarterly, 57*, 234–236.

Fullan, M. (2004). *Leadership and sustainability: System thinkers in action.* Thousand Oaks, CA: SAGE.

Gagne, F. (1999). My convictions about the nature of abilities, gifts, and talent. *Journal for the Education of the Gifted, 22*, 109–136.

Gallagher, J. (1997). Least restrictive environment and gifted students. *Peabody Journal of Education, 72*, 153–165.

Gallagher, S. (1997). Problem-based learning: Where did it come from and where is it going? *Journal for the Education of the Gifted, 20*, 332–362.

Garet, M. S., Porter, A. C., Desimone, L., Birman, B. F., & Yoon, K. S. (2001). What makes professional development effective? Results from a national sample of teachers. *American Educational Research Journal, 38*, 915–945.

Gates, J. (2007). *ADHD and/or gifted: The possibility for misdiagnosis.* Paper presented at the World Council for Gifted and Talented Children, 17th Biennial World Conference, England: Warwick.

Gates, J. (2009, September). Mistaking giftedness for ADHD. *Twice-Exceptional Newsletter*, 8–10.

Gates, J. (2011). *Total school cluster grouping model: An investigation of student achievement and identification and teachers classroom practices* (Doctoral dissertation, Purdue University). Available from ProQuest Dissertations and Theses database. (UMI No. 3479482)

Gentry, M. (1999). *Promoting student achievement and exemplary classroom practices through cluster grouping: A research-based alternative to heterogeneous elementary classrooms* (Research Monograph 99138). Storrs: University of Connecticut, National Research Center on the Gifted and Talented.

Gentry, M. (2011). *Total School Cluster Grouping national scale-up project. Year 2 report.* West Lafayette, IN: Purdue University.

Gentry, M. (2012). *Total School Cluster Grouping, Urban Pilot Project, 2 years of Controlled Study Final Report on Academic Achievement, Identification, and Teacher Practices. Technical Report.* West Lafayette, IN: Purdue University.

Gentry, M. (2013). Cluster grouping. In C. M. Callahan & J. Plucker (Eds.), *Critical issues and practices in gifted education, 2nd ed.* (pp. 107–115). Waco, TX: Prufrock Press.

Gentry, M., Carmody, H. G., Davis, L., Duncan, D., Gates, J., Kosten, M., McCoy, M., Peters, S., Pereira, N. (2011). *The Purdue simulation: Teacher in-service.* Unpublished instrument. West Lafayette, IN: Purdue University.

Gentry, M., & Fugate, C. M. (2012). Gifted, Native American students: Underperforming, under-identified, and overlooked. *Psychology in the Schools, 49,* 631–646. Retrieved from http://dx.doi.org/10.1002/pits.21624

Gentry, M., & Gable, R. (2001). From the students' perspective My Class Activities: An instrument for use in research and evaluation *Journal for the Education of the Gifted, 24,* 322–343.

Gentry, M., & Keilty, W. (2004). On-going staff development planning and implementation: Keys to program success. *Roeper Review, 26,* 148–156.

Gentry, M. & Owen, S. V. (1999). An investigation of total school flexible cluster grouping on identification, achievement, and classroom practices. *Gifted Child Quarterly, 43,* 224–243.

Gentry, M. & Owen, S. V. (2004). Seconday student perceptions of classroom quality: Instrumentation and differences between advanced/honors and nonhonors classes. *Journal of Advanced Academics, 16,* 20-29.

George, P. (1995). Is it possible to live with tracking and ability grouping? In H. Pool & J. A. Page (Eds.), *Beyond tracking: Finding success in inclusive schools.* Bloomington, IN: Phi Delta Kappan Educational Foundation.

Goldring, E. B. (1990). Assessing the status of information on classroom organizational frameworks of gifted students. *Journal of Educational Research, 83*(6), 313-326.

Greenwood, J. (1887). Principles of education practically applied. New York, NY: D. Appleton and Company.

Goertzel, V., & Goertzel, M. (2004). *Cradles of eminence: Childhoods of more than 700 famous men and women* (2nd ed.). Scottsdale, AZ: Great Potential Press.

Gross, M. U. M. (2004). *Exceptionally gifted children*. London, England: Routledge Palmer.

Gubbins, E. J., Westberg, K. L., Reis, S. M., Dinnocenti, S., Tieso, C. M., Muller, L. M., Park, S., Emerick, L. J., Maxfield, L. R., & Burns, D. E. (2002). *Implementing a professional development model using gifted education strategies with all students* (RM02172). Storrs, CT: The National Research Center on the Gifted and Talented.

Hall, G. E., & Hord, S. M. (2001). *Implementing change: Patterns, principles, and potholes*. Boston, MA: Allyn and Bacon.

Heacox, D. (2002). *Differentiating instruction in the regular classroom: How to reach and teach all learners, Grades 3–12*. Minneapolis, MN: Free Spirit.

Hébert, T. P. (2011). *Understanding the social and emotional lives of gifted students*. Waco, TX: Prufrock Press.

Henderson, N. D. (1989). A meta-analysis of ability grouping achievement and attitude in the elementary grades. Unpublished doctoral dissertation, Mississippi State University at Mississippi.

Hertberg, H. (2009). Myth 7: Differentiation in the regular classroom is equivalent to gifted programs and is sufficient: Classroom teacher have the time, the skill, and the will to differentiate adequately. *Gifted Child Quarterly, 53,* 251–253.

Hieronymus, A. N., Hoover, H. D., & Lindquist, E. F. (1984). *Iowa tests of basic skills (Form G)*. Chicago, IL: Riverside.

Hmelo-Silver, C. (2004). Problem-based learning: What and how do students learn? *Educational Psychology Review, 16,* 235–266.

Hoover, S., Sayler, M., & Feldhusen, J. F. (1993). Cluster grouping of elementary students at the elementary level. *Roeper Review, 16,* 13–15.

Jacobs, H. H. (2010). *Curriculum 21: Essential education for a changing world*. Alexandria, VA: ASCD.

Kablfleisch, M. L. (2013). Twice-exceptional students: Gifted students with learning disabilities. In C. M. Callahan and H. L. Hertberg-Davis (Eds.), *Fundamentals of gifted education: Considering multiple perspectives*. New York, NY: Routledge.

Kablfleisch, M. L., & Iguchi, C. M. (2008). Twice-exceptional learners. In J. A. Plucker & C. M. Callahan (Eds.), *Critical issues and practices in gifted education: What the research says* (pp. 707–719). Waco, TX: Prufrock Press.

Kalogrides, D., & Loeb, S. (2013). Different teachers, different peers: The magnitude of student sorting within schools. *Educational Researcher, 42*, 304–316.

Kanevsky, L. (2011). Deferential differentiation: What types of differentiation do students want? *Gifted Child Quarterly, 55*, 279–299.

Kagan, S. (1992). *Cooperative learning.* San Clemente, CA: Kagan.

Kaplan, S. (2007). Differentiation: Asset or liability for gifted education? *Gifted Child Today, 30*, 23.

Kaplan, S. (2009). The grid: A model to construct differentiated curriculum for the gifted. In J. Renzulli (Ed.), *Systems and models for developing programs for the gifted and talented* (2nd ed; pp. 235–252). Waco, TX: Prufrock Press.

Kaplan, S., & Cannon, M. W. (2001). *Curriculum starter cards: Developing differentiated lessons for gifted students.* Waco, TX: Prufrock Press.

Kaplan, S., & Gould, B. (2005). *The flip book, too: More quick and easy methods for developing differentiated learning experiences.* Calabasas, CA: Educator to Educator.

Kennedy, D. M. (1989). *Classroom interactions of gifted and non gifted fifth graders.* Unpublished doctoral dissertation, Purdue University, West Lafayette, IN.

Kennedy, D. M. (1995). Teaching gifted in regular classrooms: Plain talk about creating a gifted-friendly classroom. *Roeper Review, 17*, 232–234.

Kitano, M. K., & Lewis, R. B. (2005). Resilience and coping: Implications for gifted children and youth at risk. *Roeper Review, 27*, 200–205.

Kaplan, S. (2012, October). *Paving the way to the common core.* Keynote presented at the Orange County Council for Gifted and Talented Education's 38th Annual Conference, University of California, Irvine, CA.

Kulik, C.-L. C. (August, 1985). Effects of inter-class ability grouping on achievement and self-esteem. Paper presented at the 93rd Annual Convention of the American Psychological Association, Los Angeles, CA.

Kulik, J. A. (1992). *An analysis of the research on ability grouping: Historical and contemporary perspectives.* Storrs, CT: The National Research Center on the Gifted and Talented.

Kulik, J. A. (2003). Grouping and tracking. In N. Colangelo & G. Davis (Eds.), *Handbook of gifted education* (pp. 268–281). Boston, MA: Allyn and Bacon.

Kulik, C.-L. C., & Kulik, J. A. (1982). Effects of ability grouping on secondary school students: A meta-analysis of evaluation findings. *American Educational Research Journal, 19*, 415-428.

Kulik, C.-L. C., & Kulik, J. A. (1984). *Effects of ability grouping on elementary school pupils: A meta-analysis.* Paper presented at the annual meeting of the American Psychological Association, Toronto. (ERIC Document Reproduction Service No. ED 255 329)

Kulik, C.-L. C., & Kulik, J. A. (1985). *Effects of ability grouping on achievement and self-esteem.* Paper presented at the annual convention of the American Psychological Association, Los Angeles, CA.

Kulik, J. A., & Kulik, C.-L. C. (1987). Effects of ability grouping on student achievement. *Equity & Excellence in Education, 23,* 22-30.

Kulik, J. A., & Kulik, C.-L. C. (1991). Ability grouping and gifted students. In N. Colangelo & G. A. Davis (Eds.), *Handbook of gifted education* (pp. 178–196). Boston: Allyn and Bacon.

Kulik, J. A., & Kulik, C-L. C. (1992). Meta-analytic findings on grouping programs. *Gifted Child Quarterly, 36,* 73–77.

LaRose, B. (1986). The lighthouse program: A longitudinal research project. *Journal for the Education of the Gifted, 9,* 224–232.

Loveless, T. (2013). *The 2013 Brown Center Report on American Education: How well are American students learning? (Volume 3; Number 2).* Retrieved from http://www.brookings.edu/research/reports/2013/03/18-tracking-ability-grouping-loveless

Lou, Y., Abrami, P. C., Spence, J. C., Poulsen, C., Chambers, B., & d'Apollonia, S. (1996). Within-class grouping: A meta analysis. *Review of Educational Research, 66,* 423–458.

Luthar, S. S. (1991). Vulnerability and resilience: A study of high-risk adolescents. *Child Development, 62,* 600–616. doi: 10.2307/1131134

Maker, J. (1986). Qualitatively different: Is it a key concept in developing curricula? In J. Maker (Ed.), *Critical issues in gifted education: Defensible programs for the gifted* (pp. 117–120). Rockville, MD: Aspen.

Marotta-Garcia, C. (2011). *Teachers use of a differentiated curriculum for gifted students.* (Order No. 3477957, University of Southern California). *ProQuest Dissertations and Theses.* Retrieved from http://search.proquest.com/docview/901460589?accountid=13360. (901460589).

Marsh, H. W., Chessor, D., Craven, R., & Roche, L. (1995). The effects of gifted and talented programs on academic self-concept: The big fish strikes again. *American Educational Research Journal, 32,* 285–319.

Marzano, R. (2004). *Building background knowledge for academic achievement: What works in schools.* Alexandria, VA: ASCD.

Masten, A. S. (2001). Ordinary magic: Resilience processes in development. *American Psychologist, 56,* 227–238. doi: 10.1037/0003-066x.56.3.227

Masten, A. S., Herbers, J. E., Cutuli, J. J., & Lafavor, T. L. (2008). Promoting competence and resilience in the school context. *Professional School Counseling, 12,* 76–84.

Matthews M. S., Ritchotte, J. A. & McBee, M. T. (2013). Effects of schoolwide cluster grouping and within-class ability grouping on elementary school students' academic achievement growth. *High Ability Studies, 24,* 81-97.

McBrien, J. L., & Brandt, R. S. (1997). *The language of learning: A guide to education terms.* Alexandria, VA: Association for Supervision and Curriculum Development.

McCoach, D. B., Kehle, T. J., Bray, M. A., & Siegle, D. (2001). Best practices in the identification of gifted students with learning disabilities. *Psychology in the Schools, 38,* 403–411.

Mendaglio, S., & Peterson, J. S. (Eds). (2007). *Models of counseling gifted children, adolescents, and young adults.* Waco, TX: Prufrock Press.

Menke, C. (1993). To snare the gifted mind. *Gifted Education International, 9,* 36–39.

Miller, L. S. (2004). *Promoting sustained growth in the representation of African Americans, Latinos, and Native Americans among top students in the United States at all levels of the education system* (RM04190). Storrs, CT: National Research Center on the Gifted and Talented.

Miller, A. L., Latz, A. O., Jenkins, S. C. W., & Adams, C. M. (2011). A pastiche of outcomes for a teacher-student pair: Experiences within a reading cluster group. *Creative Education, 3,* 61–66.

Morrison, G. M., & Allen, M. R. (2007). Promoting student resilience in school contexts. *Theory Into Practice, 46,* 162–169.

Mosteller, F., Light, R. J., & Sachs, J. A. (1996). Sustained inquiry in education: Lessons from skill grouping and class size. *Harvard Educational Review, 66,* 797-842.

Moon, S. M. (2003). Personal Talent. *High Ability Studies, 14,* 5–21.

Moon, S. M. (2009). Myth 15: High-ability students don't face problems and challenges. *Gifted Child Quarterly, 53,* 274–276. doi: 10.1177/0016986209346943

Moon, S. M., Kolloff, M. B., Robinson, A., Dixon, F., & Feldhusen, J. F. (2009). The Purdue Three-Stage Model. In J. S. Renzulli, E. J. Gubbins, K. S. McMillen, R. D. Eckert, & C. A. Little (Eds.), *Systems and models for developing programs for the gifted and talented, 2nd ed.* (pp. 289–321). Waco, TX: Prufrock Press.

Moon, S. M., & Reis, S. M. (2004). Acceleration and twice-exceptional Students. In N. Colangelo, S. G. Assouline, & M. U. M. Gross (Eds.), *A nation deceived: How schools hold back America's brightest students, Vol. I*, (109–119). Iowa City, IA: The Connie Belin & Jacqueline N. Blank International Center for Gifted Education and Talent Development.

National Association for Gifted Children (1994). *Position paper: Differentiation of curriculum and instruction.* Washington DC: Author.

National Association for Gifted Children & Council of State Directors of Programs for the Gifted. (2013). *2012–2013 State of the states in gifted education: National policy and practice data.* Washington, DC: Authors.

Neihart, M. (2000). Gifted children with Asperger's Syndrome. *Gifted Child Quarterly, 44*, 222–230.

Neihart, M. (2002a). Gifted children and depression. In M. Neihart, S. M. Reis, N. M. Robinson, & S. M. Moon (Eds.), *The social and emotional development of gifted children: What do we know?* (pp. 93–102). Waco, TX: Prufrock Press.

Neihart, M. (2002b). Risk and resilience in gifted children: A conceptual framework. In M. Neihart, S. M. Reis, N. M. Robinson, & S. M. Moon (Eds.), *The social and emotional development of gifted children: What do we know?* (pp. 113–124). Waco, TX: Prufrock Press.

Neihart, M., Reis, S. M., Robinson, N. M., Moon, S. M., & National Association for Gifted Children (Eds). (2002). *The social and emotional development of gifted children: What do we know?* Waco, TX: Prufrock Press.

Neumeister, K. S., & Burney, V. H. (2012). *Gifted program evaluation: A handbook for administrators and coordinators.* Waco, TX: Prufrock Press.

Nielsen, M. E. (2002). Gifted students with learning disabilities: Recommendations for identification and programming. *Exceptionality, 10*, 93–111.

Nielsen, M. E., & Higgins, L. D. (2005). The eye of the storm: Services and programs for twice- exceptional learners. *Teaching Exceptional Children, 38*, 8–15.

Noland, T. K. & Taylor, B. L. (1986). The effects of ability grouping: a meta-analysis of research findings. Paper presented at the 70th Annual meeting of the American Educational Research Association, San Francisco. (ERIC Document Reproduction Service No. ED 269 541)

Nomi, T. (2010). The effects of within-class ability grouping on academic achievement in early elementary years. *Journal of Research on Educational Effectiveness, 3,* 56–92.

Oakes, J. (1985). *Keeping track: How schools structure inequality.* New Haven, CT: Yale University Press.

O'Connell-Ross, P. (1993). *National excellence: A case for developing America's talent.* Washington, DC: U. S. Department of Education, Government Printing Office.

O'Conner, K. J. (2002). The application of Dabrowski's theory to the gifted. In M. Neihart, S. M. Reis, N. M. Robinson, & S. M. Moon (Eds.), *The social and emotional development of gifted children: What do we know?* (pp. 51–60). Waco, TX: Prufrock Press.

Olenchak, F. R., & Reis, S. M. (2001). Gifted students with disabilities. In M. Neihart, S. M. Reis, N. M. Robinson, & S. M. Moon (Eds.), *The social and emotional development of gifted children: What do we know?* Waco, TX: Prufrock Press.

Patton, M. Q. (2008). *Utilization-focused evaluation* (4th ed.). Thousand Oaks, CA: SAGE.

Peters, S. J., & Gentry, M. (2010). Multi-group construct validity evidence of the HOPE Scale: Instrumentation to identify low-income elementary students for gifted programs. *Gifted Child Quarterly, 54,* 298–313.

Peters, S. J., & Gentry, M. (2013). Additional validity evidence and across-group equivalency of the HOPE teacher rating scale. *Gifted Child Quarterly, 57,* 85–100.

Peterson, J. S. (1997). Bright, tough and resilient—and not in a gifted program. *The Journal for Secondary Gifted Education, 8,* 121–136.

Peterson, J. S. (2003). An argument for proactive attention to affective concerns to gifted students. *The Journal of Secondary Gifted Education, 15,* 62–70.

Peterson, J. S. (2007a). A developmental perspective. In S. Mendaglio & J. S. Peterson (Eds.), *Models of counseling gifted children, adolescents, and young adults* (pp. 97–126). Waco, TX: Prufrock Press.

Peterson, J. S. (2007b). *The essential guide to talking with gifted teens.* Minneapolis: Free Spirit.

Peterson, J. S. (2008). Focusing on where they are: A clinical perspective. In J. VanTassel-Baska, T. L. Cross, & F. R. Olenchak (Eds.), *Social-emotional curriculum with gifted and talented students* (pp. 193–226). Waco, TX: Prufrock Press.

Peterson, J. S. (2009). Myth 17: Gifted and talented individuals do not have unique social and emotional needs. *Gifted Child Quarterly, 53,* 280–282. doi: 10.1177/0016986209346946

Peterson, J. S. (2012). The asset-burden paradox of giftedness: A 15-year phenomenological, longitudinal case study. Roeper Review, 34, 244-260.

Peterson, J. S., Betts. G., & Bradley, T. (2009). Discussion groups as a component of affective curriculum for gifted students. In J. VanTassel-Baska, T. L. Cross, & F. R. Olenchak (Eds.), *Social-emotional curriculum with gifted and talented students* (pp. 289–320). Waco, TX: Prufrock Press.

Peterson, J. S., & Lorimer, M. R. (2012). Small-group affective curriculum for gifted students: A longitudinal study of teacher-facilitators. *Roeper Review, 34,* 158–169.

Peterson, J. S., & Ray, K. E. (2006a). Bullying and the gifted: Victims, perpetrators, prevalence, and effects. *Gifted Child Quarterly, 50,* 148–168.

Peterson, J. S., & Ray, K. E. (2006b). Bullying among the gifted: The subjective experience. *Gifted Child Quarterly, 50,* 252–269.

Phenix, P. (1964). *Realms of meaning.* New York, NY: McGraw-Hill.

Piechowski, M. M. (1986). The concept of developmental potential. *Roeper Review, 8,* 190-197.

Piechowski, M. M., & Chucker, J. (2011). Overexcitabilities. In M. A. Runco & S. R. Pritzker (Eds.), *Encyclopedia of creativity* (2nd ed., Vol. 2, pp. 325–334). San Diego, CA: Academic Press.

Pierce, R., Cassady, J., Adams, C., Neumeister, K., Dixon, F., & Cross, T. (2011). The effects of clustering and curriculum on the development of gifted learners' math achievement. *Journal for the Education of the Gifted, 34,* 569–596.

Porcher, S. (2007). *An examination of the use of differentiated instruction practices for gifted students in an elementary cluster model classroom* (Doctoral dissertation, University of West Georgia). Available from ProQuest Dissertations and Theses database. (UMI No. 3273802)

Purcell, J. (1994). *The status of programs for high ability students* (CRS94306). Storrs, CT: The National Research Center on the Gifted and Talented.

Reis, S. M., Burns, D. E., & Renzulli, J. S. (1992). *Curriculum compacting: The complete guide to modifying the regular curriculum for high ability students.* Waco, TX: Prufrock Press.

Reis, S. M., Colbert, R. D., & Hébert, T. P. (2004). Understanding resilience in diverse, talented students in an urban high school. *Roeper Review, 27,* 110–120.

Reis, S. M., Gentry, M., & Park, S. (1995). *Extending the pedagogy of gifted education to all students: The enrichment cluster study. Technical Report.* Storrs, CT: The National Research Center on the Gifted and Talented.

Reis, S. M., & McCoach, D. B. (2002). Underachievement in gifted and talented students with special needs. *Exceptionality, 10,* 113–125.

Reis, S. M., McGuire, J. M., & Neu, T. W. (2000). Compensation strategies used by high-ability students with learning disabilities who succeed in college. *Gifted Child Quarterly, 44,* 123–134.

Reis, S. M., & Purcell, J. (1993). An analysis of content elimination and strategies used by elementary classroom teachers in the curriculum compacting process. *Journal for the Education of the Gifted, 16,* 147–170.

Reis, S. M., & Renzulli, J. S. (1992). Using curriculum compacting to challenge the above average. *Educational Leadership, 50,* 51–57.

Reis, S. M., & Ruban, L. (2005). Services and programs for academically talented students with learning disabilities. *Theory Into Practice, 44,* 148–159.

Reis, S. M., Westberg, K., Kulikowich, J., Caillard, F., Hébert, T. P., Plucker, J., Purcell, J., Rogers, J., & Smist, J. (1993). *Why not let high ability students start school in January? The curriculum compacting study.* Storrs, CT: Research Monograph, National Research Center on the Gifted and Talented.

Reis, S. M., Westberg, K., Kulikowich, J., & Purcell, J. (1998). Curriculum compacting and achievement test scores: What does the research say? *Gifted Child Quarterly, 42,* 123–129.

Reiss, P., & Follo, E. (1993). *Accelerated education methods for intellectually gifted secondary students.* Kansas City, MO: Paper presented at the Annual Midwest Educational Research Association Conference.

Renzulli, J. S. (1976). The enrichment triad model: A guide for developing defensible programs for the gifted and talented. *Gifted Child Quarterly, 20,* 303–326.

Renzulli, J. S. (1977). *Enrichment triad model: A guide for developing defensible programs for gifted and talented.* Waco, TX: Prufrock Press.

Renzulli, J. S. (1978). What makes giftedness? Reexamining a definition. *Phi Delta Kappan, 60,* 180–184, 261.

Renzulli, J. S. (Ed.) (1986). *Systems and models for developing programs for the gifted and talented.* Waco, TX: Prufrock Press.

Renzulli, J. S. (1994). *Schools for talent development: A comprehensive plan for total school improvement.* Waco, TX: Prufrock Press.

Renzulli, J. S. (1995). *Building a bridge between gifted education and total school improvement.* Storrs, CT: National Research Center on the Gifted and Talented.

Renzulli, J. S. (2002). Expanding the conception of giftedness to include co-cognitive traits and to promote social capital. *Phi Delta Kappan, 84,* 33–58.

Renzulli, J. S. (2005, May). A quiet crisis is clouding the future of R & D. *Education Week, 24,* 32–33, 40.

Renzulli, J. S., & Reis, S. M. (1991). The reform movement and the quiet crisis in gifted education. *Gifted Child Quarterly, 35,* 26–35.

Renzulli, J. S., & Reis, S. M. (1994). Research related to the Schoolwide Enrichment Triad model. *Gifted Child Quarterly, 38,* 7–20.

Renzulli, J. S., & Reis, S. M. (1997). *The schoolwide enrichment model: A comprehensive plan for educational excellence* (2nd ed). Waco, TX: Prufrock Press.

Renzulli, J. S., Smith, L. H., & Reis, S. M. (1982). Curriculum compacting: An essential strategy for working with gifted students. *Elementary School Journal, 82,* 185–194.

Renzulli, J. S., Smith, L. H., White, A. J., Callahan, C. M., Hartman, R. K., Westberg, K. L., Gavin, M. K., Reis, S. M., Siegle, D., & Sytsma, R. E. (2002). *Scales for rating the behavioral characteristics of superior students.* Waco, TX: Prufrock Press.

Renzulli, J. S., Smith, L. H., White, A. J., Callahan, C. M., Hartman, R. K., Westberg, K. L., Gavin, M. K., Reis, S. M., Siegle, D., Reed, R. E. S. (2010). *Scales for rating the behavioral characteristics of superior students: Renzulli scales* (3rd ed.). Waco, TX: Prufrock Press.

Rimm-Kaufman, S. E., & Sawyer, B. E. (2004). Primary-grade teachers' self-efficacy beliefs, attitudes toward teaching, and discipline and teaching practice priorities in relation to the Responsive Classroom approach. *Elementary School Journal, 104,* 321–341.

Roberts, J. L., & Inman, T. F. (2007). *Differentiating instruction: Best practices for the classroom.* Waco, TX: Prufrock Press.

Robinson, A. (1990). Cooperation or exploitation? The argument against cooperative learning for talented students. *Journal for the Education of the Gifted, 4,* 9–23.

Robinson, A. (1991). *Cooperative learning and the academically talented student.* Storrs, CT: National Research Center on Gifted and Talented.

Robbins, A. (2011). *The geeks shall inherit the Earth: Popularity, quirk theory, and why outsiders thrive after high school.* New York, NY: Hyperion.

Robinson, N. M., Reis, S. M., Neihart, M., & Moon, S. M. (2002). Social and emotional issues facing gifted and talented students: What have we learned and what should we do now? In M. Neihart, S. M. Reis, N. M. Robinson, & S. M. Moon (Eds.), *The social and emotional development of gifted children: What do we know?* (pp. 267–289). Waco, TX: Prufrock Press.

Rogers, K. B. (1991). *The relationship of grouping practices to the education of the gifted and talented learner.* Storrs, CT: The National Research Center on the Gifted and Talented.

Rogers, K. B. (1993). Grouping the gifted and talented: Questions and answers. *Roeper Review, 16,* 8–12.

Rogers, K. B. (2002). *Re-forming gifted education.* Scottsdale, AZ: Great Potential.

Rogers, K. B., & Kimpston, R. (1992). Acceleration: What we do vs. what we know. *Educational Leadership, 50,* 58–61.

Schuler, P. (2002). Perfectionism in gifted children and adolescents. In M. Neihart, S. M. Reis, N. M. Robinson, & S. M. Moon (Eds.), *The social and emotional development of gifted children: What do we know?* (pp. 71–80). Waco, TX: Prufrock Press.

Schultz, C. (1991). *The effects of curriculum compacting upon student achievement in fourth grade mathematics.* Unpublished Master's Thesis, The University of Northern Iowa.

Schunk, D. H., Pintrich, P. R., & Meece, J. L. (2008). *Motivation in education: Theory, research, and applications* (3rd ed). Upper Saddle River, NJ: Pearson Prentice Hall.

Sebring, D., & Tussey, D. (1992). *Local administration of progress for the gifted and talented. Challenges in gifted education: Developing potential and investing in knowledge for the 21st century.* ED:344412

Senge, P. (1991). *The fifth discipline: The art and discipline of the learning organization.* New York, NY: Doubleday.

Siegle, D., & McCoach, D. B. (2005). Making a difference: Motivating gifted students who are not achieving. *Teaching Exceptional Children, 38,* 22–27.

Silverman, L. K. (2002). Asynchronous development. In M. Neihart, S. M. Reis, N. M. Robinson, & S. M. Moon (Eds.), *The social and emotional development of gifted children: What do we know?* (pp. 31–40). Waco, TX: Prufrock Press.

Sisk, D. (1988). The bored and disinterested gifted child: Going through school lockstep. *Journal for the Education of the Gifted, 11,* 5–18.

Slade, M. J. (2012). The impact of professional standards in gifted education. In S. L. Hunsaker (Ed.), *Identification: The theory and practice of identifying students for gifted and talented education services.* Waco, TX: Prufrock Press.

Slavin, R. E. (1987a). Ability grouping and student achievement in elementary schools: A best-evidence synthesis. *Review of Educational Research, 57,* 293–336.

Slavin, R. E. (1987b). Grouping for instruction. *Equity and Excellence, 23,* 31–36.

Slavin, R. E. (1990). Achievement effects of ability grouping in secondary schools: A best-evidence synthesis. *Review of Educational Research, 60,* 471-499.

Slavin, R. E. (1993). Ability grouping in the middle grades: Achievement effects and alternatives. *The Elementary School Journal, 93,* 535-552.

Slavin, R. E. (2006). *Educational Psychology: Theory and Practice.* Boston, MA: Pearson.

Starko, A. (1986). Meeting the needs of the gifted throughout the school day: Techniques for curriculum compacting. *Roeper Review, 9,* 27–33.

Stead, T. (2005). *Reality checks: Teaching reading comprehension with nonfiction K–5.* Ontario, Canada: Pembroke Publishers Limited.

Stewart, V. (2010). Digital portfolios and curriculum maps: Linking teacher and student work. In H. H. Jacobs (Ed.), *Curriculum 21: Essential education for a changing world.* Alexandria, VA: ASCD.

Stiles, J. (1994). An interdisciplinary ecology course for gifted (and all) students. *Middle School Journal, 25,* 8–11.

Sutton, K. (2000). Curriculum compacting: Teaching science in a heterogeneous classroom. *Science Scope, 24,* 22–27.

TED (Producer). (2010). *Bring on the learning revolution!* Retrieved from http://www.ted.com/talks/sir_ken_robinson_bring_on_the_revolution.html

Teno, K. M. (2000). Cluster grouping elementary gifted students in the regular classroom: A teacher's perspective. *Gifted Child Today, 23,* 44–49.

Tieso, C. L. (2003). Ability grouping is not just tracking anymore. *Roeper Review, 26,* 29–36.

Tieso, C. L. (2005). The effects of grouping practices and curricular adjustments on achievement. *Journal for the Education of the Gifted, 29,* 60–89.

Tomlinson, C. (1999). *The differentiated classroom: Responding to the needs of all learners.* Alexandria, VA: ASCD.

Tomlinson, C. (2000). Differentiated instruction: Can it work? *The Education Digest, 65,* 25–31.

Tomlinson, C. (2001). *How to differentiate instruction in mixed-ability classrooms* (2nd ed). Alexandria, VA: Association for Supervision and Curriculum Development.

Tomlinson, C. (2004). Sharing responsibiity for differentiating instruction. *Roeper Review, 26,* 188–189.

Tomlinson, C., Bland, L., Moon, T., & Callahan, C. (1994). Case studies of evaluation utility in gifted education. *Evaluation Practice, 15,* 153–168.

Tomlinson, C., Brighton, C., Hertberg, H., Callahan, C., Moon, T., Brimijoin, K., Conover, L., & Reynolds, T. (2003). Differentiating instruction in response to student readiness, interest, and learning profiles in academically diverse classrooms: A review of literature. *Journal for the Education of the Gifted, 27,* 119–145.

Tomlinson, C. A., & Callahan, C. M. (1992). Contributions of gifted education to general education in a time of change. *Gifted Child Quarterly, 36,* 183–189.

Torrance, E. P. (1977). *Discovering and nurturance of giftedness in the culturally different.* Reston, VA: Council for Exceptional Children.

Torrance, E. P., Goff, K., & Satterfield, N. B. (1998). *Multicultural mentoring of the gifted and talented.* Waco, TX: Prufrock Press.

United States Department of Education. (1993). *National excellence: A case for developing America's talent.* Washington, DC: Author.

United States Department of Education. (2000). *OCR elementary and secondary school survey: 2000.* Retrieved from http://vistademo.beyond2020.com/ocr2000r

United States Department of Education. (2006, October 4). *Identification of specific learning disabilities.* Retrieved from http://idea.ed.gov/explore/view/p/%2Croot%2Cdynamic%2CTopicalBrief%2C23%2C

VanTassel-Baska, J. (2009). Affective curriculum and gifted learners. In J. VanTassel-Baska, T. L. Cross, & F. R. Olenchak (Eds.), *Social-emotional curriculum with gifted and talented students* (pp. 113–132). Waco, TX: Prufrock Press.

VanTassel-Baska, J., & Feng, A. X. (Eds.). (2004). *Designing and utilizing evaluation for gifted program improvement.* Waco, TX: Prufrock Press.

Van Tassel-Baska, J., & Little, C. (2011). *Content-based curriculum for high-ability learners.* Waco, TX: Prufrock Press.

Voerman, L., Meijer, P., Korthagen, F., & Simons, R. (2012). Types and frequencies of feedback interventions in classroom interaction in secondary education. *Teaching and Teacher Education, 28,* 1107–1115.

Vygotsky, L. (1986). *Thought and language* (A. Kozuin, Trans.). Cambridge, MA: MIT Press.

Vygotsky, L., & Cole, M. (1978). *Mind in society: The development of higher psychological processes.* Cambridge, MA: Harvard University Press.

Ward, V. S. (1981). Basic concepts. In W. B. Barbe and J. S. Renzulli (Eds.), *Psychology and Education of the Gifted*, (3rd ed., pp. 174-183). New York, NY: Irvington Publishers.

Webb, J. T. (2000). Misdiagnosis and dual diagnosis of gifted children. In M. Neihart (Ed.), *Symposium on cutting edge minds: What it means to be exceptional*. Scottsdale, AZ: Great Potential Press.

Webb, J. T., Amend, E. R., Webb, N. E., Goerss, J., Beljan, P., & Olenchak, F. R. (2005). *Misdiagnosis and dual diagnoses of gifted children and adults: ADHD, bipolar, OCD, Asperger's, depression, and other disorders*. Scottsdale, AZ: Great Potential.

Wang, M. C., Haertel, G. D., & Walberg, H. J. (1994). Educational resilience in inner cities. In M. C. Wang & E. W. Gordon (Eds.), *Educational resilience in inner-city America: Challenges and prospects* (pp. 45–72). Hillsdale, NJ: England.

Weinfeld, R., Barnes-Robinson, L., Jeweler, S., & Shevitz, B. R. (2005). What we have learned: Experiences in providing adaptations and accommodations for gifted and talented students with learning disabilities. *Teaching Exceptional Children, 38*, 48–54.

Werner, E. E., & Smith, R. S. (1992). *Overcoming the odds: High risk children from birth to adulthood*. New York, NY: Cornell University Press.

White, H. A., & Shah, P. (2006). Uninhibited imaginations: Creativity in adults with attention-deficit/hyperactive disorder. *Personality and Individual Differences, 40*, 1121–1131.

White, H. A., & Shah, P. (2011). Creative style and achievement in adults with attention-deficit/hyperactive disorder. *Personality and Individual Differences, 50*, 673–677.

Winebrenner, S., & Brulles, B. (2008). *The cluster grouping handbook: How to challenge gifted students and improve achievement for all*. Minneapolis, MN: Free Spirit.

Wirkala, C., & Kuhn, D. (2011). Problem-based learning in K–12 education: Is it effective and how does it achieve its effects? *American Educational Research Journal, 48*, 1157–1186.

W. K. Kellogg Foundation (1999). *W. K. Kellogg Foundation evaluation handbook*. Battle Creek: MI: Author. Retrieved from http://www.wkkf.org/knowledge-center/resources/2010/w-k-kellogg-foundation-evaluation-handbook.aspx

Wormeli, R. (2005). Busting myths about differentiated instruction. *Principal Leadership, 5*, 28–33.

Wormeli, R. (2011). Differentiated instruction: Setting the pedagogy straight. *Middle Ground, 15*, 39–40.

Yoon, S., & Gentry, M. (2009). Racial and ethnic representation in gifted programs: Current status of and implications for gifted Asian American students. *Gifted Child Quarterly, 53*, 121–136.

Yssel, N., Margison, J., Cross, T., Merbler, J. (2005). Puzzles, mysteries, and Picasso: A summer camp for students who are gifted and learning disabled. *Teaching Exceptional Children, 38*, 42–46.

Zentall, S. S., Moon, S. M., Hall, A. M., & Grskovic, J. A. (2001). Learning and motivational characteristics of boys with AD/HD and/or giftedness. *Exceptional Children, 67*, 499–519.

INTERVIEW PROTOCOL

KUWAITI YOUTH SCHOLAR TEACHER INTERVIEW PROTOCOL

Name: _____   Date: _____

Position applying for: _____

Interviewer name: _____

Instructions:
1. Introduce the program to which the applicant is applying for a teaching position.
2. Ask the questions outlined on the interview protocol, making notes of the applicants' answers. A "Keywords" box has been provided to denote words and phrases that are germane to the applicants' responses. A section has been provided under each question for rater comments.
3. Rate each answer on a scale of 1–5. Candidates with an overall average of 4.0 or above are eligible for hire.

1	2	3	4	5
Poor	Fair	Good	Above average	Excellent

Program Introduction:
The students: high intellectual ability, gifted, high-interest/passionate (intense), twice exceptional

1. Tell us about your qualifications related teaching math and/or science to elementary students.

Notes:	Comments:

Scale: 1 2 3 4 5

2. How would you teach high-ability students; also consider students who may be under-achievers due to lack of challenge and motivation. (TOF 3; TOF 4)

Notes:	Comments:

Keywords: *Independent study; provide choice activities; increase the difficulty of activities; find the students' interest, learning preferences; alternative activities*

Scale: 1 2 3 4 5

3. Why are you interested in working with the gifted, creative, and talented students in the new Kuwaiti program? (TOF 3; TOF 7)

Notes:	Comments:

Keywords: *work with GT/HA students; personal experience; desire to teach; provide new learning experiences; share knowledge of my content area; passion; enthusiasm; interaction; gain more teaching experience*

Scale: 1 2 3 4 5

4. What is your perception of the intellectual and socio-emotional characteristics of a gifted student? (TOF 7; TOF 9; TOF 10)

Notes:	Comments:

Keywords: asynchronous development; active (physically/mentally); easily bored/distracted; inquisitive; curious; intense; perfectionist; knowledgeable; critical thinking; creative; quick learner; high verbal ability; observant; takes risks; independent; keen sense of humor; varied interests; withdrawn/loner; leadership abilities; focused interests

Scale: 1   2   3   4   5

5. If we were to walk into your classroom, describe the learning environment and the types of activities we might see. (TOF 2; TOF 4; TOF 6; TOF 8; TOF 12)

Notes:	Comments:

Keywords: flexible (ability to adjust); student-centered; student choice; interactive; secure; flexible grouping; hands-on; small groups; independent study; equitable/fair; goal oriented; clear expectations; transition strategies

Scale: 1   2   3   4   5

6. Because of the gifted nature of the students, how would you handle a situation with a child who has perfectionist tendencies and has experienced a failure for the first time in your class? (TOF 7; TOF 3)

Notes:	Comments:

Keywords: one-on-one counseling; stress management techniques; find ways to learn from the experience; secure environment; fill in any knowledge gaps; student-centered classroom

Scale: 1   2   3   4   5

7. Describe what experiences you might provide for students to connect content with real-world applications both inside and outside of the classroom. (TOF 6)

Notes:	Comments:

Keywords: follow-up activities; online resources; variety of examples; independent project; hands-on activities

Scale: 1   2   3   4   5

8. Give an example of a lesson you might teach for this class and how you would integrate technology to address higher order thinking and/or creativity. (TOF 2; TOF 4; TOF 9; TOF 10; TOF 11)

Notes:	Comments:

Keywords: subject/content specific; hands-on; tiered lessons; flexible grouping; peer tutoring; experiential; student choice; one-on-one; pretesting; open-ended questions; scaffolding; higher order questioning; differentiation; brainstorming; allowing thinking time; risk-taking; web resources; software; specific technologies

Scale: 1   2   3   4   5

9. Based upon the lesson you described, how would you differentiate or what adjustments would you make for students with varying proficiency levels? (TOF 5; TOF 11)

Notes:	Comments:

Keywords: work stations; alternative activities; variety of choices; scaffolding; flexible grouping;

Scale: 1   2   3   4   5

10. You have developed a well-planned lesson, but during the class period, you notice that some of the students are off-task and are behaving in a manner that is disruptive to other students. How would you handle this situation? (TOF 7)

Notes:	Comments:

Keywords: *time out; one-on-one counseling; talk to parents; talk to counselors; provide alternative activities; encourage positive peer relationship*

Scale: 1   2   3   4   5

11. What types of final projects might you have students create for your class? (TOF 1; TOF 5; TOF 8)

Notes:	Comments:

Keywords: *high interest; choice; conceptually based; real-world application; problem-based learning; audience; independent study; small group*

Scale: 1   2   3   4   5

What questions do you have for us?

Would you hire this candidate? _____ Yes   _____ No

Overall Average: _____

TEACHER OBSERVATION FORM

PURDUE UNIVERSITY GIFTED EDUCATION RESOURCE INSTITUTE
TEACHER OBSERVATION FORM

Teacher _____ Date _____

Time _____ to _____ Room _____

____ Criterion observed
____ Criterion not observed

Rating Scale

7 – Excellent	4 – Average	1 – Unacceptable
6 – Very Good	3 – Below Average	N / O – Not Observed
5 – Above Average	2 – Poor	

Please use the seven-point scale to rate the overall quality of the instruction in each numbered category. Please check next to each category's lettered descriptors if observed in the lesson.

1. Content coverage

7 6 5 4 3 2 1 N/O

_____ A. Content is advanced for grade level
_____ B. Topics of instruction are related to other subjects / content areas
_____ C. Teacher expertise in the content area is evident

2. Clarity of instruction

7 6 5 4 3 2 1 N/O

_____ A Instructor communicates well with students
_____ B Nonverbal communication is used to enhance instruction
_____ C Handouts and instructions are clearly printed and thorough
_____ D Appropriate illustrations and examples are used
_____ E Student comprehension is evident

3. Motivational techniques

7 6 5 4 3 2 1 N/O

_____ A Teacher shows energy and enthusiasm
_____ B Variety of warm-ups, hooks, or brainteasers are used to gain student interest
_____ C Teacher encourages student enthusiasm and persistence
_____ D Multiple learning styles are considered

4. Pedagogy / Instructional techniques

7 6 5 4 3 2 1 N/O

_____ A Visual aids are used to enhance instruction
_____ B Instructional techniques are appropriately advanced for the group
_____ C Instructor avoids unnecessary repetition and drill
_____ D Instructor utilizes preassessment to prevent redundancy
_____ E Instructor provides opportunities for inquiry into authentic questions generated by the students

5. Opportunity for self-determination of activities by student

7 6 5 4 3 2 1 N/O

_____ A Adequate choices offered
_____ B Student-directed activities are available when appropriate
_____ C Individual interests are accommodated

6. Student involvement in a variety of experiences

7 6 5 4 3 2 1 N/O

_____ A Activities are based on real-world applications
_____ B A variety of assignments and/or activities are included
_____ C Problem solving and independent study processes are encouraged
_____ D Discussions, small-group activities, technology, field trips, and/or learning centers are incorporated

7. Interaction between teacher and student and student and peers

7 6 5 4 3 2 1 N/O

_____ A Interaction is appropriate to course objectives
_____ B Activities are included that promote social and/or emotional development
_____ C Teacher and students show mutual respect
_____ D Sense of order and the promotion of self-discipline is evident

	7	6	5	4	3	2	1	N/O

8. Opportunity for student follow-up on activities or topics on their own
_____ A Instructor promotes open-endedness, allowing for creativity and individual interests
_____ B Activities and assignments build upon / prepare for lessons
_____ C Extended activities are focused and purposeful
_____ D Students are encouraged and offered assistance for further study of topics of interest

9. Emphasis on higher level critical thinking skills
_____ A Critical thinking activities are included
_____ B Upper levels of Bloom's taxonomy (application, analysis, synthesis, evaluation) are evident
_____ C Metacognitive thinking is encouraged
_____ D Sufficient time is spent on open-ended discussion or other process activities

10. Emphasis on creativity
_____ A Instructor encourages risk-taking
_____ B Creative thinking skills (fluency, flexibility, originality, and elaboration) are incorporated
_____ C Instructor models creative behavior when appropriate

11. Lesson plans designed to meet program, course, and daily objectives
_____ A Lessons show a sense of planning, with flexibility
_____ B Lessons emphasize student involvement
_____ C Considerations for individual student differentiation are included

12. Appropriate use of classroom technology
_____ A Use of technology complements respective lesson
_____ B Technology advances what students already know
_____ C Instructor utilizes audio-visual materials and/or computers in instruction
_____ D A variety of technology is incorporated
_____ E Opportunities for the students to develop and employ technological skills are provided

Activities were conducted _____ in small groups _____ in large groups _____ individually.

Teacher's strengths:

Suggestions for improvement:

Additional comments:

Observer's Signature: _____ Date: _____

Teacher's Signature: _____ Date: _____

☐ Would like conference regarding evaluation. Suggested time: _____

APPENDIX C

PURDUE SIMULATION CASE STUDY EPILOGUES

STUDENT 1, NATHAN KASUN (SERBIAN)

Nikola Tesla never built a prototype, but designed and imagined his inventions in his head. He claimed to be so accurate that he never had to rethink a prototype. Nikola moved to the United States when he was 18 years old. He was robbed before boarding the ship. He arrived in the United States destitute. Nikola went to work for Thomas Edison, who made him work from 10:30 a.m. to 5:00 a.m. the next day, 7 days a week. He promised Nikola $50,000 if he could improve on his designs. Nikola made 24 different design improvements and when he asked for his money, Edison apparently laughed and told Nikola he did not understand American humor. It was then that Nikola left Edison and set up his own lab, becoming his rival. Tesla worked to design the alternating current motor. He sold his patents to George Westinghouse and went to work for him. He invented and wrote up his invention of the radio, but Guglielmo Marconi was credited with the invention, claiming he had never read of Tesla's invention. Twenty years later, Tesla sued Marconi and won. He is now credited with being the real inventor of the radio.

FURTHER READING

http://www.teslasociety.com/biography.htm
http://wwww.pbs.org/tesla/index.html

STUDENT 2, KATIE LIU (CHINESE)

Amy Tan and her siblings did deal with significant amounts of parental pressure for academic success. The Tan family did not stay in California for all of Amy's youth. Unfortunately, her father and one of her brothers both died of brain tumors within one year of each other. Mrs. Tan moved with the other two children to Switzerland, where Amy finished high school. Amy and her mother had a strained relationship that continued throughout college. Amy dropped out of her premed classes at San Jose City College and focused on English and linguistics. She earned bachelor's and master's degrees in those areas. She married and began work in a Ph.D. program, but did not complete the degree. Amy later became a successful business writer. After this phase of her career, she switched to her most notable body of work. Amy did not fulfill her mother's dreams of becoming a concert pianist or a doctor. She is, however, a widely published and recognized author. Several of her books have been on the New York Times bestseller list, including *The Joy Luck Club*, *The Kitchen God's Wife*, *The Hundred Secret Senses*, *The Bonesetter's Daughter*, and *Saving Fish from Drowning*. Her work has been translated into 35 different languages. Amy Tan continues to write, but also works extensively to raise awareness about Lyme disease. The many years she lived with this condition undiagnosed has led to her advocacy. With treatment she is now able to resume writing and traveling.

FURTHER READING

http://www.achievement.org/autodoc/page/tan0bio-1
http://www.notablebiographies.com/St-Tr/Tan-Amy.html#b
http://www.amytan.net

STUDENT 3, LOBSANG THONDUP (ASIAN)

Tenzin Gyatso, the Dalai Lama, was born in a small rural town in Tibet. He was identified as the 14th incarnation of the Dalai Lama when he was 3 years old. His formal education began at the age of 5. Much of his education has been in monastic settings. He completed the Geshe Lharampa degree, the equivalent of a doctorate of Buddhist philosophy, at the age of 25. His studies and some of the subsequent academic examinations were in the areas of logic, Tibetan culture, Sanskrit, medicine, and Buddhist philosophy (divided into wisdom, philosophy, the canon of monastic discipline, metaphysics, logic, and epistemology). At the age of 16, the Dali Lama was called to fulfill the role of Head of State for Tibet. He met extensively with Chinese and other Asian officials for the early part of his service. Just 9 years later, at the age of 25, he was forced into exile, and has remained outside of Tibet since. He has worked with the United Nations on several different occasions to try to develop an international understanding of Tibet and to create a plan for the reinstitution of Tibet. In an approach different from the previous leaders of Tibet, the current Dalai Lama has met extensively with Western leaders. He has communicated with leaders from the Catholic church, the Anglican church, and Jewish leaders. The Dalai Lama is a prolific writer, with more than 20 published works. He has received dozens of honorary doctorates and international awards for his work toward peace. He received the Nobel Peace Prize in 1989.

FURTHER READING

http://www.dalailama.com/biography/a-brief-biography
http://www.notablebiographies.com/Co-Da/Dalai-Lama.html
http://nobelprize.org/nobel_prizes/peace/laureates/1989/lama-bio.html

STUDENT 4, SANTINE BROWN (AFRICAN AMERICAN)

Farrah Gray (Santine Brown) started a business club at age 8 called Urban Neighborhood Economic Enterprise Club. He asked local businesses to donate transportation and meeting space to the club. The club raised more than $12,000. He cohosted a radio show at age 9. He founded a company called Farr-Out Foods and several other businesses between the ages of 12 and 16, and sold the Farr-Out Foods company at age 14 for $1.5 million. He was the youngest African American businessman to become a millionaire. He was also the youngest person to have offices on Wall Street. He did not attend college, but he received an honorary doctorate from Allen University at age 21.

FURTHER READING

http://www.farrahgray.com

STUDENT 5, NABHA PATEL (INDIAN)

Indira Gandhi grew up in India during the time of British control. (Her family is not related to Mohandas Gandhi). Her father was a key figure in the nationalist movement prior to India's independence. He was frequently jailed for his political beliefs. Indira left home for university shortly after her mother's death from tuberculosis. She studied at Oxford University. Indira married Feroze Gandhi, someone who shared her political convictions. They protested British control and were both jailed for 13 months for their actions. In 1945, British control in India ended. Indira and her father were instrumental in uniting the different factions that emerged to form the Indian National Congress. Indira's father was the first prime minister of India. Indira's work during this time focused on social welfare and children's needs. After her father's death, Indira moved into the role of the minister for information and broadcasting. She became the third prime minister of an independent India in 1966 and served during turbulent times until 1977. She was elected to the post again in 1979. She visited the U.S. and the USSR during her political career. Unfortunately, political unrest remained in India. Internal riots broke out among different political and religious groups. Indira Gandhi was assassinated by her some of her own security guards in 1984.

FURTHER READING

http://www.sscnet.ucla.edu/southasia/History/Independent/Indira.html
http://www.notablebiographies.com/Fi-Gi/Gandhi-Indira.html

STUDENT 6, ADA GREEN (AFRICAN AMERICAN)

Mae Jemison followed the goals she set in kindergarten. She graduated from high school at age 16. She enrolled at Stanford University that fall. She graduated with a B.S. in chemical engineering from Stanford as well as extensive study in African and Afro-American Studies. She went on to medical school at Cornell University. Following her studies, Jemison served in the Peace Corps for 2 years in West Africa using her expertise in medicine and engineering. When she returned to the U.S., she worked as a physician in the Los Angeles area.

Jemison pursued another lifelong dream after her return to the United States. She was accepted by NASA and was the first African American woman in space. She was the science mission specialist on the Endeavour mission in 1992. She left NASA in 1993 and started her own company. She continues to work in the fields of science, technology, and more specifically, medical technology. Jemison sees education as very important and started an international science camp for students age 12–16.

FURTHER READING

http://www.jsc.nasa.gov/Bios/htmlbios/jemison-mc.html
http://en.wikipedia.org/wiki/Mae_Jemison
http://www.notablebiographies.com/Ho-Jo/Jemison-Mae.html
http://starchild.gsfc.nasa.gov/docs/StarChild/whos_who_level2/jemison.html
http://www.drmae.com

STUDENT 7, DAVID COLLINS (AFRICAN AMERICAN)

Martin Luther King, Jr. attended segregated public schools in Georgia, graduating from high school at the age of 15. He received the B. A. degree in 1948 from Morehouse College. After 3 years of theological study at Crozer Theological Seminary in Pennsylvania, where he was elected president of a predominantly White senior class, he was awarded a bachelor's degree. He won a fellowship and enrolled in graduate studies at Boston University. He received a doctorate in 1955, at the age of 26. In Boston he met and married Coretta Scott.

Two sons and two daughters were born into the family. As a young child, Martin Luther King, Jr. noticed the injustices in the world, and this led him to become a key figure in the Civil Rights Movement. Although he was arrested multiple times, his home was bombed, and he was both stabbed and shot for his beliefs, he stood strong for what was right. His work with civil rights took him over 6 million miles during the years of 1957–1968. He spoke over 2,500 times, wrote five books and multiple articles. He was the leader of many civil rights activities and his "I Have a Dream" speech is regarded as one of the best speeches of the 20th century. He won the Nobel Peace Prize for his tremendous efforts. He was 35 at the time, the youngest man to have received the award. Although he was killed for his beliefs, his legacy lives on as he is remembered as one of the most influential Civil Rights leaders.

FURTHER READING

http://www.nobelprize.org/nobel_prizes/peace/laureates/1964/king-bio.html

http://www.biography.com/people/martin-luther-king-jr-9365086

STUDENT 8, JANICE PHILLIPS (CAUCASIAN)

Jane Goodall spent much of her childhood in London and the more rural setting of Bournemouth. Her parents divorced when she was 16; she then moved with her mother and sister to her grandmother's house. Following high school graduation, Jane's mother did not have enough money to send her to college. Jane worked as a secretary. After 4 years of working office jobs, a friend of Jane's invited her to visit Kenya. Jane worked as a waitress to earn the money for the trip. It was during that first African trip that Goodall met Dr. Louis Leakey, an anthropologist and paleontologist. He hired her to work as an assistant and secretary at a fossil dig in Africa. It was Leakey that proposed the idea of studying chimpanzees. He had been looking for the right person to do intensive observational research. Jane accepted the job and began her study in Tanzania. During this first period of research, Goodall observed the chimps using tools. This discovery was groundbreaking for the time and caused a shift in the way researchers regarded primates. National Geographic documented much of her research (and she ended up marrying a photographer from that organization). In order to gain more credibility and respect among scientists, Goodall pursued a Ph.D. at Cambridge University. She was one of a very small number of people admitted without a college degree. She earned her Ph.D. in animal behavior in 1965. She is often cited as one of the early scientists to recognize personalities, emotions, and other features in animals. Goodall and her then-husband founded the Gombe Stream Research Centre to provide a place for researchers and graduate students to study chimpanzees. Although she no longer does field work, she is still associated with the Centre. She travels extensively to raise awareness of environmental issues and to bring attention to the interactions between people, animals, and the environment. She has published extensively. Goodall also started the Jane Goodall Institute to raise awareness, help those living in poverty in Africa, and support her educational program Roots and Shoots.

FURTHER READING

http://www.notablebiographies.com/Gi-He/Goodall-Jane.html
http://www.webster.edu/~woolflm/goodall.html
http://www.janegoodall.org/study-corner-biography

STUDENT 9, ANGELA BAEZ (HISPANIC)

Sonia Sotomayor (Angela Baez) overcame many obstacles in her childhood. In addition to her family's financial struggle and her diabetes, Sotomayor's father died when she was just 9 years old. She took comfort in books, further developing her love of reading. Nancy Drew books were a favorite. Sotomayor did well in school, graduating as the valedictorian of her high school class. Her high school debate coach told her about Ivy League schools. Sotomayor followed his educational path, earning a scholarship to Princeton University. She graduated summa cum laude and was a corecipient of the highest award Princeton grants to undergraduates. She went on to Yale University for law school. She served as editor of the *Yale Law Journal*. Following graduation, Sotomayor became an assistant district attorney in New York City. After 5 years in that role, she entered corporate law and became a partner at her firm after 4 years. In October 1992, President George H. W. Bush appointed her to the United States District Court for the Southern District of New York. She was the youngest member of the court. She served for 6 years before becoming the first Latina appointed to the U.S. Court of Appeals for the Second Circuit by President Bill Clinton. In 2009 she became the first Hispanic person and the third woman to serve on the

United States Supreme court after her approval by Senate following President Barack Obama's nomination.

FURTHER READING

    http://www.biography.com/people/sonia-sotomayor-453906

    http://www.cnn.com/2009/POLITICS/05/26/sotomayor.bio

    http://www.whitehouse.gov/the_press_office/Background-on-Judge-
       Sonia-Sotomayor

STUDENT 10, JAMES WILLIAMS (AFRICAN AMERICAN)

After some changes at home, Benjamin Carson began to succeed in school, and by the sixth grade he was at the top of his class. He went on to graduate from high school with honors and earned a degree in psychology from Yale University. He attended medical school at the University of Michigan and is now the Director of Pediatric Neurosurgery at Johns Hopkins Hospital. Dr. Carson is known for developing an innovative surgical technique to separate conjoined twins, prenatal surgeries, and others. He is also a bestselling author and motivational speaker.

FURTHER READING

Carson, B. (1990). *Gifted hands: The Ben Carson story*. Grand Rapids, MI: Zondervan.

Lewis, G., & Lewis, D. S. (2009). *Gifted hands, kid's edition: The Ben Carson story*. Grand Rapids, MI: Zondervan.

STUDENT 11, MARK MATHESON (CAUCASIAN)

Albert Einstein did change schools at the age of 10. He continued to excel in mathematics, completing calculus by age 15. After he completed college, he was not able to get his dissertation accepted. He worked 6 days a week in a patent office. During this period he wrote four revolutionary papers in theoretical physics. One described light as both a particle and a wave. Secondly, he proved the existence of atoms and molecules. The third paper dealt with relativity. And finally, he published his famous formula relating energy and matter (E = mc squared). Einstein later won the 1921 Nobel Prize.

FURTHER READING

http://www.bbc.co.uk/history/historic_figures/einstein_albert.shtml
http://einstein.biz
http://www.history.com/topics/albert-einstein

STUDENT 12, WILLIAM HORN (CAUCASIAN)

Bill Bradley is a former United States senator, NBA player, and Olympian. He attended public school through high school graduation. He went to Princeton University for his undergraduate degree and then to Oxford as a Rhodes scholar. He won an Olympic gold medal in the 1964 games in basketball. He played for the New York Knicks for 10 years. Bradley was then elected as a senator from the state of New Jersey. Some of his work involved tax law and finance reform. He was also involved in the Javits bill, which was one of the primary sources of funding for gifted education before being removed from the 2011 national budget. He served as senator 18 years before running for president in 2000. Since that time, Bradley has worked as a consultant, served on several not-for-profit boards, and acted as a visiting professor. He has a weekly radio show and has published several books. He was inducted into the New Jersey Hall of Fame in 2008.

FURTHER READING

http://www.billbradley.com
http://www.pophistorydig.com/?tag=bill-bradley-biography

STUDENT 13, CALEB RAMSEY (NATIVE AMERICAN)

Sherman Alexie was born on the Spokane Reservation in Wellpinit, WA, where he attended school through the eighth grade. Sherman made the decision to attend high school in Reardan, WA, in order to obtain a better education. After graduating from high school, he went into premed at Washington State

University (WSU) but, after a fainting spell in his anatomy class, soon made the decision that medicine was not the right career choice for him. While at WSU, Sherman attended a poetry workshop and quickly realized his passion. His first two poetry collections were published one year after his college graduation. Battling alcoholism soon after starting college, Sherman stopped drinking at the age of 23. Since then, he has gone on to publish numerous collections of poetry as well as short stories, novels, and screenplays. He has been honored with several awards, including the 1993 PEN/Hemingway Award for Best First Book of Fiction for *The Lone Ranger and Tonto Fistfight in Heaven*; two prizes at the 1998 Sundance Film Festival for his first screenplay, *Smoke Signals*; and the 2007 National Book Award in Young People's Literature for *The Absolutely True Diary of a Part-Time Indian*.

FURTHER READING

http://www.shermanalexie.com

http://www.poetryfoundation.org/bio/sherman-alexie

http://www.articlemyriad.com/biography-sherman-alexie

RECOMMENDED DIFFERENTIATION AND GIFTED EDUCATION RESOURCES

GENERAL DIFFERENTIATION RESOURCES

Advancing Differentiation: Thinking and Learning for the 21st Century
by Richard Cash

This book goes beyond the basics of differentiation to explore more advanced strategies that will help teachers move to the next level. It includes plenty of classroom examples, reproducible handouts, and a unique take on several older differentiation strategies used in the past.

Available from: Free Spirit Publishing; http://www.freespirit.com

Byrdseed

Byrdseed is a great source of information and professional development on differentiated instruction for gifted learners. Topics include language arts, math, creativity, and technology. Access to videos on these topics can be purchased for a small fee.

Available from: http://www.byrdseed.com

Curriculum 21: Essential Education for a Changing World
by Heidi Hayes Jacobs

The author of this edited book presents a framework for reexamining the curriculum and instructional strategies used in today's schools in light of technological advancements made in the 21st century. Practical and innovative ideas for revamping today's classrooms are presented.
Available from: ASCD; http://www.ascd.org

Curriculum Compacting: The Complete Guide to Modifying the Regular Curriculum for High-Ability Students
by Sally Reis, Deborah Burns, & Joseph Renzulli

Everything teachers need to understand, justify, and implement curriculum compacting for advanced learners.
Available from: Prufrock Press; http://www.prufrock.com

Curriculum Starter Cards: Developing Differentiated Lessons for Gifted Students
by Sandra Kaplan & Michael Cannon

A collection of cards with differentiated learning experiences that emphasizes depth and complexity and includes independent study, student products, and higher level thinking.
Available from: Prufrock Press; http://www.prufrock.com

Developing the Gifts and Talents of all Students in the Regular Classroom
by Margaret Beecher

This is an innovative K–12 curriculum model designed to reach all students in heterogeneous classrooms. It combines the Enrichment Triad Model with differentiation strategies.
Available from: Prufrock Press; http://www.prufrock.com

A Different Place

This website provides basic knowledge about differentiation as well as activities in all content areas.
Available from: http://www.adifferentplace.org/index.html

The Differentiated Classroom: Responding to the Needs of All Learners
by Carol Tomlinson

In this book, Tomlinson provides a definition for and guiding principles of differentiation as well as easy-to-implement instructional strategies to help teachers make it a reality in their classrooms.

Available from: ASCD; http://www.ascd.org

Educating Gifted Students in Middle School: A Practical Guide
by Susan Rakow

Not many resources currently exist specifically targeting gifted middle school students. This book helps teachers better understand the unique needs of the gifted middle school student and provides practical ideas for meeting those needs.

Available from: Prufrock Press; http://www.prufrock.com

How to Differentiate Instruction in Mixed-Ability Classrooms (2nd Edition)
by Carol Tomlinson

A practical guide to addressing the diverse needs of students in mixed-ability classrooms.

Available from: ASCD; http://www.ascd.org

The Schoolwide Enrichment Model: A How-To Guide for Educational Excellence (2nd Edition)
by Joseph Renzulli & Sally Reis

The authors present a collection of instruments, charts, checklists, taxonomies, assessment tools, forms, and planning guides designed to help educators organize, administer, maintain, and evaluate the Schoolwide Enrichment Model.

Available from: Prufrock Press; http://www.prufrock.com

Strategies for Differentiating Instruction: Best Practices for the Classroom (2nd Edition)
by Julia Roberts & Tracy Inman

This book offers practical differentiation strategies for teachers to use in the classroom, including many example Think-Tac-Toe samples.

Available from: Prufrock Press; http://www.prufrock.com

Tiered Instruction Example Lessons
Tiered activities in math, language arts, and science for grades K–12 are available free for download.
Available from: http://www.doe.in.gov/achievement/individualizedlearning/
    tiered-curriculum-project

Understanding by Design
by Grant Wiggins & Jay McTighe
This book provides a wonderful way to differentiate curriculum through the planning of different outcomes with similar or overlapping learning tasks.
Available from: ASCD; http://www.ascd.org

SPECIFIC CONTENT AREA RESOURCES

LANGUAGE ARTS
Center for Gifted Education: Language Arts Curriculum Units
Units that develop students' skills in literary analysis and interpretation, persuasive writing, linguistic competency, and oral communication, as well as strengthen students' reasoning skills and understanding of the concept of change can be purchased here.
Available from: William and Mary's Center for Gifted Education; http://educa-
    tion.wm.edu/centers/cfge/

Cummings Study Guides
Study guides for great works of world literature, including all the plays and poems of William Shakespeare, can be viewed online for free.
Available from: http://www.cummingsstudyguides.net

Differentiating Instruction With Menus: Language Arts
by Laurie Westphal
This book can save teachers countless hours developing their own choice menus for differentiated instruction in language arts. Three versions are currently available: K–2, 3rd–5th, and 6th–8th.
Available from: Prufrock Press; http://www.prufrock.com

Junior Great Books

This is a literature program designed to develop essential literacy skills and deductive reasoning through shared inquiry discussions.

Available from: http://www.greatbooks.org

Michael Clay Thompson: Language Arts Curriculum

Thompson's books are both inspiring and engaging, full of language activities including grammar, vocabulary, poetry, writing, and literature.

Available from: Royal Fireworks Press; http://www.rfwp.com/mct.php

The Schoolwide Enrichment Model Reading Framework

by Sally Reis, Elizabeth Fogarty, Rebecca Eckert, and Lisa Muller

This enrichment-based reading program for young students has been shown through research to increase students' interest in reading and as well as overall reading achievement.

Available from: Prufrock Press; http://www.prufrock.com

Some of My Best Friends Are Books

by Judith Halsted

This book can be used to aid in choosing appropriate reading materials for students. It contains over 200 pages of annotated bibliographic references organized by grade level with plot summaries and discussion ideas.

Available from: Great Potential Press; http://www.greatpotentialpress.com

Suppose the Wolf Were an Octopus Series

by Michael Bagley and Joyce Foley

Questions targeting all six levels of Bloom's taxonomy have been carefully created for dozens of commonly used books for children and young adults. Four versions are currently available: K–2, 3rd–4th, 5th–6th, and 7th grades.

Available from: Royal Fireworks Press; http://www.rfwp.com

Teaching Thinking Skills Using Non-Fiction Narratives Series

by Don Barnes and Wyman Fischer

This series of books will help teachers utilize more nonfiction texts in the classroom as mandated by the new Common Core Standards. The following versions are available: 3rd–4th, 5th–6th, and 7th–8th.

Available from: Pieces of Learning; http://www.piecesoflearning.com

MATHEMATICS

10 Things All Future Mathematicians and Scientists Should Know
by Edward Zaccaro

Over 50 stories are included that show children the strong connection between mathematics and science in the real world.
Available from: Prufrock Press, http://www.prufrock.com

Chi Square, Pie-Charts and Me
by Susan Baum, Bob Gable, & Karen List

This book will help students differentiate between real-world research and report writing. It also clarifies and elaborates on the different kinds of research and the specific steps necessary to conduct a research project.
Available from: Royal Fireworks Press; http://www.rfwp.com

Differentiating Instruction With Menus: Math
by Laurie Westphal

This book can save teachers countless hours developing their own choice menus for differentiated instruction in math. Three versions are currently available: K–2, 3rd–5th, and 6th–8th. There is also a version for Algebra I/II.
Available from: Prufrock Press; http://www.prufrock.com

Figure This!

This site contains math challenges for the whole family that focus on real world problem solving.
Available from: http://www.figurethis.org

Historical Connections in Mathematics Vol. 1–Vol. 3
by Wilbert Reimer, Luetta Reimer, and Brenda Dahl

Have your students ever asked you how a famous mathematical theory was developed? Lessons are presented that help the students discover the answers to these questions through hands-on activities.
Available from: AIMS; http://www.aimsedu.org/

Khan Academy

This website has hundreds of free short video tutorials that allow students to self-pace through the math curriculum.
Available from: Khan Acadmy; http://www.khanacademy.org/

Mentoring Mathematical Minds

Project M3 presents challenging and motivational math units for grades 3–5 that concentrate on communication, reasoning, connections, and problem solving.
Available from: http://www.projectm3.org

National Council of Teachers of Mathematics: Illuminations

The NCTM website contains resources that can help improve the teaching and learning of mathematics for all students.
Available from: http://illuminations.nctm.org

The National Library of Virtual Manipulatives for Interactive Mathematics

A library of uniquely interactive, web-based virtual manipulatives or concept tutorials for K–12 math instruction are available to use for free.
Available from: http://nlvm.usu.edu/en/nav/index.html

NRICH

This site contains free mathematics enrichment resources for pupils of all ages.
Available from: http://nrich.maths.org/public

Open-Ended Assessment in Math

An explanation for how to create open-ended math problems for students is given as well as several hundred examples.
Available from: http://books.heinemann.com/math/construct.cfm

SCIENCE

Center for Gifted Education: Science Curriculum

These units available for purchase challenge students to analyze real-world problems, understand the concept of systems and design, as well as conduct scientific experiments.
Available from: William and Mary's Center for Gifted Education; http://education.wm.edu/centers/cfge/

Differentiating Instruction With Menus: Science
by Laurie Westphal
This book can save teachers countless hours developing their own choice menus for differentiated instruction in science. Three versions are currently available: K–2, 3rd–5th, and 6th–8th. There is also a version for Biology.
Available from: Prufrock Press; http://www.prufrock.com

Exploratorium
This site has extremely engaging science experiments on hundreds of different topics.
Available from: http://www.exploratorium.edu/

FermiLab's Science Adventures
Problem-based learning activities with a technology emphasis can be experienced for free.
Available from: http://ed.fnal.gov/index.shtml

HowStuffWorks
This site shows kids how dozens of objects, processes, and living things work. Pyramids, the human brain, and the iPhone are just a few examples.
Available from: http://www.howstuffworks.com

Rader's Kapili.com
This webpage is a portal to introductory science sites on chemistry, biology, geography, physics, and the cosmos.
Available from: http://www.kapili.com

Science Brainstretchers: Creative Problem Solving Activities in Science
by Anthony Fredericks
Critical and creative thinking skills are developed through lessons exploring the life sciences, Earth and space science, and physical science.
Available from: Good Year Books; http://www.goodyearbooks.com

SOCIAL STUDIES

Center for Gifted Education: Social Studies Curriculum

Social studies units are available for purchase that emphasize primary source analysis, critical thinking, and concept development to help students develop understanding of high-level social studies content in key areas.

Available from: William and Mary's Center for Gifted Education; http://education.wm.edu/centers/cfge/

Differentiating Instruction With Menus: Social Studies

by Laurie Westphal

This book can save teachers countless hours developing their own choice menus for differentiated instruction in social studies. Three versions are currently available: K–2, 3rd–5th, and 6th–8th.

Available from: Prufrock Press; http://www.prufrock.com

Famous People Puzzles: Exercises in Inference and Research

by Carolyn Powell

Students are shown what was found inside the pockets of a famous person. Using these clues, students must discover who the mystery person is. Research, inference, and writing skills are developed and emphasized.

Available from: Prufrock Press; http://www.prufrock.com

Kids Guide to Social Action

by Barbara A. Lewis

This book shows kids how to write letters, conduct interviews, make speeches, take surveys, raise funds, and get media coverage to solve some of today's social problems.

Available from: Free Spirit Publishing; http://www.freespirit.com

The Learning Page

Access to over 100 collections in the Library of Congress' American Memory Project can be found here.

Available from: http://www.loc.gov/teachers/index.html

Quotation Quizzlers: Puzzling Your Way Through Famous Quotations
by Philip Steinbacher

Students are given a challenging code to crack revealing a quotation from a famous person. Brief biographies of these famous individuals are included as well.

Available from: Prufrock Press; http://www.prufrock.com

INTERDISCIPLINARY

Interact

Ready-to-use interdisciplinary simulations that encourage K–12 students to learn in a variety of ways are available for purchase.

Available from: http://www.interact-simulations.com/

Smithsonian

A variety of free interdisciplinary lessons for K–12 students can be downloaded.

Available from: http://smithsonianeducation.org

WebQuest.org

This site contains over 2,500 webquests and a search engine to find exactly what you want!

Available from: http://webquest.org/search/index.php

HIGHER LEVEL THINKING SKILLS RESOURCES

Edutopia – Project-Based Learning (PBL)

The process of conducting problem based learning in the classroom is explained with activities and examples from multiple grade levels.

Available from: http://www.edutopia.org/projectbasedlearning

Exploring the Environment: Teacher Pages

Excellent background information on PBL, plus sample modules for grades 5–12 are available.

Available from: http://www.cotf.edu/ete/teacher/teacherout.html

Independent Investigation Method
by Cindy Nottage & Virginia Morse

    This book presents a teacher and student-friendly research process, adaptable to your own curriculum and differentiated according to your students' grade level and abilities.

Available from: http://www.iimresearch.com

PETS: Primary Education Thinking Skills Series
by Jody Nichols, Dodie Merritt, Sally Thomson, and Margaret Wolfe

    Using engaging stories and fun activities, young children are taught important thinking skills they will use for the rest of their lives. The following versions are available: Kindergarten, 1st, 2nd, and 3rd.

Available from: Pieces of Learning; http://www.piecesoflearning.com

Questioning Makes the Difference
by Nancy Johnson

    Strategies and methods for using questioning as a teaching tool are presented. Multiple examples in math, reading, and social studies are included.

Available from: Pieces of Learning; http://www.piecesoflearning.com

The Research Book for Gifted Programs K–6
by Nancy Polette

    The author presents a framework students of all ages can use to conduct high-quality research on almost any topic.

Available from: Pieces of Learning; http://www.piecesoflearning.com

SOCIAL AND EMOTIONAL NEEDS OF THE GIFTED

The Essential Guide to Talking With Gifted Teens
by Jean Peterson

    Discussion starters and lessons for addressing social and emotional issues with gifted teens are presented. Topics include identity, stress, and relationship issues.

Available from: Free Spirit Publishing; http://www.freespirit.com

Guiding the Gifted Child: A Practical Source for Parents and Teachers
by James Webb

This excellent book focuses on social and emotional issues that gifted children often encounter.

Available from: Great Potential Press; http://www.greatpotentialpress.com

Learning to be a Durable Person
by Mary Hennenfent

Practical strategies and ready-to-use lessons for helping young students deal with common social and emotional issues are presented. This book is especially useful for young gifted students who often experience life with more intensity than their peers.

Available from: Prufrock Press; http://www.prufrock.com

The Social and Emotional Development of Gifted Children: What Do We Know?
by Maureen Neihart, Sally Reis, Nancy Robinson, and Sidney Moon

This is a comprehensive guide to the social and emotional lives of gifted children and youth covering issues related to underachievement, sensitivity, depression, and loneliness.

Available from: Prufrock Press; http://www.prufrock.com

What to do When Good Enough Isn't Good Enough
by Thomas Greenspon

This book about perfectionism is written for kids, not for their parents or teachers. It is written in a kid-friendly, fun way that will help students better understand themselves and how to deal with the stresses of being gifted.

Available from: Free Spirit Publishing; http://www.freespirit.com

SPECIAL POPULATIONS

GENERAL RESOURCES

Special Populations Network

Dedicated to increased recognition of gifted students from special populations, this network of the National Association for Gifted Children provides a variety of opportunities and resources for parents, teachers, and researchers.
Available from: National Association for Gifted Children; http://www.nagc.org

Special Populations in Gifted Education: Understanding Our Most Able Students From Diverse Backgrounds

by Jaime Castellano and Andrea Frazier, Editors

This book is focused on the unique needs of gifted students from diverse backgrounds. Topics on identifying and servicing a variety of special populations in programs for the gifted are addressed including profoundly gifted, twice-exceptional, culturally and linguistically diverse, and female students.
Available from: Prufrock Press; http://www.prufrock.com

Special Populations in Gifted Education: Working with Diverse Gifted Learners

by Jaime Castellano, Editor

This insightful book provides educators with the tools needed to address the needs of a diverse population of gifted students.
Available from: Pearson; http://www.pearson.com

TWICE-EXCEPTIONAL STUDENTS

2e: Twice-Exceptional Newsletter

The 2e Newsletter is a valuable resource for teachers and parents alike. This bimonthly newsletter is available by subscription and delivered via e-mail as a PDF. The newsletter includes articles, profiles of experts in the field, resources, the latest research, book reviews, news, and upcoming events.
Available from: http://www.2enewsletter.com

ADHD and Education: Foundations, Characteristics, Methods, and Collaboration
by Sydney Zentall

This book provides research-based strategies for addressing the needs of the ADHD child in the classroom.
Available from: Pearson; http://www.pearson.com

Bright Not Broken: Gifted Kids, ADHD, and Autism
by Diane Kennedy, Rebecca Banks, & Temple Grandin

For teachers and parents, this book provides insight into the lives of these twice-exceptional children, the potential for misdiagnosis, and what families and educators can do to address the needs of gifted students with ADHD and Autism.
Available from: Jossey-Bass; http://www.josseybass.com

Misdiagnosis and Dual Diagnoses of Gifted Children and Adults: ADHD, Bipolar, OCD, Asperger's, Depression, and Other Disorders
by James Webb, Edward Amend, Nadia Webb, Jean Goerss, Paul Beljan, and F. Richard Olenchak

Addresses the potential for misdiagnosis of specific learning and/or behavioral disorders in gifted students.
Available from: Great Potential Press; http://www.greatpotentialpress.com

Spotlight on 2e Booklet Series from 2e: Twice-Exceptional Newsletter

This informative series of easy-to-understand booklets includes titles such as *Understanding Your Twice-Exceptional Student*; *Parenting Your Twice-Exceptional Child*; and *The Mythology of Learning: Understanding Common Myths About 2e Learners.*
Available from: 2e: Twice-Exceptional Newsletter; http://www.2enewsletter.com

Twice-Exceptional Gifted Children: Understanding, Teaching, and Counseling Gifted Students
by Beverly Trail

This book guides educators through the development of a collaborative team of educators to identify twice-exceptional students in their schools, their unique needs, and the development of a comprehensive plan to meet those needs through enrichment, modification, and accommodation.
Available from: Prufrock Press; http://www.prufrock.com

Uniquely Gifted

This website provides a comprehensive list of resources, designed for families of gifted students with special needs. Informative articles provide parents with a more complete understanding of twice exceptionality, while personal stories from families and twice-exceptional children give insight into the experiences of these students. Included are also links for online support groups, information on specific learning needs (e.g., ADHD, Autism, Dyslexia), and much more.
Available from: http://www.uniquelygifted.org

GIFTED GIRLS

Failing at Fairness: How Our Schools Cheat Girls
by Myra and David Sadker

Failing at Fairness demonstrates the gender bias that, when it is present in the classroom, can lead to decreased identification of learning/behavioral differences, less attention from teachers, and underachievement.
Available from: Scribner; http://www.simonandschuster.com

Smart Girls: A New Psychology of Girls, Women, & Giftedness (**Revised Edition**)
by Barbara Kerr

This book takes a comprehensive look at the extant research on gifted girls and reviews the lives of women who became eminent in their fields.
Available from: Great Potential Press; http://www.greatpotentialpress.com

Tips for Parents: Ten Tips for Parenting Gifted Girls
by Sylvia Rimm

This informative article provides parents with practical tips for building confidence and decreasing chances for underachievement in gifted girls.
Available from: Davidson Institute for Talent Development; http://www.
davidson.org

Work Left Undone: Choices & Compromises of Talented Females
by Sally Reis

Dr. Reis examines the choices, attitudes, and stereotypes that gifted girls and women face and how these factors affect the directions they take in life.
Available from: Prufrock Press; http://www.prufrock.com

CULTURALLY, ECONOMICALLY, AND/OR LINGUISTICALLY DIVERSE

The Absolutely True Diary of a Part-Time Indian
by Sherman Alexie

This exceptional work of semiautobiographical fiction gives the reader insight into the life of a bright young Indian boy growing up on the reservation. This is a must read for young adults and adults alike.
Available from: Little, Brown; http://www.littlebrown.com

Culturally Diverse and Underserved Populations in Gifted Education
by Alexinia Baldwin & Sally Reis

Part of the Essential Readings in Gifted Education series, this book addresses issues of underrepresentation of culturally and/or economically diverse students in gifted programs.
Available from: Corwin; http://www.corwin.com

Bright, Talented, and Black: A Guide for Families of African American Gifted Learners
by Joy Davis

Offers suggestions for teachers and parents to help gifted, African-American students reach their potential.
Available from: Great Potential Press; http://www.greatpotentialpress.com

Identifying and Serving Culturally and Linguistically Diverse Gifted Students
by Lezley Collier Lewis, Anne Rivera, & Debbie Roby

A practical guide for educators, this book examines practices for identifying culturally and linguistically diverse students and evaluating programs that serve them.
Available from: Prufrock Press; http://www.prufrock.com

Reaching New Horizons: Gifted and Talented Education for Culturally and Linguistically Diverse Students
by Jaime Castellano & Eva Diaz

Addresses the needs of gifted, bilingual/multicultural/ESL students.
Available from: Pearson; http://www.pearson.com

Teaching Culturally Diverse Gifted Students
by Donna Ford & H. Richard Milner

Part of the Practical Strategies Series in Gifted Education, this book examines effective teaching strategies as well as a list of resources for teaching gifted students from diverse backgrounds.
Available from: Prufrock Press; http://www.prufrock.com

GIFTED EDUCATION AND ADVOCACY

RESOURCES FOR TEACHERS

Critical Issues and Practices in Gifted Education: What the Research Says **(2nd Ed.)**
By Jonathan Plucker & Carolyn Callahan, Editors

Each of the 50 chapters of this volume focuses on an important topic in gifted education. The chapter authors provide a review of the research and a guide for applying the research to gifted education and gifted children.
Available from: Prufrock Press; http://www.prufrock.com

Enrichment Clusters: A Practical Plan for Real-World, Student-Driven Learning
by Joseph Renzulli, Marcia Gentry, & Sally Reis

The authors present a step-by-step guide on how to set up a student-driven enrichment cluster program with exciting opportunities for students to explore areas of strong interest.
Available from: Prufrock Press; http://www.prufrock.com

Fundamentals of Gifted Education: Considering Multiple Perspectives
by Carolyn Callahan and Holly Hertberg-Davis, Editors

This book provides educators with a comprehensive view of the history of gifted education, issues of identification and effective programming, curricular models, and the needs of specific gifted populations from the perspective of experts in the field.
Available from: Routledge; http://www.routledge.com

Hoagies Gifted Education Page

This is a comprehensive website with links to full text articles on a wide variety of topics concerning gifted education.

Available from: http://www.hoagiesgifted.org

Identification: The Theory and Practice of Identifying Students for Gifted and Talented Education Services

By Scott L. Hunsaker, Editor

This book helps practitioners demystify the identification of gifted students by providing viewpoints from experts in the field on a variety of topics including theory, practice, underserved populations, and instrumentation.

Available from: Prufrock Press; http://www.prufrock.com

Looking for Data in All the Right Places: A Guide for Conducting Original Research with Young Investigators

by Alane Starko & Gina Schack

This book guides teachers how to transform students into disciplinarians through the process of teaching students how to conduct real research.

Available from: Prufrock Press; http://www.prufrock.com

Multicultural Gifted Education

by Donna Ford

As our country becomes more and more diverse, it is important to ensure our classrooms are meeting the needs of all students, not just those from the dominant culture. This book provides tools for accomplishing this task.

Available from: Prufrock Press; http://www.prufrock.com

Multiple Intelligences in the Elementary Classroom: A Teacher's Toolkit

by Susan Baum, Julie Veins, & Barbara Slatin

Designed to help classroom teachers create effective curricula to meet the diverse needs of the students in their classrooms, this book serves as a guide for The Pathway Model. Through this model, educators gain an understanding of multiple intelligences (MI) theory, goal setting, and planning for the implementation of MI in the classroom.

Available from: Teachers College Press; http://www.teacherscollegepress.com

The National Association for Gifted Children (NAGC)

NAGC is an organization that advocates for gifted education at the national level and has affiliate chapters in all 50 states.

Available from: http://www.nagc.org

A Nation Deceived: How Schools Hold Back America's Brightest Students
by Nicholas Colangelo, Susan Assouline, & Miraca Gross

This is a national report on the practice of acceleration and its effects on students.

Available from: http://www.nationdeceived.org

National Research Center on the Gifted and Talented

The National Research Center disseminates information on research-based best practices in gifted education.

Available from: http://www.gifted.uconn.edu/nrcgt

Systems and Models for Developing Programs for the Gifted and Talented
by Joseph Renzulli, E. Jean Gubbins, Kristen McMillen, Rebecca Eckert, & Catherine Little, Editors

This edited book is a must have! It includes chapters explaining the most well-known and effective models/programs in gifted education today written by the creators themselves (e.g., Sandra Kaplan, George Betts, Francoys Gagne, Sylvia Rimm, Carol Ann Tomlinson).

Available from: Prufrock Press; http://www.prufrock.com

Teaching Young Gifted Children in the Regular Classroom: Identifying, Nurturing, and Challenging Ages 4–9
by Joan Smutny, Sally Walker, & Elizabeth Meckstroth

This is a practical, easy-to-read guide for teachers about how to develop talent in young gifted students.

Available from: Free Spirit Publishing; http://www.freespirit.com

RESOURCES FOR PARENTS
Davidson Institute for Talent Development

Links to information for and about gifted students, their parents and educators, including young scholars and fellows programs are provided.

Available from: http://www.davidsongifted.org/

Exceptionally Gifted Children (2nd Edition)
by Miraca Gross

This book of case studies of 15 profoundly gifted students follows their academic, professional and social experiences over a 20-year time period, highlighting the potential pitfalls that exist for these students including underachievement and social isolation.

Available from: Routledge; http://www.routledge.com

Genius Denied: How to Stop Wasting Our Brightest Minds
by Jan and Bob Davidson

This book provides practical advice from founders of a nonprofit organization that assists gifted children.

Available from: http://www.geniusdenied.com

How to Parent So Children Will Learn (3rd Edition)
by Sylvia Rimm

Dr. Rimm provides advice based on decades of experience working with children and families on how to raise happy, achieving children.

Available from: Great Potential Press; http://www.greatpotentialpress.com

Light Up Your Child's Mind: Finding a Unique Pathway to Happiness and Success
by Joseph Renzulli and Sally Reis

Drs. Renzulli and Reis present parents with practical advise on how to motivate and help bright children reach their potential for gifted behaviors by tapping into their intelligence, task commitment, and creativity.

Available from: Little, Brown and Company; http://www.littlebrown.com

The Mile Marker Series: Your Road Map to Successfully Support Gifted Children (2nd Edition)
By the National Association for Gifted Children (NAGC)

This CD-ROM from NAGC provides an interactive tour of the five "Mile Markers" that represent different components of nurturing gifted children.

Available from: National Association For Gifted Children's Bookstore; http://www.nagc.org

Parenting with Love and Logic
by Foster Cline and Jim Fay
    Love and logic is a method for providing parents with strategies that encourage children to develop problem-solving skills while minimizing friction and power struggles between parents and children.
Available from: http://www.loveandlogic.com

Supporting Emotional Needs of the Gifted (SENG)
    SENG is an advocacy group with a focus on social and emotional needs of gifted individuals.
Available from: http://www.sengifted.org

PROGRAMS FOR GIFTED YOUTH

Gifted Education Resource Institute (GERI) at Purdue University
    Purdue University's Gifted Education Resource Institute offers enrichment programs throughout the year for Pre-K–12th grade high-ability students.
Available from: http://www.geri.education.purdue.edu/youth_programs/index.html

Center for Talent Development (CTD) , Northwestern University
    CTD conducts a Midwest talent search for highly able youth, provides challenging online courses for students in grades K–12, and offers summer and academic year programs for students in grades Pre-K–12.
Available from: http://www.ctd.northwestern.edu

Continental Mathematics League
    This is a mathematics problem solving competition for students in grades 2–12.
Available from: http://www.continentalmathematicsleague.com/

Destination Imagination
    This afterschool program focuses on the process, art, and skill associated with problem solving.
Available from: http://www.destinationimagination.org

Duke University Talent Identification Program (TIP)

TIP conducts a talent search in the Southeast region for highly able youth in grades 4–7, provides challenging online courses for students in grades 8–12, and offers summer programs for students in grades 7–12.
Available from: http://www.tip.duke.edu

The Education Program for Gifted Youth (EPGY) at Stanford University

EPGY provides computer-based distance-learning courses for high-ability students of all ages addressing a variety of subjects at levels ranging from kindergarten through advanced undergraduate.
Available from: http://epgy.stanford.edu/

Future Problem Solving (FPS) Program International

FPS is a creative problem-solving program that stimulates critical and creative thinking skills and encourages students to develop a vision for the future.
Available from: http://www.fpsp.org

Invention Convention

This program gives students an opportunity to think creatively, experiment, and work with data as they invent a new product or process.
Available from: http://www.eduplace.com/science/invention/overview.html

Johns Hopkins University: Center for Talented Youth (CTY)

CTY conducts a talent search for highly able youth in grades 2–8, provides challenging online courses for students in grades K–12, and offers summer programs for students in grades 2–12.
Available from: http://www.cty.jhu.edu

Math Olympiads

This is a mathematics contest for elementary and middle school groups.
Available from: http://www.moems.org

Mentor Connection

The University of Connecticut offers this 3-week summer program for high school students who work on creative projects and research investigations under the supervision of a university mentor.
Available from: http://www.gifted.uconn.edu/mentor

Odyssey of the Mind

Odyssey of the Mind is a creative problem-solving program for K–12 students that challenges them to apply their creativity to solve problems ranging from building mechanical devices to presenting interpretations of literary classics.
Available from: http://www.odysseyofthemind.com

Science Olympiad

This is a science contest with an emphasis on teamwork, problem solving, and hand-on/minds-on constructivist learning practices.
Available from: http://www.soinc.org

University of Iowa, Belin-Blank Center

The Belin-Blank Center conducts a talent search for highly able youth in grades 2–9, and offers summer and academic year programs for students in grades 2–12.
Available from: http://www.education.uiowa.edu/belinblank/Students/

INTEREST AND LEARNING STYLE INVENTORIES

If I Ran the School

This free survey was designed to identify areas of interest among students in order to help the teacher plan differentiated activities.
Available from: http://www.gifted.uconn.edu/siegle/curriculumcompacting/
    sec-imag/ranschol.pdf

Interest-A-Lyzer Family of Instruments: A Manual for Teachers
by Joseph Renzulli

Students learn best when they are interested in the topic. Six interest assessment tools, in sets of 30, as well as a teacher's manual are available for purchase.
Available from: Prufrock Press; http://www.prufrock.com

Multiple Intelligences and the eSmartz Aliens

This tool uses eight aliens in the form of trading cards to teach your students about Gardner's Multiple Intelligences. Students are asked which alien is most like themselves in order to help them determine their own strongest areas. It can be purchased for $0.99.

Available from: http://www.podls.com/strategies/view/?ID=10832342

Scholastic Interest Inventory

This is a free interest inventory from Scholastic appropriate for upper elementary students.

Available from: http://teacher.scholastic.com/LessonPlans/unit_roadtosuccess_invent.pdf

PROFESSIONAL DEVELOPMENT RESOURCES

Developing Student Strengths and Talents: Professional Development by GERI

This online professional development series contains nine intensive learning units that can be purchased for a single user or as a site subscription.

Available from: Gifted Education Resource Institute; http://www.geri.education.purdue.edu

Becoming a Learning School

By Joellen Killion & Patricia Roy

This is a soup-to-nuts manual for nurturing a culture of professional learning in your school.

Available from: Learning Forward; http://learningforward.org

Edutopia

This website/online community from the George Lucas Educational Foundation provides a wealth of resources and sharing opportunities focused on six core strategies: comprehensive assessment, integrated studies, project-based learning, social and emotional learning, teacher development, and technology integration.

Available from: Edutopia; http://www.edutopia.org

Powerful Designs for Professional Learning (2nd Ed.)
By Lois Brown Easton, Editor

This is a comprehensive handbook that explains 21 distinct approaches to professional development, including lesson study, classroom walk-throughs, tuning protocols, and many more. Includes a CD-ROM with 270 pages of handouts in PDF.

Available from: Learning Forward; http://learningforward.org

Protocols for Professional Learning
By Lois Brown Easton

Part of the Professional Learning Communities series from the Association for Supervision for Curriculum Development, this book is a guide for using 16 different protocols for engaging in critical discussion about specific components of the teaching and learning process.

Available from: Association for Supervision and Curriculum Development; http://www.ascd.org

Teaching Channel

A free website dedicated to professional development for teachers. Here you will find high-quality videos of real teachers and classrooms sharing ideas and strategies for a variety of topics, as well as a community of teachers with whom you can connect for professional networking.

Available from: Teaching Channel; http://www.teachingchannel.org

ABOUT THE AUTHOR

Marcia Gentry is the director of the Gifted Education Resource Institute and professor of educational studies at Purdue University. Her research has focused on the use of cluster grouping and differentiation, the application of gifted education pedagogy to improve teaching and learning, student perceptions of school, and nontraditional services and underserved populations.